GROUNDS

FOR

DIVORCE

GROUNDS FOR DIVORCE

MEL HUCKRIDGE

You're mad!

A statement that I can't really find reasons to disagree with.

My wife, family, friends, Romans and countrymen have all said words to that effect.

Where ever football is being played, and I am in the near vicinity, there is an innate compulsion on my part to view whatever game is taking place. This can take the form of looking over my shoulder at the television, visiting stadia all over the planet or just kids playing in the park. (Though since the conviction, I've been advised to keep clear of these areas.) Like Peter Sellers' character 'Chance' in the film 'Being There', 'I like to watch.'

This vice of mine not only includes an all encompassing passion for everything Queen's Park Rangers, but virtually every facet of association football, as it is never now referred to.

To instantly contradict myself this is not strictly true.

It's often not about the actual game in question, but about the whole experience, the culture, or even the lack of it, that surrounds 'the beautiful game.'

Believe me this game does not seem so beautiful at say, Boundary Park, home of Oldham Athletic, in January, when you are three down and the wind from the Pennines is blowing the rain into your face. The only person apart from the handful of you huddled together who wants to be as far away from this windswept hell as possible, is your goalie, who having made a gaffe worthy of inclusion in a Christmas DVD, is getting deserved abuse from the followers of his own team, in addition to coping with the howls of laughter from the home crowd.

It's an obsession without rhyme or reason. Something unfathomable drives you on, but often when you are there, you question why? Or is it just O.C.D.? It's train spotting with an acceptable face.

Nick Hornby touched upon it with 'Fever Pitch' and good author as he is, for me and many people like me, his book should have instead been titled 'Passing Interest'. Wild horses wouldn't keep me from being at a match where my team has the prospect of winning the league title just because I didn't have a ticket.

A far closer representation would be the brilliant 'Golden Gordon', an episode from the Terry Jones/Michael Palin '70s series 'Ripping Yarns'. If you've never seen this, then I suggest you do, not because it will necessarily give you an insight into my viewpoint, just because, in my opinion, it's the funniest thing ever produced on screen about football.

Everything written hereon in, was done so, pretty much, without the benefit of hindsight, so if I predict a heavy defeat and am justified shortly after, all this signifies is that I should be working for the pools panel, or more accurately the honest realisation that my lot are in fact, useless.

The summer had been quite an eventful one so far.

Jobless, but not penniless, fatherhood had reached me on the 8th June, with an 8lbs 6oz play station, we named Jake. Born at 9.45 on a Monday morning, which seems fair enough to me, as like his forty five year old 'im'mature dad, he already shows a reluctance to leave the warmth of the womb early that leaves his father proud.

Another thing that, at first, seemed quite considerate was that he decided to not inconvenience my hedonistic lifestyle too much by entering this world during pre-season.

Well thanks for trying Jake, but next time think it through some more, as your birth clashed with England's WC qualifier in Kazakhstan. Surely, you realised that I wanted to go?

A few Morse code messages from inside the womb to indicate when you would be arriving would have been extremely useful. Especially as it turned out, the return flight from Almaty that I'd mentally booked, landed at Heathrow at eight o'clock that very morning, which would not have caused been a problem. A fifteen minute cab journey to Hillingdon Hospital and voila, enough time for a caffeine injection to combat jet lag (which would have been irrelevant as I was up all night anyway) and there in ample time for the birth.

Surely, there is no way my wife, Bea, would have had any reason to object?

That game, and the subsequent unappealing Wednesday walkover against Andorra at Wembley, pretty much draws a line on the season that was 2008-9.

Thankfully these days, if football is what you want you don't have long to wait until it dominates our nation's psyche once again. Cricket and music festivals are often fantastic substitutes as long as the weather decides to play ball, which this year, overall, it hasn't.

If you are lucky, and you plan it right, you may be fortunate enough to catch a game abroad, or better still, your own heroes playing half-heartedly against the background of an Alp or a tropical sunset.

QPR were lined up to play exactly such games in Croatia and Slovenia. Unfortunately the club decided against notifying the hoi polloi until about a week before the matches were due to take place. This leaves little time to find cheap flights or to beg your other half for good behaviour time off.

I had to make do with the Exit music festival in Novi Sad, Serbia and looking around the ground of Vojvodina, the local team. This in itself was a minor coup, bribing my wife in May whilst she was heavily pregnant and short of cash in the hairdressers and agreeable to most anything. Using Machiavellian techniques are common place when away travel is concerned.

July 21

Pre-season, from a spectating perspective, can often be a complete waste of time. In the past I've walked out on what are effectively training sessions played under the pretext that both teams are trying, when all they are doing is prizing your hard earned from you that could be better spent on other activities that involve alcohol.

This year was no different, however itchy feet finally draws me to a fixture in Gloucestershire, at Forest Green Rovers, with the added prospect of going somewhere new. Ask most people where they actually play and you will most likely receive blank looks, myself included. A bit of research reveals that it's near Stroud, which I know, in Nailsworth, which I don't.

No one I speak to is up for a Tuesday night in the Cotswolds, even the wife, especially the wife, so I post on the internet to see if I can ponce a lift from someone as foolish as me.

The website I sometimes use is 'Loft for words', run by the indomitable Clive Whittingham, a young man wiser than his actual years. This is one of several QPR supporters' websites running. These should not always be sneered at as they often serve a useful purpose. Camaraderie between followers of the same team is commonplace, your own football free masonry without dodgy handshakes and one trouser leg raised knee high. Of course you are much more likely to scratch the back of one of your own than one of the other bastards, whoever those particular bastards happen to be.

It has invaluable uses. I bought Jake's buggy via a friendly 'R's fan Pete in St Neots, and many people I've met via this site have since become good friends to the extent that they attended my wedding.

There is quite a big BUT though, many posters on the chat forums are self obsessed, sad, lonely, vindictive cyber warriors with the mental, as well as the actual age of eleven. This sounds bitter on my part but is borne of arguments held with faceless typists over such wide ranging topics as politics, religion along with the plusses and minuses of playing a 4-5-1 formation at home. This is just a self portrait.

Today however is more positive, as Dave from Ruislip agrees to be my chauffeur, and meet me at Ruislip Gardens station. I arrive wearing a pink carnation and a bowler hat as agreed, but without the necessary essentials on a journey such as this, for me at least, tins of beer.

An uneventful journey is suddenly made into an occasion by Dave's Renault packing up on a B road about seven miles from our destination. My two concerns are being stranded, and more importantly not having time for a pint. Dave is on the blower to the breakdown service, whilst I try to catch cars that pass by, salivating like a rabid dog. Thankfully, unbelievably, I manage to hail a car down, the only one I've ever seen with a QPR sticker actually on the front windscreen. The driver 'Lee', unselfishly turns around us for us, obviously realising that I'm gagging for a pint, and gets us to 'The New Lawn' near to match time.

When you approach, you half expect to arrive at Gloucestershire County Cricket Club rather than a football ground.

Like John Mills' character from 'Ice Cold in Alex', I dive into 'The Green Man', the bar which is built into the stand, even though the game has already started. It is pretty underwhelming watching friendlies, much like watching the reserves or the youth team or frequently, Serie A.

Eventually I stroll in and survey a three sided ground, with only one side open on this summer's evening, a lovely playing surface though. We win by a couple of goals, one scored by the phrase only used pre-season, 'A Trialist'. You've got to say that playing in the Conference looks likely to be Forest Green's limit. It is too small to ever be league worthy, but a nice place to visit in the cup though.

We are none the wiser about our chances for this season, Lee drops us home, too late for the pub, but not too late for the fridge.

July 24

On a roll now, the offer of a lift to Oxford is hard to decline. A Friday night fixture as well, normally a no no, but when football starvation takes a grip, any excuse will suffice.

Most of us haven't been here since the Manor ground days. Try and picture that old style ground hosting Premiership games now. These days they are battling to get out of the Conference, and now play at the Kassam Stadium. What a dreadful name? The eponymous donor is no longer involved, though he still is the owner of the ground, yet the club is lumbered with a legacy of his surname. Likewise John Madjeski down the Thames Valley at Reading, perhaps naming a tank or an aircraft is understandable, underlined in cases such as 'Enola Gay', but an arena? The Sycophant Stadium or the You Gotta Look at Me Ground seems more appropriate.

As an outsider it seems that somewhat dubious practices got this site developed, whereas the previous attempts had failed.

Driven here by Paul Finney, originally from Belfast but now based in London, along with Chris Hewitt, a fellow seasoned England away traveller.

We meet other Rangers at The New Inn, a couple of miles from the ground, now located in Cowley. It certainly doesn't have the feel of going to a football match. Plenty of time for more beer near the ground in The Priory opposite, it's difficult to imagine how much trade this establishment managed to get before the ground was built, or for that matter when there's no match on. In this day and age of public house closures it would seem to be a prime candidate to me.

Here I meet Tom Jacobson, Oxfordshire based Rangers old friend, and I suspect, secret U's fan. He seems to think that Oxford merit their pre-season status as favourites for a return to former league status, then maybe they can build a fourth stand behind one of the goals, rather than just the fence there at present. After a two all draw that under whelms us, we head back to urbanisation and to a fortieth birthday party for Spurs mate Richard Procter. This sees me get indoors at six in the morning. I feel dreadful all day as we go to Ascot races, Diamond Day, to celebrate our first wedding anniversary, complete with gate crasher, Jake. Seven weeks old and he's now been racing but has yet to go to Loftus Road. I think I've got my priorities wrong. My wife agrees with this, but I've a sneaky feeling that this may be for a different reason.

That is it for my early season ornithology. A family wedding in Poland next weekend curtails any flights of fancy that I may have had, though in it's defence, if you've never been to a function like this, let me just say that 'vodka frenzy' is probably the most accurate description.

August 7

My wife stays in Central Europe allowing me two important pleasures, sleep, and unchecked freedom. Here I'm sounding like John McCarthy just released from his Beirut kidnapping hell, but when you've spent much of your life doing as you please, it's nice to do the same once again, without getting a bollocking.

Armed with a selection of credit cards, and overbearing football wanderlust, I plot.

It is paramount that I'm here for Saturday and Tuesday, fortunately the German fixture Gods have, in conjunction with the German television Gods, thrown up a fixture to my liking.

A six o'clock kick off enabling me to catch a flight back the same evening.

Oberhausen is the venue, a small city in the Ruhr, for a second division game against the mighty Union Berlin, the first of their season. Here, my intention is to meet mein Deutsche Freund, Bernd Breitkopf with others, a few beers and back home. All the best laid plans.

Some background here, Union are, or were, an East German side. Champions of the German third tier last term, where I only managed one visit, a two nil victory at Braunschweig, during their all conquering season.

This year, against bigger and better opposition, I promise more attendance, to myself at least.

Bernd with another Anglophile, Oliver, were on a football trip to London when they met loads of us in a pub by Victoria returning from Selhurst Park after an FA Cup 5th Round defeat against Wimbledon in '98.

After putting up with the typical Nazi gags they still stick around drinking with us for the rest of the night and the next day before their flight home.

Bernd then comes over to Rangers a couple of times, and I eventually reciprocate as Union Berlin, a third division side, reach the German Cup Final in 2001, losing unluckily to Schalke 04. Result apart, a great day, one of the highlights being the air raid siren smuggled into the Olympiastadion. I would like to say that when it was activated, half the crowd ran under the stand fearing squadrons of Lancaster bombers passing overhead. This was false, but it was funny nonetheless, how on earth did they get it in the ground? It weighed a ton, albeit a metric one.

In addition Bernd has travelled to England games in Bratislava and Vienna, the former of which ends up with his picture all over the papers, comically surrounded by riot police, watching the match, after they had needlessly baton charged us. It is quite unusual a German following England, but handy when the World Cup is held in Germany. It's not as if the Krauts don't like a drink!

In the morning I potter about, knowing that I have ample time to get to Heathrow for my flight to Dusseldorf at 1.25pm. Passport, credit cards and Euros, no jacket required as it is warm and I'm hard, and stupid.

The tube is straight forward enough, but sloth gets the better of me, so I book a minicab. It was about the time when I am deciding what T-shirt to wear that my wife sends a text asking for me to urgently send a replacement express breast pump as she's broken the other one. From calm to panic in an instant.

The cab is late, there's a queue in Boots, and the man from the penny arcade is in front of me in the Post Office. The result of which sees me get to Terminal 5 a risky thirty five minutes before take off. As I haven't checked in online and the flight has closed, no amount of shouting or grovelling will get me through security. Fuck.

The BA staff manage to placate this sweaty, cursing man by talking to another employee who says that there's a flight at three I can get for another £171. It may have been a bit cheaper, but I booked with BA miles with no refund.

Instead of spending the day sulking, I reluctantly hand over a credit card and pay the extra.

It would have been easier to have hand delivered the fucking breast pump, or have bought a diamond encrusted one made exclusively for the Prada baby range!

The sympathetic ground crew let me go and stew in the business lounge, where I consume as much free Heineken as is possible before the flight, though without a jacket or bag, I can't smuggle out any extra.

Of course, the plane sits on the tarmac longer than I want, and we arrive late.

Deutsche Bahn doesn't let me down though, and a taxi from Oberhausen station gets me to the Niederrheinstadion ten minutes before half time. Ten Euros later and I'm walking into the away terracing, and just as I get to the back of the stand, Union score.

Nonetheless, with half time approaching, we queue for a large amount of beer, which you are allowed to drink anywhere in this unremarkable ground, a running track spoiling your view.

Union manage another couple, in a fine three nil win to get their season up and running, and I say my auf wiedersehns lively to get back to the airport for a Flybe trip to Gatwick.

Even though I get there forty five minutes before the departure time, somehow I still nearly manage to miss check in at a nigh on deserted airport.

A pre-booked cab at Gatwick gets me back to my local comfortably before closing time at midnight.

My brother, Miles, asks how long I was actually in Germany.

'About four hours'.

'You're fucking mad!'

He's not wrong, and poorer, wiser though, remember to check in online and let my wife sort out her own breast implements next time. I'm sure Jake prefers au naturel anyway, as do the rest of us.

August 8

The new domestic season, no Premiership for another week, but apart from the self publicists at Sky, most of us don't care. I can hardly recall an opening day that isn't bathed in sunshine. The powers that be may be able to ruin most things that we hold dear to do with football, but they haven't been able to mess with the weather. Yet I've now got visions of cloud bursting chemicals being used on cup final day.

All the old faces are out for the first game, with the exception of those whose other halves have conveniently booked two weeks in Majorca, leaving at three o'clock this afternoon.

A disappointing 1-1 draw against our old boy Ian Holloway's Blackpool and that courtesy of a fluke equaliser. We may have had most of the possession, but this highlights our need for an out and out finisher. Everyone knows this except it seems our board.

Irrelevancies aside, like the actual game, the post match aftermath turns into the mother of all benders. After terrorising much of Shepherds Bush and Ealing, a motley crew pile back to the den of iniquity that is my place, all through the night and the most of the next day.

Amongst the events the can be recollected include the revelation that one of the party has a different coloured member to the rest of his body. I will change the names to protect the innocent, and only give the internet monikers of some of those involved, including 'GanjR', 'Rodney'sgongger', 'StrangeR', 'The Ram' and, Mr.A.Sharp, hailing from Maidstone, Kent, who is now known as 'le coq noir.'

We haven't laughed so much since Iniesta's late leveller against Chelsea in last season's Champions League semi final.

In the morning, pre-boozer opening, there is a chill out zone in my back garden, with auditions for the world bollocks talking championship taking place. With various corpses strewn about, my neighbour Steve looks over the garden fence and says to my brother, 'Mel's wife still away then.'

This all sounds very immature, because it is, but highlights an important feature of football watching. The match may last ninety minutes, but a dog is for life, not just for Christmas.

August 11/12

By Tuesday I've recovered sufficiently to be on my way from Paddington to Exeter for whatever they call the League Cup these days, tie. A visit to a 'new' ground, with the added bonus of seeing your own team. I find a B & B near the station, quickly dump my bag in the room, a Mexican shower, and back to the station to head for the first event of the day, Newton Abbot Races.

Horse racing then football on a glorious day, a perfect way to lose a pocketful of readies.

Friends have used this time wisely to have family holidays in Devon, especially as we are at Plymouth on the coming Saturday. This is much more convenient than a break in Majorca.

Several others make a day of it like me, though with much more luck than me on the nags.

Idiotically, I don't even back a horse with red and black hooped silks, our 'Dennis the Menace' away strip, which, predictably for everyone else, romps home.

Luckily, being a big fan of drowning sorrows, or joys for that matter, I've already made inroads into my self inflicted misery with best man/best mate Danny Gristwood. We are dropped off in Exeter by his wife Fiona, who departs back to their Dartmoor retreat, leaving us to the difficult task of being blokes.

A minor backstreet pub crawl ensues, gradually gathering fellow day trippers, until the unfortunate incident of a football match breaks out.

There seems to be a fair crowd in St James's Park, especially in the away end, where it is fifteen pounds to stand in a cramped terrace. The Grecians have done remarkably well in the last few seasons since relegation from the Football League in 2003. They were the first team to be automatically demoted without finishing bottom. Now owned by the fans, they have just celebrated two successive promotions, and must be looking to consolidate this season.

A dire first half only accentuates my continuing thirst, and having now ticked off the ground, mates Beefy, Jimmy Naughton and Graysie don't take much convincing in joining my quest for refreshment.

A naïve copper thinks that we're leaving for a brawl, but the old heads there from the Met know better and allow us to proceed to The Wells Tavern just around the corner. We're not the first in there who've left, or didn't bother going in, so after about half a pint there's a loud cheer when it appears on SSN that we are one nil up. Another minor roar before we've finished that pint, and just as a second round is ordered Routledge has completed his hat trick. Drinking up to move on elsewhere, we get a fourth. This has now become comic.

It is not until about half an hour later that now drinking with people who actually saw the whole ninety minutes that I find out it was actually five!

A long day is completed in the company of Brian Kirk amongst others, at 'The Old Firehouse' which is open until two. He found out that handily there is a direct flight from his home, in Belfast, to Exeter so he gets to an unexpected away game. I bail out at closing. I simply cannot drink another drop and stumble into a cab back to the hotel.

There's a knock at the door, 'Mr Huckridge, are you OK? We're worried about you.'

Glancing at my watch it's a quarter past eleven, I've missed breakfast, but it has been well worth it for another couple of hours of undisturbed kip.

Showering quickly and trying to leave on tiptoe to not incur the wrath of the owner, I get collared.

'You should have vacated by eleven.'

'Yeah, sorry.'

Strange people I usually find private hoteliers are, and here is no exception. They give you a look like you've started a dirty protest in your room. When it is only vomit in the bed. The previous occupant's vomit.

Thankfully I'm on an afternoon train and can take my time. A late brekkie, followed by a stroll around this historic city.

Near the cathedral, I notice a couple of lads wearing hideous bright green 'Aviva' training tops with what looks like a budgie for a badge. Further on, a few more are similarly attired, then the birdseed drops that they are the Norwich City squad.

Unable to stop an impulse, and referring to the seven goal home defeat they suffered on Saturday I yell 'Colchester' as they pass. One of the players gives me a glare of daggers. I return the compliment, bring it on you turnip. I've never forgiven Norwich for our defeat at Carrow Road in '76 that ultimately cost us the League title. There is no further incident, they melt. (Bryan Gunn is sacked on the Friday)

Plenty of time to kill before my train home, so I stroll back to the St David's area of the city and a building catches my eye, which conveniently turns out to be a Wetherspoon's public house, 'The Imperial'.

Once it was a grand hotel with a huge arch window, now a perfect place to relax on a humid day such as this. Pear cider is the order of the day, and then, as I try the unusual St Helier Elderflower and Lime variety, I have my Eureka moment. This is as opposed to an Ulrika moment that from what I have imagined, quite a few blokes have experienced.

Now at a crossroads in my life, this is more commonly known as a mid-life crisis. I decide that football, and its related culture is what I think I know, so in my best Bronte style gentle reader, this is what I'm going to write about.

The wife isn't back for a while, so she can't put the mockers on it yet.

Normally England's friendly against Holland would have taken precedence over both my club and I. However Amsterdam does not appeal once you have visited there what feels like a hundred times. Rotterdam as the venue would have made a change.

It is encouraging to hear Fabio Capello's comments regarding the possible selection of goalkeeper Manuel Almunia to the England squad.

'Almunia for me is Spanish, and plays for Arsenal.'

Quite right too, though double check on Zola Budd's availability, and Tony Cascarino is definitely Irish, so that's him ruled out.

Our poor defending is exonerated only by Defoe's finishing, it's only a friendly, but at least it's not a defeat.

August 15

Today is the big one. It's Burton Albion's first home game as part of the ninety two. If this is your first experience of the big time, then this is quite a big deal.

My lot are away at the Janners, and typically, I get offered free match tickets, but have already made plans to attend the Pirelli Stadium, and the chance of a few beers to increase the radius of my spare tyre. Sorry about the poor quality rubber gag there.

There are a friendly bunch of West Brom supporters on the train from St Pancras on their way to Nottingham Forest. Involved in the usual banter you'd associate with people on their way to football. For me at least, this isn't always easy, often I just can't help being Mr Correct. This would normally be in the form of overhearing a conversation in which a fellow passenger would say to another that Quito is Ecuador's most populous city, or more poignantly a statement where a game finished two-nil. No it isn't, and it didn't. It is Guayaquil, and it was two-one, and for the record, the second goal was three yards offside!

Today however, after a late night out at my mates' bar 'The Flowerpot' in Camden, I'm not in the mood for football chat, in fact if it was the Hugh Hefner Playboy branch of the QPR women nymphomaniac supporters club train football quiz challenge, with sexual favours as prizes, I would still struggle.

Changing at Derby for Burton on Trent, here I meet Anthony Robinson, Preston Knob End fan, who likes nothing better than a new ground, and a Jack Daniels.

Discovering that the ground is in walking distance, we set off allowing a couple of hours for pub exploration which finds us in two terraced house boozers, 'The Albert', and 'The Derby Arms', both serving decent ale, and so they should in a brewery town.

Hence, Burton has the cool nickname of 'The Brewers', certainly an admirable one for a football club, along with the likes of 'The Gunners', or 'The Blades'. Better than 'The Cottagers', or 'The Silkmen'. Certainly if you were considering a tattoo, you would be unlikely to pick the latter.

Completely unconnected I've always thought that Bury have the best nickname with 'The Shakers', who could double up as a sixties covers band.

Fifteen quid gets a reasonable half way line seat in a small functional ground where the days' opponents Morecambe, hold up a banner welcoming their hosts to the Football League, which they are fairly new to themselves.

A lively start sees three goals in opening quarter of an hour, great for a neutral. It's a lot easier to watch a game such as this when you do not favour either side, only developing bias as a result of the events that unfurl before you.

Great too, is the half time snack of faggots and mushy peas, which you certainly wouldn't see available at most stadia, certainly not anywhere south of the Watford Gap. Superb.

Five two, is the final score, surprising, mainly because we manage to see all the goals. A disappointing crowd though for an opener, only 2742.

One last pint before heading home where we take in the final scores. I learn that Rangers have conceded a late equaliser at Plymouth. Wankers.

The main talking point of the weekend is the goal that never was at Bristol City. Freddie Sears' strike for Crystal Palace was clearly in to everyone but the referee and linesman. This is a turnaround from the 'goal' that never was last season for Reading at Watford. Disbelief is understandable for both of these. For once you can't moan at Neil Warnock for moaning. In both instances, referees Rob Shoebridge and Stuart Attwell respectively need have only looked for the reaction of the players for an indication of what had occurred. It's their reluctance to admit a mistake or change the decision that gets me. They cannot have a proper feel for the game. If you ask them to kick a football towards you they would no doubt toe punt it. The one goal not given, but in, the other not even vaguely in, but allowed. The humorous fact about the latter is who is credited with scoring? It is listed as an own goal, but as a player you would fairly pissed off if it was you credited with it!

Should we show respect? You would have so much more if for once, a referee would come clean and say for the record, 'I cocked it up.' With these exact words, and be made to officiate his next match dressed as a chicken.

August 18

Side tracked during the day, I leave it too late to go to Ashton Gate, to watch us probably lose at Bristol City. (They do 1-0.Wankers)

Instead, I make the short trip to Kingston, or Norbiton to be exact, to watch the newly promoted AFC Wimbledon. Now they are only one division off their quest to rejoin the elite. Will they enjoy it when they get there?

They share with Kingstonian, a non league team once of note, at Kingsmeadow, and to the outsider, it seems a case of poacher turned gamekeeper. Wimbledon now own the ground after, it seems their original hosts were stiffed, as seems common these days.

Wimbledon, are the football fairy story with a twist. Since their reincarnation in 2002, they've been relentless in their upwardly mobile desire to get back to where they feel they belong, though they only caught the public imagination in the '80s, culminating in their FA Cup triumph in 1988. The cynic in me wonders how many of the followers here, would say they were there then, in the same obtuse way that nobody voted for Thatcher in the same era. Nonetheless, the football going public want them to succeed, like they want their bastard son, MK Dons, to fail, and you can't blame them.

I'm not sure why, but I always feel that many non league followers have a kind of Slavic one thousand yard stare. This is not helped tonight by the fact that Salisbury City, with the same back to back promotions as Wimbledon, has the useful Matt Tubbs up front. His unfortunate surname forces my mind to wander to the 'League of Gentlemen' adage that I can adapt for non league purposes that it is for local people. Which of course it is, because they will never receive national coverage, it still remains the lifeblood of football.

Often though, I cannot but help sometimes feeling superior, like a Manchester United supporter would probably feel that they lord over me. Football snobbery, I hate to admit, is now engrained in our psyche more than ever, and this caste system is widening all the time. Smaller clubs will be happy with their occasional day in the sun, but the big boys are now predefined as being BIG worldwide. The trouble is, they are. To break in to this inner sanctum you need a sugar daddy of immense influence, time and patience. Oh, and a serious amount of hard cash.

I cannot see a 'Wimbledon' ever being victorious in the FA Cup again.

Smaller battles get won however, and they are on the up, perhaps like Albania, whose badge theirs seems to resemble, I think. It wouldn't surprise me these days if King Zog's family were the clandestine owners, claiming that they've always been true fans, because Norman Wisdom had once lived there!

A good crowd of 3591, with the 'home' Temple End full, this only allows a maximum of six rows deep, telling me that if their progression continues they will have to move on, which I'm not sure logistically they can. I cannot think where their new stadium could be located. Plough Lane perhaps?

One up at half time, courtesy of a great strike from Luke Moore, no relation to the Baggies player, whose brother Stefan, played for QPR, of whom I can confidently say he is one of the worst I've ever seen don my beloved hoops, and couldn't hit a dry dock oil tanker with automatic rivet welder. (You get the idea.) He managed to see his full contract out though. Just a minor rant at the mention of his surname.

Four goals to the good at the end, good luck to them, and to Kingstonian, as well as to Salisbury, who are suffering from another curse, the ten point deduction for entering administration.

August 22

Making the most of being loose from my shackles, the last of my BA miles is used for a return flight, the first leg to Zurich to indulge in one of my other great passions, travel.

The benefit of having several obsessions is that you can incorporate watching football with most of them, pretty much anywhere in the world. Even the sex tourist can get a game in. Recently, this popularity (not for sex) was highlighted by the game played in the Galapagos Islands, where Chile's Colo Colo played in the South American Cup. Have you seen the away end? Huge carved stone heads. As they have in Norfolk. That is what you call intimidation.

If England had played there, we would have got the blame for the disappearance of the giant tortoise. Not extinct, but with our help this shouldn't be a problem.

Switzerland always strikes me as a place where you would want to bring up your kids. They'll more than likely grow up well rounded individuals, but as interesting as a piece of toast.

This, of course, is very unfair on a nation that has kept many generations alive, by not being daft enough to join in many wars, albeit turning a blind eye when financing them.

The Swiss rail network, SBB, like its German equivalent, is flawless. Our now privatised narrow gauge money maker pails into insignificance against them. With all our rail history, Stephenson to Brunel, the Rocket to the Mallard and massively important, the football special, count for nothing. Beeching, and Thatcher's privatisation have a lot to answer for.

Nostalgia isn't what it used to be when recalling the days of the supporters train. We were stuffed on the lowest grade available rolling stock, left sitting in the sidings whilst the regular service is allowed to pass through to your destination, getting there in half the time that you or your ugly followers will. Then running out of food and drink with no chance of replenishment for several hours. The coup de grace was losing all of your weeks' wages to a card sharp, and the real dot on the card the unavoidable defeat.

For the young an adventure, for the older and world weary, a long day. My memory doesn't paint these outings in such a glamorous light, though if pressed then I would have said they were superb. They weren't.

The appearance, as I pull into Zurich main station, of a Junkers Ju52 tri-motor transport plane flying overhead adds to the romance of being away. This was probably used in transporting Nazi gold bullion to Argentina.

Not long to wait, I change trains to travel lakeside to Sargans.

From then, outside the station, a number 12 bus transports me to another nation's capital, and only city, Vaduz.

At least in this tax haven, the national side actually play their matches within its boundaries.

Flanked by the Rhine on one side, and Austria on the other, my hour in Liechtenstein was as uneventful as an episode of 'Songs of Praise'.

Been there, not concerned about obtaining the passport stamp available at the Post Office, done that.

Now back to Sargans and a train to St Gallen to watch the Swiss play a game. Funny really in a nation that has the control of both European and world football that no one seems to take an interest in theirs.

Surprisingly to me, St Gallen are the second oldest team in continental Europe, 1879, but more importantly knocked Chelsea out of the UEFA Cup in 2000. Got to be worth homage for that alone!

The Swiss League is weird, only 10 teams, but thankfully they don't have to wear skis.

As you've seen stereotyping is all too easy here, especially as we, England, managed to avoid the 2008 Euros, and so the chance to help try and change the perception of another much ridiculed or possibly misunderstood nation was missed.

Located outside the city centre, a free bus ride, ie don't bother buying a ticket, takes me to the AFG Arena. The cost of 25 SFR to stand, in a 20,000 capacity ground which is only a year or so old, with a passion of which I had not expected.

As mentioned, Switzerland is home to the two most important football federations in the world, it passes you by that they may be human like us, in a footballing sense at least.

One thing that I wonder about, is, as I watch the home end singing in German, is if all the team's following here sings in the same language. My last time here saw us watch England beat Argentina in Geneva, or would have done if my brother and I hadn't left at 2-1 down, only for Owen to get two late goals. This was in Geneva, a French speaking area, at the ground of Servette. Surely a language difference would create more than just rivalry? Or would you not know what the opposition are singing about? Or would they completely nonplussed by it all? Taking a neutral stance?

An unusual 5.45 kick off time is not the only odd custom here. They adopt the credit card system for buying refreshments, obviously designed to stop fraud, and if anyone should know about this, you would imagine it is here. Bit of a pain though, if you only visit the once, as you are likely to have credit remaining, so I have two beers and two hot dogs just to make sure.

To my left in the corner of the usual seats, there's the unusual spectacle of a sofa bang in the middle of the stand, probably for a competition winner. You'd rather win the actual sofa though.

The host's kit is green and white hoops, more Sporting Lisbon than Celtic, and they send the crowd home happy with an unconvincing goal late on, the only one of the game against Aarau, a town from the east of the country.

I've got to say that it was a lot livelier than I expected naïve of me not to think so, Hopp St Gallen indeed.

A quick look around St Gallen's 'Aldstadt', then cross canton to change at Buchs, which is, for an hour while I wait for the sleeper, full of the cast of the Swiss version of 'High Street Musical'. Let's see how passionate the Italians really are as I look to cross the Dolomites.

QPR, after being a goal ahead at home, allow Forest to fight back for a point. Wankers.

August 23

It's difficult to sleep in a sleeping compartment on a train.

Being 6' 3" doesn't help. Once, on a summer journey from Prague to Budapest in the upper berth, I remember my feet semi-dangling out of the window, and in my half slumber, being concerned that their dismembering would be like a shark bite is meant to feel, just a warm sensation. Then later, I'd wake up screaming when noticing their absence.

I was in the buffet car at the time.

Alcohol usually gives you a fake sleep that you make do with. That is until you get woken up by passport control, or a noisy bunch of drunks stumbling in to the wrong compartment, or as is the case tonight, I kid you not, two German speaking girls, who are sharing a cabin with me. They get on at a stop further down the line. The sight of me lying in boxers with my hairy back prominent plainly inspires these Teutonic shot putters to not stop talking all fucking night. Whispering in an enclosed space is not whispering, even if it is dulled by the sound of a moving train, with its endless jolts and shudders.

Needless to say, that at six in the morning, when we arrive in Villachs, Austria, I haven't had much sleep and this isn't because I was hoping for a threesome.

After three quarters of an hour wait in the cafe outside the station, the rest of the journey is to be continued by bus to Udine. (Pronounced like the escapologist.)

General tiredness increases my irritability, especially with a Venice day tripper woman, who insists on parking her considerable bulk next to me because it is her designated seat number, when there are plenty of pairs of spare seats all around. Stupid cow. You get people like this at football too. Always it seems, next to me.

A scenic journey that includes some seriously engineered tunnels, is assisted by the Ipod shuffle option throwing up a good selection of the 5000 tunes encrypted thus, not much need for the fast forward button,

Gun Law – The Kane Gang
Everything in its right place – Radiohead
Caramel – Suzanne Vega
Bruce Forsythe – Derek & Clive
Make another world – Idlewild

Jacob's ladder – Rush
Colours in waves - South
Robot sympathy – The Flaming Lips
The Fix – Elbow
Revol – Manic Street Preachers
Bullet with butterfly wings – Smashing Pumpkins
Harvester of eyes – Blue Oyster Cult
Work, work, work – The Rakes
You are the sunshine of my life – Stevie Wonder
Mammoth – Interpol
Nah' mean, Nah'm sayin' – The Herbaliser
Summer Breeze – The Isley Bros

Poignantly, Mr Blue Sky – ELO, have you ever met anyone that doesn't like this song? How uplifting is the outro?

Included on my player are very few songs with a footballing theme. World in motion is the only really credible tune ever written with this in mind. Apart from Hoddle and Waddle's 'Diamond Lights', this goes without saying.

Just pulling into Udine and the live version of a proper rock song, Highway Star by Deep Purple ends my daydreaming.

I should remember not to play air guitar in public places, and to unplug my air amp before departing the tour bus.

As it's only just gone eight in the morning, I wonder if I can check into a hotel without paying for a pre-night booking.

The first wants sixty Euros, as does the second, but noticing my reluctance, immediately makes me a better offer of fifty, not surprising as virtually every key seems to be in the rack. Too good to turn down and too knackered to haggle, I concur and grab a few hours.

A shower and lunch later, and off out to see the sites. To be honest, there don't seem to be too many here and it seems to be a bit of a ghost town on a Sunday. On a day as beautiful as this, perhaps everyone has headed down to the coast, surely though many will be back to see their local team for the first game of the season? As we're constantly reminded Italians are passionate about calcio.

By chance, I'm introduced to Spritz, an aperitif of Aperol or Campari mixed with

Prosecco or sparkling white wine, soda and a slice of orange. Much like Pimms and lemonade, on a hot day, it hits the spot.

This weekend, Usain Bolt again makes other sprinters look like they're running the three legged race, I also receive a text from Danny whilst sipping on my new liquid friend that Steve Harmison is on a hat-trick to win the Ashes. Great, but will it be MBEs all round? These may have to be upgraded to OBEs for Strauss and the like as they have them from last time. Didn't take the gongs back when they lost five nil in Oz did they?

My cynicism does not end here. Sitting in the land of the World Cup holders, won, albeit with a very ordinary side, a country that is meant to eat, drink, and sleep football. Scratch the surface and all is not well. Attendances for Serie A are now only the fifth highest in Europe, behind the Bundesliga, the Premiership, La Liga and believe it or not the Championship (Division two to most people.)

Apart from derby games, tickets over here are easy to come by, certainly I've never previously had a problem in Genoa, Milan, Rome, and Turin.

From a nation where everyone seems to have an opinion on everything calcio, this is now more likely to emanate from television coverage than from behind the goal.

Much has changed since the days of Channel Four's live matches. English and Spanish sides now dominate UEFA competitions, the fear factor that once prevailed when playing an away leg here, is now much diminished.

Then there is the seemingly constant scandals and corruption, that shouldn't surprise anybody with a country that has Berlusconi as a President, with or without the Axl Rose headscarf.

My evening appointment, Udinese, on the other hand, have been a relative success story, qualifying for the UEFA Cup and then the Champions League in recent seasons.

Recalling as I do the Stadium Friuli from the 1990 WC, with three of its sides uncovered, a huge arch down on one side, and where three matches took place, and I've always fancied coming here. This is in a strange, that would be an unusual ground to visit sort of way, that people like me tend to suffer from.

I get to the ground early, as the stalls are setting up outside, which is just as well as I try to buy a ticket only to be refused as my I.D is not sufficient. I should have known better, last year at Empoli, slunk in on a romantic weekend in Florence, they checked my passport at the same time you bought the ticket and then once more as I gained entry to the stadium, but I didn't take enough heed of it. An Italian inquisition takes place, a helpful Tom Hanks lookalike speaks to his boss, then the stewards, the police and anyone else with an opinion, but the fact remains that I'm obviously a seven nation army and can't be trusted to watch the game without starting a white riot, thus I must first prove who I am. Next time, I'll leave the balaclava behind.

Jumping back on the bus, my pidgin Latin works wonders for two more free journeys from and back to the stadium. 15 Euros finally gets me in the Curva Nord revealing another municipal stadium with an eight lane running track in a state of disrepair.

An unimpressive crowd (15383) with a paltry following from Parma, back in the top division after a season's absence, with as many flags as supporters it appears. They are even more of success story than Udinese. Winners of both the Cup Winners Cup and the UEFA Cup in the '90s. The collapse of Parmalat, their generous sponsor, didn't aid their quest to continue with these feats though.

A game not without incident, the home side hit the bar after ten minutes, but just on half time by my watch, Parma take the lead. The arbitro (ref) probably added at least a minute for the time it took the players to celebrate the goal. Virtually the whole team run over to the small pocket of fans. You know the drill, over advertising boards across the track and clamber onto the fence. At home it would be yellow cards all round, but here, a blind eye is turned.

Ironically, this costs them the lead. Udinese miss a good chance, have a penalty appeal turned down and then gets awarded one. In all likelihood, in the time that Parma wasted poncing around celebrating, the spot kick would not have been awarded. Di Natale scores by chipping straight down the middle, a method that makes you look stupid if you miss.

Parma dominates the opening quarter of the second half and go ahead from a headed set piece. The crowd get on the black and white shirted home teams backs until a late, great strike from the old warhorse Di Natale earns a point.

Final score, due – due.

The same bus driver checks every ticket, but waves the mad Englishman on board almost as if I'm a now regular with a freedom pass.

The temptation of a late night pizza, with kebab meat, is too hard to resist. Cin cin.

I crash out watching a late night football show surprised to see two famous names now in management, Roberto Donadoni, the Napoli manager whose curls have turned grey, and former keeper Walter Zenga, now the Palermo manager, bald as a coot.

August 24

Up early, to get the train to first Venice, then Bologna, and finally to the seaside at Rimini.

I wile away the journey with the daily pink paper 'La Gazetta Della Sport'. Not the Italian Gay Times for those of you who are uninitiated in daily papers that are not 'The Sun'. This rag is totally dedicated to footie, with a few minor sports tagged on at the end just to make the numbers up. Even though my Italian is poor, I can usually get the gist of what's written. This is not always the case however, this morning, looking through the foreign section a stray across the headline

'Dramma Davenport rischia l'amputazione.' This most definitely seems to be lost in translation.

I manage to decipher the words '26 anni' (Why do they always have the age?) and police, and the like from the main column, but amputation? Bloody hell. This refers to West Ham's Callum Davenport, but as to what has exactly has happened I'm left stumped until I return.

On a lighter note, I get to Rimini, and quickly find a reasonable hotel. Then wait for the bus for a fifty five minute uphill excursion to the picturesque nation of San Marino, which transpires to be a haven of duty free and tat. En route I meet a couple of fellas who have been to a rock 'n' roll weekend further down the coast, and with whom I share a beer after a brief look around complete with obligatory photo. That's another country coloured in on my map of Europe.

Returning to Rimini, I catch some late afternoon rays and dip my toe in the Adriatic. The ludicrously packed shoreline is a sea of sunshades and private beach areas which I wouldn't recommend.

A couple of beers, a calzone, a gelati and a shower later, and off to the station for the short trip to Cesena, who conveniently, are playing Reggina in a Serie B match, one of only two fixtures taking place in Italy tonight. Having seen the Stadio Dino Manuzzi from the train tracks when passing by earlier, I waste no time in having to ask the usual 'Scusi, sloppy Giuseppe, where is the calcio, grazie? This never normally gets me anywhere but nowhere.

A quarter of an hour later and I'm in their boozer next to the stadium 'Bombonera', as in the nickname of Boca Juniors ground. This appears to be where their 'ultras' go, the WSB. I assume this stands for West Side Boys or something similar, but it's 'Weiss Schwarz Brigade' after the teams colours, but in German? Even my basic grasp of the lingo would mean it would be 'bianco nero'. It turns out it is out of respect for former player Walter Schachner, an Austrian hero who played here in the early '80s.

Cesena are newly promoted from Serie C to B, and they once had a certain Marcelo Lippi as manager when they were last in Serie A. Reggina, located on the toe of Italy, are just relegated, and the game starts at a lively pace. I instantly like the ground, similar in style to some of ours, my opinion is shaped by a noisy crowd, and the fact that there is no athletics track to spoil the view and ruin the atmosphere. Of course my bias is tempered further by the fact I paid eleven Euros for the pleasure of standing. Here I get chatting to spectators around me, thankfully one of them, Marco, speaks decent enough English, and so he gives me a potted history of the Seahorses, a great nickname. With a bit of prompting by yours truly, there is a constant stream of sorties to the back of stand to the vendor serving Moretti lager, which here, you can drink whilst watching the match.

Unfortunately for Cesena, the away side score a well worked headed goal near the end, but the 11000 home support give their heroes a generous round of applause for effort.

As the game hadn't kicked off until 8.45, I don't get back to Rimini until gone midnight, and even though it is a Monday, this is tourist resort so everywhere stays open until late, more than enough time for several nightcaps to end an enjoyable evening.

August 25

Back to Blighty, looking forward to seeing my wife and son, also back today, Jake's probably over six feet tall by now.

At Bologna airport passing through security, I notice several sporty looking blokes all wearing burgundy polo shirts. Closer inspection reveals that they are indeed the Reggina squad flying back to the south. Their flight is departing on the berth next to mine, so I ask if anyone speaks English. One does fluently, thus I explain that I was at last night's game and would like to meet the goal scorer. He duly obliges pointing him out, and I get to shake hands with one Nicolas Viola, who happily lets me have a photo taken with him. Marco, who I met last night, gave me his business card so I'll email this photo to him. Hopefully he has a sense of humour.

If you land at Gatwick as I do today, a little travel tip, unless you are in a rush, don't get the 'Gatwick Express', board the slower train, which only takes about ten minutes longer, and may well be the first train out anyhow, getting to Victoria before the licence to print money train does. You can get a return which you won't use, but has a six zone travelcard included for you to use anywhere on the tube network, as I will tonight, and it is considerably cheaper than the former. They don't advertise this freely.

My wife seems pleased to see me, but not so happy when she discovers that Rangers are at home tonight.

It's the second round of the League Cup and we're at home to Accrington Stanley. Exactly.

That famous milk advert is the extent of most people's knowledge of the Lancashire club.

After they folded in 1962 they pretty much disappeared off the football radar, but made a welcome return forty four years on.

The prices tonight are reduced to a tenner, though most of us would have much rather visited their ground. I've now seen every league team play, but have yet to complete all the stadia.

The few regulars attending tonight's tie at Rangers, chat as though the match is incidental, which actually it is. The League Cup, our only significant trophy, has been devalued to a serious extent.

Tom reckons that there are 132 Accrington fans in the School End. Mainly because he bothered to count them. This highlights how gripping the proceedings are. We just want to go through, and they are hoping for a shock. Worst of all would be extra time and penalties, leaving hardly any time for a post match beer. No longer do you get replays in this competition. At least the previous round used to be played over two legs, and gave you the chance to visit somewhere novel.

Every credit to the small gathering in the away end. They produce a large St Georges flag bearing the legend 'STANLEY ULTRAS', however, it seems, that not enough people volunteer to help in holding it aloft, keeping us all amused. To a certain extent I know the feeling. You buy one of these, with the logic the bigger the better, but often less is often more.

Mine, bought for three hundred quid, and made a successful debut at Hillsborough in 2004 on the day we got promoted. It was draped over the front of the top tier of the Leppings Lane End, a name that we all unfortunately know too well.

Since then, with a couple of exceptions, it is often more of a hindrance than, well, it is always a hindrance. You drag it around like Linus's blanket from Charlie Brown, bar to bar, city to city.

The best exception though was at England v Paraguay in Frankfurt in the first group game of World Cup 2006. Two friends, Wiggy, and Pat, who is sadly no longer with us, managed to get tickets for the Paraguayan section. As usual the stadium was filled with all manner of red crossed flags, although Danny and I could not stop laughing when ours is held aloft amongst the only area of the ground not Anglican.

This may not seem hysterical to you, but it is images of Neil Armstrong, or the GI's finally overcoming the fierce resistance at Iwo Jima. More appropriate for us would be Edmund Hillary, Agincourt or Waterloo.

In an era of relative peace, we still cling, subconsciously or otherwise, to our tribal instinct and our inner need to belong. Plus there is a good chance your mates might see you when they watch it on the telly.

The final score is 2-1, thankfully no extra time to make us feel guilty about going to the pub early.

Looking forward to Saturday's draw, someone decent but beatable, at home, this is what most would like, but we are very unlikely to get.

The same evening there's trouble at West Ham v Millwall. Well that is a surprise. Tea at 'The Ritz' it is never going to be.

It would be more surprising if there was no violence at all. Watching the footage, it did seem that the Hammer's fans looked somewhat upset. The rumour had got out that one of their own had been stabbed, this was incorrect, but there is nothing like a Chinese whisper to create an angry mob. This is also a rumour.

UEFA, being the omniscient presence that they are, charge Eduardo, he of the ninety degree shin, with diving whilst conning a penalty against Celtic. This has worms written all over the side of the can. Would the same action be taken if the offence had happened in a less important area of the pitch?

August 29

There's an episode of 'Red Dwarf' from Series eight, episode six that goes something like this.

Kryten, the android, in regard to a collection of humans frozen in time says 'I've never seen such a thing. A group of people who show all normal life signs, but seem totally incapable of movement.'

Holly, the computer with the deadpan face replies, 'Never seen QPR away from home then?'

To the non Ranger this does not mean much, but to me this was a moment when you splutter coffee or something stronger over all and sundry as you explode with a mixture of laughter and surprise. It is not as if I can disagree. At times, on our travels over the years, we have been pitiful, especially 'Oop North'.

I can picture the conversation in the snug bar at 'The Whippet and Wife Beater' before a match in early December.

'Who've we got today Postlethwaite?'

'Queen's Park Rangers, Southern softie shandy sipping shitters.'

'Great, that's a sure-fire win then, by at least three clear goals.'

'Aye, they should wear frilly blouses and bonnets instead of shorts and jerseys. Probably play better an all.'

''Appen they would.'

This is what it is usually like to waste your day going away with us, knowing deep down, that you will lose.

Today however, buoyed by the fact we have loaned a forward, Jay Simpson, unproven, but a forward nonetheless, I decide to make the journey to Scunthorpe. My last visit here was two seasons ago, an enjoyable drunken day out. Coach stops in Doncaster on the way up, and Retford on the return, a two all draw, no grief, I counted them all in, and I counted them all back again. Scunny were relegated that season but managed to return via a play off final victory over Millwall in a thrilling match which I also attended courtesy of free ticket. Every credit should be given to Nigel Adkins, the physio turned manager, who has done a fantastic job here, although they are one of the favourites to be relegated once again.

Travel today involves the quick, if too expensive train to Peterborough from King's Cross, where I'm collected by Paul Pickwell, who hails from Peterborough, and who we call Peterborough Paul, being the articulate and original name givers we are. Scott is also in the car; he follows Motherwell, but is coming with us for the day out, and is known as Scott. I hope this is clear, however irrelevant.

An easy drive gets us to Glanford Park, which, as far as I am aware, was the first of the 'new' grounds, replacing the 'Old Show Ground' in 1988. Coincidentally, along with London Road, Peterborough, they are the only grounds left in the top two divisions to have terracing remaining; no doubt this will have to be adapted to accommodate seating in following the league regulations within the next couple of seasons. A case of sit down shut up. Parking is easy enough, as it's situated on an edge of town entertainment complex with all the charm of napalm, as does 'The Old Farmhouse', the Wacky Warehouse pub where we are forced to go for a drink.

Contradicting my earlier Rangers are shit away from home and are bound to lose comments, we don't, and hold on for a win after taking an early lead through our skilful Moroccan loan star Adel Taarabt.

Afterwards, the three of us get a beer in the late afternoon sun at 'Frankie and

Benny's' one of a chain of flat pack American bar/diners, which is next to the ground's gates. These are decorated with the logo of 'The Iron', you would hope this is made of the same, or more than likely stainless steel, imported from a factory in China chances are.

The ground and surrounding car parks have cleared fairly quickly and it no time it appears that we are virtually alone. I cannot envisage anyone wanting to come here on Saturday night, or any other night for that matter, especially having to travel out of town. However, most modern stadia are built with at least these features as minimum criteria. It seems this is the only way that planning permission is granted, as long as you can watch a movie and eat a taco. In this place though you'd only get a pizza, as I can't see any trace of a cinema, maybe it wasn't the proviso in the early days of seeking approval. We head south and I hope for the locals for whom these services are provided, that this is what they want, as I find that more often than not, the public wants what the public gets.

August 31

The last bank holiday until Christmas day, when up until recently there used to be a full programme of footie, giving police forces around the country, especially the ones on coastal resorts, a month's worth of paperwork on one day. Certainly the 80s were an era where this seemed as usual as wearing a Pringle diamond cut jumper did at the time. I recall getting a split lip at Southampton in '83 as a green nineteen year old with my blood all over the collar of my Adidas 'Ivan Lendl' t-shirt, though it probably looked like part of the pattern.

No chance of that today however, mainly due to the fact that the rozzers have had a word with the fixture setters and kiboshed those days to the history books, certainly for the bigger teams.

Other options today include the Notting Hill Carnival of which I am not a fan. For a while I lived in the area off Ladbroke Grove, it's non stop bass lines, people blowing whistles and showing how wild they are blowing marijuana smoke in the direction of a dancing copper, give me a rock festival through the streets instead, as if that would be allowed.

However, attending a game in West London today is still possible.

Sloping off before two, saying that I'll be back by six, with Bea none the wiser, and not suspecting that there are any matches today.

Wealdstone FC is who I surreptitiously sneak to see, my 'non League team'. These days now playing at the old ground of Ruislip Manor, finally settling here after a nomadic existence for nearly twenty years after their original ground, Lower Mead, was sold to make way for a Tescos, under very dubious circumstances.

This is commonplace all over the country, but seems more prevalent in the London region, where land prices are high. Without having to give too much contemplation, just in what is now left of Middlesex, teams such as Edgware, Enfield, Hendon, and Southall have all lost their homes over recent seasons, and are now either defunct or ground sharing.

They all have a proud history, and Wealdstone, are up there with some of the most famous non league sides, in the last years before automatic promotion to the fourth division, they just fell short of election to the Football League. They did the non League double in '85, defeating Boston United in the Trophy Final, who themselves have since flirted with professional status, but in a manner similar to the Stones, pretty much are back to a level to where their conquerors that day are now. Stuart Pearce, Vinny Jones and more recently Jermaine Beckford are renowned former wearers of the shirt, underlining their pedigree. Well some of it, make your own minds up here.

The Ryman or Isthmian League is always a tough one to get out of, an enigma for most to fathom, certainly for the pyramid plotters of the football hierarchy. Today's opponents Sutton United, one time conquerors of Coventry City, at the time FA Cup winners only two seasons before, underline this fact.

The Stones are managed by Gordon Bartlett, for what feels like an eternity. It's a tenner to get in, I add to what turns out to be a bumper crowd of 480, and look for a comfortable barrier to lean on and watch proceedings. The new ground 'The Vale', former home of Ruislip Manor, is not great compared to previous locations, but it's now home, and much deserved, even if it is a compromise that their followers must accept reluctantly.

Looking around to see if I can identify anybody, immediately I nod at faces that I know but not exactly sure where from, or you're unsure of their names, until I meet Dave Jones, an old friend.

A half time pint reveals a poster in the club house of a friendly in '78 against Udinese, then on a par, coincidental for me, and a marker of what can be achieved with dedication, and a good side.

I recognise the voice of Peter John Baptiste, as the half time announcer, England follower and avid Stones fan. Where in league football would you still hear 'Rip it up' by Orange Juice over the loudspeaker? A song a quarter of a century old, and not even on re-release? This is not a criticism; all you'll get elsewhere is some vacuous cover by an embryo from 'X' Factor. Maybe I'm just being nostalgic, but I like the fact that this can still happen.

Sutton take a second half lead, but are pegged back late on, giving rise to a frenetic finish in which Wealdstone score to win 2-1, where, it seems that half the players end up in the net in their efforts to either prevent or force the ball in.

Last minute winners, the raison d'etre of going to watch football live. Nothing can equal the feeling of elation shared jointly amongst everybody around you, who celebrate without a hint of embarrassment in whatever way they deem suitable. The previous 89 minutes become irrelevant instantly.

David Platt, Alan Sunderland, Ole Gunnar Solskaer are the three scorers, from off the top of my head, of late, late goals that should need no introduction, and fall into the category of 'jump around' or 'let's go fuckin' mental'. Less noted, but no less important, is my particular favourite, that of the then Carlisle United keeper Jimmy Glass. This works on several levels, firstly the fact that he is the nutter between the sticks who actually manages to score is a novelty in itself. He only played three games in his loan spell, but scored the only senior goal of his career. This goal kept the Cumbrians in the Football League in 1999. The build up of forty six matches hinging on that one moment.

Best of all, is the reaction of the supporters. Brunton Park goes ballistic, and invades the pitch. I did have this goal on video, and once replayed the celebrations over and over, each time focusing on a different fan's reaction. If you get the chance watch it, especially the bloke in the white top who dives on the ref. Brilliant. Only a Scarborough supporter, whose team were sent down as a result of the goalie's half volley, would have hearts hard enough not to enjoy it. A heart of glass?

In my local, the Black Horse, the warm weather has made the beer garden almost a crèche, and my wife is there showing off our little man. I'm home before she's noticed that I've been away. Until now!

September 3/10

We board a Boeing 777 bound for Tobago on a family holiday that was booked in advance of the young Huckridge being with us. We're a bit nervous about taking a twelve week old baby to the Caribbean, as I'm certainly no Dr Benjamin Spock, or Leonard Nimoy for that matter. Jake is, I suppose, what would be considered a 'happy' baby, and despite the horror stories I've been told, is fine on the flight, the BA staff are good in situations like this, the crib is prepared if you want it. It's funny for my hypocritical self, previously cursing crying offspring on night flights as the devil's spawn, but now, a shrug of the shoulders is a sufficient apology to any dissent when your flesh and blood ruins their slumber. Put your headphones on, I gesture, with mock apology, watch the films, I'm sure one of them is decent, knowing full well that the stewardess will always side with the family unit in the event of any disturbance. Thankfully none of this is necessary. Jake is a good baby. Of course he is, he's mine. No blinkers on here.

No football this week insists my beautiful wife, and she's right, it's international week and there is nothing to be remotely concerned about.

In the taxi from the airport to our resort, I can't help but notice a sign for the town of 'Bon Accord', the team at the receiving end of the world record defeat I recall. No! Don't. Switch off from all thoughts football based. Thirty six nil they lost, against Arbroath. Probably a team of fishermen, more than likely playing their wives, only seven of 'em, covered in haddock, eleven of the goals were offside, and one went through a hole in the net, if indeed there was a net, if indeed there was a goal frame, jumpers probably the order of the day. Jumpers made out of fishing nets and being towed by a trawler. The second half was played on the shore, with Mrs McKipper in goal, up to her knees in sea water, with starfish for gloves. Captain Ahab was the referee, with Moby Dick main boy for the home side.

I've only been away a day and already I'm suffering from withdrawal symptoms.

Our resort, Turtle Beach, is not at all bad, with our room actually on the beach, not much cop in the event of tsunami my wife points out, though thankfully the television has BBC World which makes everything hunky dory in my eyes.

The first piece of news that I glean from this medium, is that Chelsea have received a one year ban from UEFA for 'tapping up' Lens youngster Gael Kakuta two seasons ago. This is as unexpected as it is pleasing, and not just because it is happening to Chelsea, although it helps.

Anybody with half a brain knows that this goes on, not just in football circles but in life. Here it seems that one of the larger clubs has been caught with their fingers in the till, or should that be with a player trying on their kit?

A pleasant break ensues, though it is pretty hard to go wrong in the Caribbean. I leave my phone switched off, and proceed to get a tan in this beautiful tropical paradise.

Of course, Tobago is the smaller of the two islands that make up the nation that most shorten to Trinidad.

England played T & T in Nuremburg on a hot late afternoon during the 2006 World Cup, where we ended up that night in the nice town of Bamberg drinking the local smoked beer, a novelty for me. The match earlier is infamous for Peter Crouch's goal, a header where he yanks the dreadlocks of centre half Brent Sancho which is pretty clever in my opinion. Clever if you get away with it. The same could be said of the more infamous Maradona 'Hand of God' goal in Mexico, twenty years earlier. Except that this was cheating, as it was against us.

More recently, the same fixture was played as a friendly just over a year ago, and careful of what I write here, not, of course, to curry favour with Jack Warner, the FIFA Vice President and President of CONCACAF, to assist with vote for the 2018 World Cup bid. Many used the opportunity to have a holiday and go to the match as a sideline. This actually works out just as cheap, if not cheaper to do this when a game is in such a location, but because of our impending wedding, this was not possible for us. When I say us, I mean me. If I had gone the whole deal was off. We have though previously managed to combine the two when England played in Macedonia, taking in the Greek sunspots of Skiathos and Thessaloniki on the same trip. This has a down side, when your better half finally realises that it is not just about the fixture, more about being there. In Skopje, Bea had to inform me that Crouch had scored what turned out to be the only goal, as I was otherwise involved at the bar, for about twenty five minutes.

Eventually I find out the results from Saturday, England have won their friendly against Slovenia, and Northern Ireland and Scotland still have slim play off chances at least. Studying the permutations, it could be that Argentina won't qualify after a home defeat to Brazil. This, of course, is not going to happen. They will. The dice are loaded in most of the WC qualifying groups; it can be argued that Europe and perhaps Africa are the only ones that are not. Not as much.

T & T have lost 4-1 in Honduras, so Mr Warner's travel company look unlikely to be making money on tickets for this coming World Cup, eh Jack!

It's good to be away, browsing the news on BBC World underlines this.

A woman in Sudan is being prosecuted for wearing trousers. Israel is taking liberties on the West Bank. Potential compensation for IRA victims from Libya, blaming the gun not the perpetrator, I Wish hadn't switched it on.

Looking at the forthcoming fixtures from around the globe, I discover gleefully that T & T are at home Wednesday. Further investigation reveals that this game is easily doable. Frankly, Bea is more than happy to get rid of me for most of the day whilst she and Jake take a tour around Tobago.

Another plus point is the Caribbean Air airbridge service between the islands. Just 24 US Dollars each way, booking at any time, flights roughly every hour or so until about eleven at night.

In the early afternoon the turboprop Dash 8 flies me for about twenty minutes on the sort of route that you wish you could always fly.

It is with a small amount of trepidation that I take a taxi from the airport to Port of Spain, the capital. Although any tales of Trinidad's potential terrors are unwarranted in my case. The taxi fare costs more than the return air fare, but with little time or choice, I arrange for the cabbie to pick me up later.

After a quick mosey around, I take a stroll towards the stadium named after the islands most famous son, Hasely Crawford, the Olympic 100 metres champion from 1976. Brain Lara may have since eclipsed his fame since, and Dwight Yorke has a smaller stadium named after him on Tobago, but the original 'man' is Hasely.

Passing a couple of decent hotels en route, I pause to see if England v Croatia is being shown anywhere. In one, Northern Ireland v Slovakia is on live, and although I don't know it until returning back to London, I get chatting to football agent Eric Walters. He's obviously here protecting his interests, or on a jolly. Turns out he's agent for several of the QPR players too, only putting two and two together later does the total add up to four. Wish I'd asked him for a complimentary ticket, as purchasing a ticket soon after sets me back the equivalent to thirty quid, costly, for out here.

The ground is, in fact, more like a three in one sports centre, incorporating tennis and basketball, with the back of each stand becoming the front of another. Pressing on across the road to Movie Towne, the sort of modern entertainment complex that is now commonplace Nationwide and it seems worldwide. I am not interested in watching a movie, or having an authentic Mexican food experience, surely what is left of the game is on somewhere? Alex and Darren, two Aberdonian oil industry workers, have the same idea, and are searching for the Scotland v Netherlands match. We settle on a restaurant/diner called Zanzibar which seems to be showing every worldwide qualifier except the ones we want. The first round of bottled Carib is ordered, and before I've had two mouthfuls a second is lined up in front of me. I like these blokes already. (For the record, Stag is a better local beer.)

As the beer flows, we keep half an eye on the wall of screens in front of us for updates. The news filters through that England have banished the memory of the Scott Carson/Steve McClaren umbrella disaster to the record books by beating Croatia 5-1. Northern Ireland and Scotland are not so lucky and go out. More live South American qualifiers are shown as we drink and talk, having to force ourselves to make the short walk via the inevitable pit stop at Burger King and make kick off at the strange time of 7.11.

A big uncovered stadium as one would expect in this climate, but only one third full. The excessive price can't have helped, as can the lack of followers from the World's richest nation, who clearly haven't embraced the concept of the away day to the same extent as we have.

Still thirsty, I go to get a round in, and am offered a deal for twelve small tins for the price of ten with a free cooler bag thrown in by the buxom Carib girls. Alex also takes advantage of this never to be repeated offer, so we have enough to last the ninety minutes.

The incessant drumming tries to inspire the SOCA Warriors, who, on the face of it have some decent players, Kenwyne Jones, Carlos Edwards, J Lloyd Samuel, Jason Scotland and the like. However, a local boy catches the eye, Hayden Tinto, a diminutive winger whose runs fail to materialise into goals, giving you the feeling that T & T just don't have the belief in themselves to go on and win.

As we lounge about, chatting with anyone who'll care to listen and share a lager, I can't help myself from singing to myself 'North American Scum' by LCD Soundsystem. As I suspected, the Septics get the goal they don't look like getting, and will be heading to the World Cup.

We head back to my pre-booked taxi; the driver knows that I've got to get back to the airport for the last flight. The Scots lads are staying at a hotel on the way, so I agree to drop them off, but we have to wait about fifteen minutes for another passenger who the cabbie has also booked. I think that we are cutting this fine, especially as we have to now negotiate the traffic.

Eventually our surrogate fare arrives, of all people a Jewish New Yorker. He is as unprepared for us as we are for him, and we lie in ambush for him to say the ultimate blasphemous word, soccer. There is no special relationship in the world of football. To be fair he knows his stuff, so we relent with the interrogation and I give him a beer as he is one of the only Yanks to have made the effort, there is a direct flight to Port of Spain from New York.

After dropping everyone off, I am just in time; Mr Taxi driver then proceeds to ask for more than I'd originally been charged on the inward journey, and asks if he can have the cool bag. What a piss taker, already having collected from our Yankee buddy, keeping me waiting all that time. There is always someone that can ruin an enjoyable day. I throw the cash at him, and kind of hope he will make a scene, but surely knowing he is in the wrong, he doesn't. Leaving me to swear and rush to the gate. The security doesn't seem too concerned that I have an unopened tin, and I drink it on the plane.

A cab, for a fairer price at the other end, and I'm back at the resort earlier than I get home from a night game at the Bush.

September 12

Reluctantly returning from out of the tropics to a home game against Peterborough. No disrespect to the 'Posh' but it's hardly awe inspiring. The sun is still shining at least, but that is about the highlight. Sporting a tan, that you forlornly hope an Indian summer will keep up throughout September, or at least until long sleeves are required.

Most of our players look like they've been away somewhere, and play like they are still there. We get away with a one all draw, when for the last quarter we are holding on, and they look to have had a perfectly good goal disallowed in the last minute.

Darren Ferguson's team are still without a win since their promotion, elsewhere his old man's lesser known team teach Tottenham a lesson. It makes you wonder how far the spouse would have got without 'help' from the elder. Nepotism, present in most walks of life, throws up no distinct pattern within the game. For every step forward given by a well meaning father, many careers have gone two steps back because they are expected to live up to the hype the family name brings.

Racking my brains for father/son combinations that emphasise the benefits of having a dad who could play a bit, I soon realise that they throw up as many club feet as golden balls. For every Frank Lampard Jr, there is a Chris Hollins, though for every Kenny Dalglish there is a Terry Owen. (Father of Michael)

One thing is clear that any sibling of a maverick player is unlikely to make it, both because they'll have to have a real talent to equal their father's antics, and will always be constantly be compared. If George Best's son, was any good or not, would never have stood a chance in the pro game.

Surely a university study could have spent a vast amount of time and money to conclude that a leg up of a famous surname opens a few doors as a junior, it might not be of much help as an adult.

Saved millions there, telling you absolutely nothing, a bit like watching Soccer AM.

September 15

There are many conspiracy theories over the course of history; the most notorious include the moon landings, and the assassination of John F Kennedy. None though can eclipse the pub thought out explanations as to why QPR versus Crystal Palace was postponed. In all my football going years, I cannot recall a match being postponed because of weather, in London, and in September. OK, so it has rained today, but it hasn't been bucketing down all week, and, I stress, it is not December.

Before the game was postponed, we had messages saying that Rangers had watered the pitch, even though it was pissing down at the time. A team out of sorts, a few injuries, don't fancy this tonight, let's get this called off, by exploding silver iodide in the atmosphere, causing the opposite effect to what the Russians have done in the past for the May Day parades and the 1980 Olympics.

Of course, none of this may be true, but it will soon be fact, as it deflects the attention from our omniscient chairman, whom has resigned as Renault F1 boss over the blind spot Singapore crash scandal.

We were touted as the richest club in the world with the backers we've had over the last two years, it is beginning to look like that old adage, if it looks to good to be true, then it usually is.

As Notts County, I feel, may soon discover.

Remember, all the above is fact. Tell your friends.

September 19

In theory, organising a coach trip should be as simple as drawing a map for a woman on how to get back from the shops. They don't seem to need directions for the route there.

A standard executive coach seats roughly fifty people, and to a man, as soon as they climb the stairs a metamorphosis takes place that changes everyone into an adolescent teenager. If you get a full coach you can grab yourself a few quid, but believe you me, its money well earned.

Originally, I had a no birds or kids rule, but this is neither clever nor profitable. We don't show porn on the screens any more. This is a shame, as it normally quietens down a noisy bus, and large bets were taken on who would be the first to make for the toilet. Last time it was the driver.

In addition there are the no shows, the late comers, the chaps who know the route better than the driver, and others who feel that the coach is solely run for their benefit. The toilet will inevitability overflow, normally about ten minutes after setting off, Friday night's curry is deposited in the liquids only khazi.

Usually they return without a major incident and more often than not when watching Rangers, without a victory. Ever since running my first coach to Liverpool for the Milk Cup semi final in '86 as a twenty one year old, I've orchestrated irregular journeys that are normally based on demand, distance and drinking. Rowdiness over the years that can be mentioned herein includes, the locking of the bar staff in their own toilets in Gotham near Nottingham, the sister coach hijacking the driver so as to not let him leave without us on the way back from Leeds, crashing a wedding on the retreat from Wolverhampton, and once in Blackburn, whilst negotiating with the police to release some drunk and disorderlies for the trip back, the whole double-decker went for a drink. We were parked outside of the nick at the time. All this can make the organiser's lot not a happy one, but the devil inside can make you complicit in the anarchy that ensues. In general, you count them all in, and count them all back again.

A lot of coach companies won't do football, I can't see why?

Always do the collection for the driver on the outbound leg of the journey, for two reasons. He'll get more money, people are likely to be asleep or skint on the way home, and if the whip raises say, one hundred quid, he almost has no choice but give you an unscheduled beer stop in an unsuspecting village coming back.

This is the third time I've arranged a day out to the capital of Wales, and at three different venues. The now defunct Ninian Park, the Millenium Stadium, and the novel and imaginatively titled, Cardiff City Stadium.

There is no love lost between the Bluebirds and ourselves, and as we cross the Severn Bridge, I pay £16.30 for the coach and check the passports for visa expiry. A stirring speech is given from Henry V as 'we happy few, we band of brothers' go for a drink in Chepstow. This driver is earning his tip today.

Two other coaches along with mine populate the boozers of this pleasant town, and we head off in good spirits but late to our destination with Owain Glyndwr.

The police escort pick us up outside of the city and lead us into the car park of the sanitised stadium. It's an all ticket affair, when there is no need, and some of the lads, ticket less, and unable to get in do the next best thing and find the nearest pub.

A quick slash before taking my seat results in missing our opener. Understandably thirsty, just before the interval we pop downstairs for some alcoholic Eurofizz, happy with what we've seen or heard about, and to cap it all, we score another, which I miss, as I'm queuing at the bar, in order to miss the half time rush. At least I've got a drink while I'm informed about the goal!

This is the most assured we've looked so far this season, and Wales finest look far from promotion contenders, and don't threaten in any shape or form, leaving us comfortable winners.

A deserved round of applause then back to the waiting coach, a victorious team photo and the Heddlu move us out on the double. Too quickly in fact, as the two unfortunates, Alex and Streety, who saw the game from the lounge of a pub, have to catch us up in a taxi when we can finally shake the escort.

A winning bus is a happy bus, and the celebrations deserve at least one more gallon, so we turn off in the South Cotswolds, Junction 18 on the M4, to The Compass Inn at a place called Tormarton, which is quite near to Badminton. A quaint rural pub/hotel/restaurant, a perfect setting for forty plus geezers to be as loud as it is humanly possible to be. The look on the faces of the regulars as we all pile in is worth all the days hassle alone. As we have won, our collective bark is worse than our bite, but why let that get in the way of a minor bit of panic for the bar staff.

There are no further incidents, and we all return without any discussions with plod, of whom, if you are mad enough to run a coach, you are meant to advise them of such, they don't half get the needle when you don't.

September 20/21/22

Hung over, I get to the Easyjet check in desk at Gatwick just two minutes before closing. Why is it that flying with Stelios doesn't grate in the same way that boarding a Ryanair flight does?

My wife and son also fly to see her family before she returns to work. Tyre fitting is quite an exhausting profession. Especially when she's based at the airport.

Toulouse is my destination, home of the Airbus, which I'm flying on increasingly more these days. As we land I perk up, and expectantly, keep an eye out for a glimpse of rows of the new super jet A380, but I'm kidding myself.

The fall out from yesterday's drinkathon, has resulted in my camera being 'borrowed', by one of the lads on the coach, and in a drunken fit of pique, me smashing my phone on the ground. What an idiot.

Luckily, I've got a new one, minus several hundred numbers, which will now result in any calls I receive getting the 'who is this?' treatment.

As I wait at a wet Blagnac Airport the messages I receive all relate to the collateral damage from yesterday, missing jackets, keys and wives missing their husbands, not in the pining sense.

Accompanying me today is my friend Clark Malone, ex pat, who is driving down from his home in Bergerac. Four years ago we came over to visit, and visited St Emilion and surrounds, where we drunk our fill of Grand Cru, arguably the best area for red wine on the planet. We got a game in as well, Girondins de Bordeaux v Paris St Germain.

When we meet he is gagging for a beer, and is as usual for a couple of liveners in somewhere new, we find ourselves adrift in the seedier part of town. Known as the 'Pink City' because of its red brick architecture, not a gay parade, although because of the incessant rain we are not inspired to be even vaguely cultural.

There is no escaping the fact that this is a rugby town, so we're not expecting too much as we get Joe Le Taxi to the 35,000 capacity Stadium Municipal. It's out of the centre, and because of this there is nowhere obvious to drink, certainly in close proximity. Clarky, eager to show off his range of linguistic skills shouts 'Oi, Jean Claude, quelle est le coup, si vous plait' which manages to get us a cheap deal on a couple of complimentary tickets, and thus we find ourselves inside the complex, where England lost to Romania in WC '98.

Catching up, discussing the relative merits of Huggies over Pampers, we fail to notice that the screens are showing the Manchester derby live until the last quarter, that said it's worth watching. Two great Craig Bellamy goals, only for City to be flattened by Michael Owen's 195th minute finish.

Les Violettes, managed by the wonderfully named Alain Casanova, who had a good away Europa League result in Belgrade on Thursday, are today facing Le Mans, where there are more hours in the race than travelling fans. The roof reminds me of the iconic Mount Stand at Lords, however, the 13072 here to witness a two nil home win, are symbolic of the Gallic attitude to football, even if it is the most popular sport in the country, with great national success, it just feels apathetic.

Put two wheels on it and you'll get a better response.

Clark sniffs out an Irish bar on the walk back to town, where a few stouts later we're now friends with the locals and go on a crawl.

Thankfully, a few pints in, eating makes the agenda at a great restaurant, probably a chain in France, L'entrecote.

Just steak, chips, salad and wine is the take it or leave it complete menu, bloody good though, on a par with what I've eaten in Buenos Aires. Mind you, a kebab would work right now. Often, I use the maxims that if you don't eat on the day, have twice as much the day after, so large amounts of catching up to do from the South Wales trip yesterday.

We finish off in a crazy rock bar, L'Autan, wishing that we had found this place earlier and soberer.

Clark rings me shortly after leaving the hotel to inform me that the French bastards have broken into his van, and have stolen the gas tanks he uses for his plumbing business. They will cost 1000 Euros to replace.

Au revoir to Clark and to France, only just, luckily catching the minibus after going to the wrong pick up point, taking me to the remaining principality I've yet to visit, Andorra.

The journey is unremarkable, mainly because rain is obscuring the view, and a headache is obscuring my eyes. Four hours over the Pyrenees, and we're in La Vella, green and out of skiing season. I'm not really sure what to expect, an abundance of duty free shops, Franco Spanish Darby and Joan equivalent trips, and little else is the answer.

Opting for temperance, I decide to go to the cinema to kill a couple of hours, and see Tarantino's 'Inglorious Bastards' with one hitch; they've over dubbed the sound into Spanish! This is the least important of the mistakes that I've made.

Up early next morning, for the trip to Barcelona. Nearing the airport, we pass the brand new Estadi Cornella-El Prat, only inaugurated last month and home to RCD Espanyol. This rubs salt into my self inflicted wound, as the fixture I had planned to see here tonight has been moved until tomorrow. My back needs a good whipping; I didn't take any heed to my own advice and double check.

It'll cost over a oner to change my flight to later today, so at 32 degrees I might as well stay the night, find a cheap bed, and spend roughly the same amount on pleasure seeking.

On my previous visits, I've left disenchanted, probably due to the time of year I've visited, November and March, as much like London when the sun is shining, the city becomes alive.

Completely at peace with myself, I ramble on where ever my human compass guides me, only new DNA techniques can link me to the kidnapping in '85.

Walking around the port, I set myself a target of a cocktail at the new W Hotel I can see on the horizon, striking a similar resemblance to the Burj Al Arab in Dubai. My amble there is peculiar to say the least, in the region that gave us Dali, Gaudi, and Picasso, I shouldn't be in the least bit shocked.

First up, I encounter the naked cyclist. An old boy, stark bollock naked and riding a bike.

Next, along the beachfront, ahead of me, a one legged man puts his crutches alongside and proceeds to stretch out in the afternoon sun, again naked, there are two stumps on show.

Then, the baywatch adventure, a windsurfer gets into trouble on the choppy Med, and after what has just gone before me, I'm hoping for the most surreal rescue ever. In one respect I'm not let down, as when the fat bloke with a moustache is saved, instead of concern and sympathy, his friends stand around laughing, not in the least bit concerned that he had to be dragged from the cruel sea, and not by Pamela Anderson either, more like Iain Anderson from Jethro Tull.

After all this entertainment, I arrive at my destination badly in need of a caipirinha, only to discover that it is not open until next month, by this stage I'm half expecting it to be a mirage.

It's time to head to the seedy Las Ramblas for the night, an area on a par with Leicester Square for all its allure, but like a moth to the flame, we tend to be drawn there.

Some sangria and tapas later, I find a bar showing the Leeds v Liverpool LC tie, which partially clashes, time wise, with Barca away at Santander. Nonetheless they keep the English game on, annoying the young Catalans who come in to watch what turns out to be another devastating Messi display, the ball appears tied to his left foot at times.

Spain, goes to bed late, and before you know it, you realise you better go and get six hours sleep, tomorrow could be a long day.

September 23

Early the next morning, I rush to the El Prato airport to get a BA767 flight back to Heathrow, and head out with a spring in my step. Today is our derby, Chelsea at Stamford Bridge, or as my dad calls them, North Battersea.

Fame and fortune have changed this fixture considerably, both the clubs and the supporters. As it's a cup tie we are allocated 6000 tickets, with demand for more, when thirty years before we would be lucky to have taken more than 600. Ironically, we have now been allocated what was the home, Shed End, and ticket prices have been reduced to just less than a score.

Much as I hate to admit it, their ground is now quite decent; previously the monolithic East Stand seemed ridiculously out of place. The construction of such nearly pushed Chelsea into bankruptcy, which eventually saw Ken Bates, a QPR supporter as a youngster, buy the club for just £1. Twenty years later, with club on the verge of administration, the fairy godfather appeared in the shape of Roman Abramovich, rumoured to have been turned down by Spurs, and moved on to the next available club, convenient for everyone involved. The lucky, lucky bastards.

The limitless supply of roubles has brought prosperity, but alienated many of my Chelsea mates, (yes, I have got some) with a dislike of 'new' fans, the type who start booing if they haven't scored after ten minutes, add to this the extra cost, inconvenient kick off times, and every other game being televised, then the demographic alters to a multi-cultural, wealthy and fast food supporter.

Of course, most of these nouveau patrons, as will many of the elder ones, view Rangers as just an irritation; despite during much of 70s, 80s and 90s we were much more than that. Our 6-0 victory on Easter Monday '86 is fondly remembered by those old enough, as is the 3-1 win early on in the '87-'88 season, when we were top of the table with Chelsea were lying in second. Gary Bannister scored hat-trick in both matches, possibly some sort of record?

Outside the confines of West London, the majority of Home Counties based Blues only feel disdain or pity, they have bigger fish to fry. Plainly, in places like

Guildford, Tonbridge and Crawley, an encounter with Man United is regarded as a derby.

Back to this evening's fun, a lot of the boys are out in force, early doors, as big Ron would say. Years of being bullied by support of the 'harder' London teams has turned full circle, it's quite some time since we fitted the bill of a little family club that some would prefer. The image makers won't appreciate this, but truth in football is seldom a concern with the powers that be, making decisions on our behalf but without our consent.

Eventually, we all disperse, after the constant police surveillance in Hammersmith, and via the North End Road we converge on Fulham Broadway. Beer and bugle fuelled scuffles break out on all sides of the Fulham Road, with the darkening sky making it difficult to make out who is who.

We play well, but inevitably lose by a single goal. Rangers make things tough enough for Chelsea to bring on John Terry to shore up their defence. I'll bet he wishes they didn't. For fully ten minutes, he is subjected to our vitriol, the whole Rangers end chorus of, 'John Terry, your mum's a thief.'

In vindication of this unscheduled outburst, it is merely statement of fact, no expletives are used and he is fair game. Not so sure the liberal majority would agree, but they are in a minority amongst us.

The gap between us and them is now of Grand Canyon proportions, in realisation of this we trudge back to our constituencies and get extremely wasted, safe in the knowledge of the three C's we were taught to avoid as kids. No Conservatives, cottaging or Chelsea. The night is long, so much so that my brother doesn't surface until late the next afternoon, still wearing the velvety jacket that he was so critical of at closing time.

September 26

Making the most of my free time, and foregoing the Tykes at home, Ryanair have the pleasure of transporting me to Riga. To be honest my sole reason for going to Latvia is simply because it completes the trio of Baltic States I've visited along with Estonia and Lithuania, and I'll get a sneaky game in while I'm here as well. It has become a popular stag destination, and because of such has seen an increase in prices, as I find out trying to grab a hotel. The currency, the Lat, is one of the few that is stronger than the pound sterling on a one to one basis. After being quoted ridiculous amounts for a room, eventually I find a side street hostel, that charges 17 Euros for a clean, spacious double room, and a friendly enough welcome, to give them a name check, Ala Hostel.

Setting out, I reluctantly forego a visit to the Museum of War due to time constraints, and walk the backstreets until I arrive at the Skonto Stadium.

This also doubles up as the national arena, which for a country of only just over two million inhabitants hardly comes as a shock.

Greeting me is a huge banner of Kaspars Gorkss, QPR and Latvia centre half. Although Marian Pahars, the useful former Southampton forward is probably the nation's most famous player. The only human life here is the grounds man, who is marking out the pitch. I'm early it transpires, but Igor assures me that there's a game on, 'Da'.

The season here runs from March to November, so is in full swing, playing in January you would need skis. Current Champions, Ventspils, have made it through to the Europa League group stage, and play these matches here to fulfil UEFA requirements.

Fed and watered five minutes walk away, I return for Skonto v Jurmala VV, and spend three lats (£4) for a seat in the main stand, the other three are empty, it's like watching the reserves, you can even hear the slaps from the players as they shake hands.

Jurmala, a coastal resort only 25km away, equalise on the half time stroke, and as I grab a coffee, the silence is still echoing. It is here that I get chatting to Anton Joore.

My, bought at a reduced price from Tesco, plastic backed notebook, has led him and others into thinking that I'm a scout, in fact all I was putting down on paper was doodles, and world domination plans, with big Bristols.

The Dutchman turns out to be an interesting character, manager of smaller Riga side, RFS Olimps, but in the same division. His brief synopsis of the Latvian game is that only a few teams are in contention, and that his side are virtually nothing much more than a feeder club. Judging by the 250 hardy souls watching the nation's biggest club, there can't be too much money in it.

Then we talk about his playing career with NAC Breda in Holland, all the time we speak I keep my amateur goal scoring exploits under wraps. Whilst I was being kicked up in the air by big Brian from Hanwell, he was, he explains, a few years earlier, trying to catch Bob Latchford and Cyrille Regis, and a real blast from the past, Ronnie Goodlass. Unsure of my motives for being in this football backwater, he gives me his number in case any jobs surface. If you happen to know of any positions that may be suitable, give him a call on 0031 629 500000, and tell him Mel, the gobby London match assessor told you to ring.

3-2 to the red shirts of Skonto, in the meantime it seems I've missed a cracker at Loftus Road, my friend Ian Furey, has been texting me score updates, we have beaten Barnsley 5-2, he tells me to 'not come again' if this is what happens in my absence. Once again I miss five goals. Typical. Wankers.

Later, I get drinking with a group of Brummies in the city centre, which is now geared to foreigners flush with weekend cash, and because of such has lost the charm I'm guessing it once had. A trip to fire a Kalashnikov isn't reason enough to venture here. Tallinn, in Estonia, is a far prettier venue

If you do happen to spend some spare time there, ask for Elizabeth at Miss Pussywhip's Olde Smoking Emporium. Remember to bring your own salt, if you would prefer the lashes to be accentuated by the addition of sodium chloride rubbed into the weals in your back.

September 27

Bus number 22 coughs its way to the airport, where the most ludicrous queue to security in world history has stretched over half the length of the terminal. This is causing much consternation, as it appears half of Riga is departing.

It is considerably cheaper to fly to Belgium today than head for home, and contrary to popular opinion, it is actually not as boring as it is made out to be, even if Monty Python did state otherwise. Anywhere that has the selection of beers available here can't be that bad. I prefer the comment by old big nose De Gaulle, about Belgium being created by the English to annoy the French, which should sit should better with us.

Naming famous Belgians has now become easier with success of the tennis girls, Clijsters and Henin, to add to Eddy Merckx, Audrey Hepburn, who shares the same birthday as me (as if you care) and as good old Plastic Bertrand said, 'Ca plain pour moi'.

Charleroi, which featured in two of England's games in Euro 2000, is a 13 Euro coach ride from Brussels, which leaves frequently, right outside arrivals, and then takes you to the Gare du midi.

Some of the hotels near the terminus are rotten, eventually, I settle for one off the Avenue de Stalingrad that has less mould than the others I've inspected.

A glorious end of the summer day, and the impressive Grand Place is bristling with visitors, I've no inclination to see Mannekin Pis again, and Jake does an equally good version of this every day.

St Guidon is the Metro station stop for Royal Sporting Club Anderlecht, 'the' team of Belgium. This has the feel of home, the Constant Vanden Stock Stadium is located in a residential area, the place is a buzz, and I get all tearful when I notice a few drunken lads taking a leak behind trees and walls. It's re-assuring to see our culture exported without prejudice, and as Al Murray would say, 'It makes you proud to be British'.

Fortunately, I'm here early enough to get a ticket (22Euros) for what looks like being a sold out match, most of the queue are buying tickets for the midweek Europa League fixture against Ajax, which is, effectively, Brussels v Amsterdam, so not much love lost here then. There is no real local Brussels derby as such, so these matches and games against sides from Bruges and Liege are the tastier ones.

Outside, a cold but tasty beer in hand, I'm intrigued by a burger bar, which, apart from the bleeding obvious, is selling snails, three Euros for ten. Not tempted myself, I wonder who might be. Twenty minutes without any takers, then a rush near kick off, which is at six o'clock. Unsure of escargot's aphrodisiac qualities, I don't want to make a mess of my jeans when I see the cheer leaders, so they remain a delicacy untried at a game by yours truly, mussels later on is a better bet methinks.

Inside, the crowd are partisan, without the berets. It has, in part, a Villa Park feel about it.

Germinal Beerschot are the lambs to the slaughter today, of whom I confess I know little, except their great name, and now, that they wear fluorescent green away shirts. I learn that former Belgian International and prodigal son Bart Goor, is now plying his art in their disgusting away strip. For the second Sunday on the trot, a team is wearing purple as a first choice strip. If I soon go and watch Fiorentina then that is all the major mauve teams ticked off, if not at all interesting.

Anderlecht stay top of the league, their support is tremendous, raucous, even the trumpeters near me in the ground are in tune, more than the England supporters band normally are. The scorer of the games only goal is a sixteen year old, Romelu Lukaku, a handful at this early age, and he could be on the way to greatness, watch this space.

Just off the Central Square, I settle down for late evening beer tasting, including DeuS, an 11.5% champagne beer, Waterloo, a mere 7%, served in a glass that gives the impression that it is from 1815. Quite a tough one to nick though.

Several more, including Bush, 12%, making Honduras v Hungary, which I'm watching through one eye, in the World Under 20 Finals taking place in Egypt, extremely enjoyable. The Central Americans look very good and are three up as I write. Perhaps this is the Delirium Tremens I'm sinking, but the elephant in the holding roll in midfield is definitely not pink!

September 28

Dusseldorf is somewhere I could live. If you haven't already got inkling, my fondness for things Germanic, extends not just to the wunderbar game. As a baby I vaguely recollect the milkman being named Gunther, but think this is just a coincidence. In the early '70s, I was in the Hitler Youth or Boys Brigade as it has since become known. These days, I often attend themed parties with Max Mosley, where I can bring the house down with my impersonation of Herman Goering.

So it should come as no surprise when I pop into the Rhineland the next day, this has been done before with greater force.

A two hour Deutsche Bahn ICE train to Cologne, 42.20 Euros, much cheaper if I had booked in advance, then change for a slower service further up the Rhine to the north. This route takes me past the vast Bayer works, and early season pace setters, Leverkusen. They are hoping for fortune similar to their near success under the management of the eccentric looking Klaus Toppmoller at the start of this century.

Cologne itself is a decent enough place, with the imposing Gothic Cathedral 'dom'inating the skyline, once the tallest building in the world. I've spent many nights here drinking its unique beer, Kolsch, in contrast to the dark ale served in my destination city.

It is true that the 2006 WC changed many people's perceptions of the Fatherland for the good, and, personally, I never want to hear the 'ten German bombers' song again. If you like football this region, North Rhine Westphalia, the powerhouse of Germany, is where it's at.

Immediately I make for the Aldstadt, once sufficiently fed and watered, I'm pointed in the direction of the tram trains, and told to get U78. This is not to the submarine pens of Das Boot. Besides, the crew were followers of Schalke if you recall!

Tonight's match is bigger than I anticipated, as I speak to young Aachen supporters on the U-Bahn, who estimates they'll have over 4000 here tonight.

They sell me a spare 11 Euros ticket, which, judging by the queues saves me a lot of Sven hassle.

One, who hardly speaks English, still manages to enquire, 'Are you a ground hopper?'

'No, well yes, sort of.'

They've got them here as well then, says I tucking his shirt into his high waistband trousers, and attaching more tape to the side of his National Health spectacles.

Fortuna, who were promoted behind Union Berlin last season from the third division but have a proud history and loyal following, their last home game of '08-'09 attracted a record third division crowd of 51000.

The Esprit Arena only five years old, has nearly 30000 tonight, it was unfortunate to be passed over as one of the WC venues, just too many large stadiums in the same geographic location.

Null-null is the final score, in an evening only made interesting by the away following. Aachen who also have a brand new arena, demonstrate against seating, and to prove the point, throw loads into the moat for good measure. The stewards provided by Knoblich Security, you can't make it up, do little to prevent this vandalism, it appears this is acceptable behaviour; the heavies don't bat an eyelid.

I'm tempted to join this minor anarchy myself.

Back to town with the rowdy Aachen lot, even on a Monday it's still busy. I round the night off with a schweine brotchen, essentially a hot pork roll. Fantastisch. It must be difficult being a vegetarian in Germany, and I'm 99% sure that it has been scientifically proven that vegetarians don't like football.

It's a pity that there is no Anglo-Deutsche Cup for teams like mine, or people like me, with a two legged final at Wembley and Berlin. Or just go to the Oktoberfest and be done with it.

Air Berlin fly me back to Stansted for only thirty quid, and I wait an hour to greet my wife back from Poland that earns me some brownie points.

Not enough to take me to St James's Park, Newcastle the following night, our first visit in fifteen years, even if you are stuck up in the seats of the Gods. I'll bet Alan Whicker didn't have to babysit. We earn a creditable 1-1 draw.

Portsmouth's new owner, Sulaiman Al Fahim, has not paid this month's salaries; didn't you just know that something like this was going to happen? His eyes are too close together or something similarly shifty, and my gut feeling is that there are more excuses to come in the near future.

October 3

Fill in your own expletive here. Sometimes following your team can border on hatred. The love isn't forthcoming when you feel let down.

Finally, the pieces of the puzzle are starting to come together, the feeling of optimism isn't just blind faith, it's borne from a belief that the corner has been turned, we are ticking the right boxes, and any other cliché that fits the bill. Basically, Rangers are playing quite well, so, when in your heart of hearts you know that you've thrown away three points, you feel like you've been stood up by a lover, sitting at a table for two, looking at your watch, knowing it'll be a good night if she turns up, but she doesn't.

What a load of shit. That's the last time I ask Ian Holloway for some literary input.

About eight o'clock, ten of us are waiting at the Target Roundabout to be picked up for the second trip in two weeks to South Wales, though with another forty miles each way on the journey to Swansea. A curious historic pub stop at 'Ye Olde Wine House', Pyle near Bridgend, sees us leave in good spirits bound for Abertawe, pronounced in my best Max Boyce accent.

The Liberty Stadium was inaugurated in 2005, regrettably it is another example of an anodyne, headache inducing Ikea flat pack arena. Vetch Field may have passed its sell by date, but at least it was distinctive.

Gone are the days when just by watching a game on television you could discern which ground it was after seeing a throw in or a corner. Now like a line up of terraced houses in Manchester, they all look the same, he says, adjusting his Zimmer frame.

To the match itself, fast forward to the interval, and a pint of Eurofizz. The game is goalless, but we all believe that Rangers will up the ante in the next forty five. When it restarts, we are still downstairs in the bar, but the monitors have the game on live, so no need to rush back. Then, as predicted, we put the pressure on, and this looks to have paid dividends when Routledge's shot loops into the net. Actually it doesn't. A trick of the light gives the impression that the ball was in, but by that time I'd thrown what was left of my beer in the air, and was jumping about before realising that there was no goal, and that in the next passage of play, our captain, Martin Rowlands had dived in late, and was receiving a second yellow card. Within the space of less than ten seconds there was a shift of cosmic proportions. A nailed on win, has now become holding on for a point, which of course, we don't. Fifteen left, the Jacks score, then we are reduced to nine men, and to cap it all, and that big dollop Lee Trundle even manages to net one. It is a long way home. Wankers.

Sir Alex Ferguson complains about the fitness of referee Alan Wiley after the game at Sunderland. In international week, I wonder if we are going to complain about the fitness of players who will conveniently withdraw from the squads they are selected for, only to miraculously recover for matches in a fortnight.

Jack Warner opens his mouth again and the FA collectively wince. He said our 2018 bid is 'creeping along, when it should be galloping', before reiterating that we'll still get his vote. I'm sure they are reassured, wishing that what happened to the original JW, Dixon of Dock Green, in the 'The Blue Lamp', could happen to this one. Sir Trevor Brooking could take the place of Dirk Bogarde.

Flavio Briatore is under scrutiny from the FL under the 'fit and proper persons test'. His lawyers will no doubt get to work to fudge any allegations as they will do on the Formula One appeal.

October 8/9

I've been looking forward to this trip since the draw was originally made, my first visit to the bread basket of Europe, so many images are conjured up by the thought of the Ukraine.

Just under four hours flight time to Kiev and its Great Gates, which only ever existed in the design stage, and in music, but it sounds good nonetheless.

Thankfully we no longer require a visa for entry, one of the major drawbacks of travelling to Russia, due to cost and inconvenience, and the legalised con of the letter of introduction. This doesn't mean however that you waltz through customs; we are there over two hours, the result of which is that by the time we get to the Hotel Ukraine it is dark. Day or night, there is no way you can miss where we are staying, it is a landmark building slap bang in the middle of the city, located looking down on The Square of Independence, the scene of the celebrations when the Orange Revolution took place. The hotel is more impressive on the outside than in.

Taxi fares vary wildly, the same journey taken four times gives assorted prices, ranging from 250 to 50 hryvnia, pronounced greevna. That is just the way things are out here.

It is a shame that the match is not taking place here in the capital; Kiev's main stadium is being renovated to host the final of Euro 2012. It once held 100000 spectators.

After a McDonalds, I know I shouldn't, but at least you know what you are getting in an unfamiliar surrounding. Often it's a case of nutritional value nil, enjoyment factor ten. Unfortunately you never see the franchise of the superior Wendy's outside of the US any more. We unsuccessfully stroll around in search of friendly watering holes, but retire to the hotel for a nightcap. Here there are two bars, the usual hotel fare, and a more specialist outlet, Bar Velvet. (From hereon I have the old folk/ rugby club tune 'The Mayor of Bayswater' constantly humming through my head. You know the verse, 'I smelt it, I felt it etc)

With no fee to move from lobby to lazy lob, we saunter into this den of iniquity to be swamped by scantily clad girls. Being a star of the 'Lynx' ads, it is water off a hairy back to me, but to some of the other cagey cretins in the dark room, you'd think they had never seen a girl with natural breasts smile at them from an angle of ninety degrees before.

One barely legal nymph, from hereon in who shall be known as Dave, takes a shine to my pocket asking if I will buy her a drink, and if I would like a private dance for forty Euros. Why would I want to part with my spending when I can see it all for free in a minute when you do you stint on the pole?

Dave questions me, 'You are Engleesh, yes?'

'Yes love.'

'You go to watch football, yes?'

'Yes darling.'

'I will go to your room for one hundred Euros, or I stay with you for weekend for three hundred?'

Now, this is a good deal. Trouble is none of us are single, and there are no spare tickets available for the game. That may have swung it, and if she could have named the 1970 WC squad. The thought of a team concubine sends me to bed with a smile on my face, glad that is the only thing I have to feel guilty about.

This smile has gone three hours later with a vodka hangover at the train station. A cock up on the ticketing front leads us to not being able to board the seven am train, and after much deliberation we have to the get the one o'clock instead. This will take two hours longer than the earlier express one; it will get to Dnipropetrovsk at nine pm. Now I'm not a morning person at the best of times, but today is not a time to test me. Sorry travel company rep for shouting at you and making you shake, it was Johnny's fault after all.

As we never actually checked out, it's back to the hotel, and piss off the cleaners who've already changed the sheets. I'll leave them a drink, but a couple of hours shut eye is better than nothing.

First class for just over thirty quid, hardly Orient Express standard, but you can lie down, which for the long trek ahead is essential. The Soviet built locomotive trundles across miles of wheat fields and woodland, punctuated by the occasional farmhouse, dacha, or tethered goat. Staring out of the compartment window, I can't shake from my musings Carl Davis's evocative music from 'The World At War', with Larry Olivier saying 'the Ukrine'(sic) in the way only he could, along with black and white footage of Nazis, 88mm guns and T-34 tanks.

Their are six of us, Fleetwood Town Paul, DJ Kev from Leicester but an Everton fan, Steve the Man. United two and a half hour marathon man, and two Blackburn lads Ian, the General, along with Chas, and like a cross section in a Gallup poll, me, the token Londoner. Other lads in and around our carriage include some Bristolians, and a chap from Sunderland who's route to get this far make Marco Polo's travels look a trip to the shops. Between us we down several bottles of local lighter fluid, which must have been laced with LSD from what takes place a couple of hours from our final station stop.

Pulling into a large junction called Piatykhatky, (this was not easy to find out) at first, I notice a couple of stalls selling cuddly toys and don't think anything of it. The train comes to a stop and we stretch our legs. You've never seen anything like this unless you've worked in a Chinese toy factory. The whole length of the platform, which is vast, is selling all manner of teddy bears, giant pandas and stuffed animals. Is this the orange revolution in action? Not having much use for a furry lion, I go in search of recognizable food only to encounter even more extras from Alice in Wonderland. It is not often you are offered pike, eels, and crayfish on a plate, still wriggling. A sandwich? Neit.

Finally crawling into Dnipro, we are greeted outside by students eager to hand us details on how to behave, and others just intrigued to see at first hand the mad England fans.

Later, we meet up with the lads in a bar called Reporter, lively enough, but with techno so loud that you have to shout to make yourself heard. Anthony and Sean from Preston, Leicester Jon, wee Glasgae Gregor, and Dan with the Carlisle lads have made a week's pilgrimage to Europe's lesser known hotspots including Moldova and Transnistria, a Russian buffer state that you are not recommended visiting by the Foreign Office. These secret locations are well worth searching out, but you have to leave a few unvisited in case we are drawn there one day, Armenia and Bosnia being amongst the great unexplored and as of yet by the Three Lions, untarnished.

October 10

On the morning of the game, we go cultural and try to visit to the Dniproges Dam. Apparently this is one of the seven wonders of the modern world, better than the day trip available from Kiev, the happy face of the past, Chernobyl. Four of us venture forth in search of transportation, easier said than done. We may as well have been asking taxi drivers for directions to Narnia. My kerbside descriptions don't fare any better. Using a trickle of water to represent a river, and then drawing a line with a stick to halt its flow, one would assume to be a universal way of portraying a dam. A big dam. Eventually we have an audience the size of a non league game, with onlookers and translators. Because of this we are found a cab prepared to take us the three hour return excursion for a wallet busting forty quid, for all of us! Off we go, pleased to not be ripped off, but we'd quite happily have paid more.

When we finally find a vantage point overlooking the dam, we are underwhelmed to the point of being downhearted. Is this it? Even the cabbie laughs in disappointment. We had expected a big dam, like, what you expect a big dam to be, dominating the mighty Dnieper River. Don't get me wrong, it's not just a weir, but not really up there in the category of world wonders.

On the return leg, we stop on the hard shoulder for a photo alongside a sign stating, 'Place of the forced crossing over the Dnipro by the Soviet troops in 1943.' This was the next passage of combat after the Battle of Kursk, lesser known to most in the West, the Lower Dnieper Offensive, it lasted for four months, and combined casualties are estimated at over two and half million. That is warfare at its most extreme. Don't ever think you've got it tough.

Returning to what was once a closed city, Dnipropetrovsk, once, before glasnost, the USSR's leading missile production base. Presently, it is a leafy metropolis that wouldn't look too out of place in the Home Counties. Our driver waits for us at the hotel, while we grab the tickets and jackets, and then drops us near the Dnipro

Arena for no extra charge. We give a £20 tip and he's made up.

Not finding a suitable watering hole, we're standing on a corner like sore thumbs, when an old boy motions to us to join the crowd lurking down the side street. Normally this would be a recipe for a row, but since no animosity has been shown to us since our arrival, we agree to their hospitality, and we're immediately handed a cup of vodka. As alcohol is a known Babel fish, and this tongue loosener will clean silver, it's not long before we're all best friends. The Ukrainians tell us that it is an honour for their city to host England, especially as the stadium won't be used for Euro 2012, as it is not suitable for UEFA requirements. This is a must win game for them in the race for a WC play off place, why should we want Croatia to nick it after the Euro 2008 disaster?

An extremely noisy ground, with more flares than the night the Titanic sunk, sees us lose by the odd goal in one, and Rob Green has the dubious distinction of becoming our first national goalie to be sent off.

We bump into our local friends in ebullient mood afterwards, and offer to take them for a drink, they say the bar is too expensive, and we should go to their house. We won't take no for an answer, and insist. Three hours of detente later and with more beer and vodka downed than you can shake a shot glass at, Fleetwood and I settle the bill. Extortionate. Roughly twenty quid.

The train back to Kiev is an early morning red eye, and most of us stay up in our hotel bar all night. The six hours pass with a snoring and dribbling contest, and my brief rest in the arms of Morpheus somehow involves Kate Bush's 'Babushka', the tune, not her grandmother, which is stuck in my head for the rest of the way home.

Our remaining currency is spent at Boryspil International Airport, and we all agree that we hope we return here in two and a half years time for a more detailed look.

Bea returns to work at the steelworks, leaving me to be a house husband. Just Jake, Sky Sports News and a clueless father. Channel 83 on my set up, puppet meerkats, bulldogs, and Kasabian's 'Club Foot' bass intro. This is really all there is, repeats of Will and Grace don't really find my inner gay, and watching Jeremy Kyle is almost as bad as appearing on it, though a bit of channel hopping will usually reward you with a programme about Hitler that you've only seen a couple of times. Horrible Histories and Shaun the Sheep on Cbeebies are pretty damn good as well.

October 14

Wem-ber-lee. Home of In-ger-land. The most famous stadium in the world, it is. As an outdoor arena it has no peers, certainly in the fame stakes. It has to be said that new visitors would be disappointed with their first impressions of the area when they walk down the high street. Growing up nearby, the area has seen a downturn in prosperity in the last thirty years, so much so that you would now be unlikely to linger longer than is strictly necessary.

Monumental as the new stadium is, don't you think that it should have had the capacity of a round hundred thousand? It should go without saying what the crowd is for the FAC Final, if not for the League Two Play Off. Just three or four more rows on top would in all probability have been adequate for the magical one hundred thousand. Presumably, at an extra cost of a quarter of a billion, especially if Multiplex are involved.

Another question that has remained unanswered satisfactorily, is, what does the roof that doesn't close actually do? Can you believe that they built half a roof? What was the fucking point? Is it a covering or an umbrella? A sham more like.

Other drawbacks of the new era include the security response teams strutting around with their blue bibs waiting to pounce and manhandle any unsuspecting wrong doer who puffs on a sneaky fag or stands up once too often.

The Mexican wave also entertains the young and the stupid, though old school England fans refuse to indulge.

Belarus, minus the anagram like Hleb, are easily beaten three nothing and we can look forward to a southern hemisphere journey next June.

After all the fake scares, many of the top nations still qualify. No Swedes, Poles, Czechs, Turks, Romanians but several countries have a second bite at the WC cherry.

FIFA surreptitiously seeded teams according to ranking, with no reason other than the more fancied countries with bigger populations and potentially higher generation of TV revenues will not be drawn against each other, and therefore are more likely to qualify. This is a disgrace. Public opinion usually favours the underdog, none more so than now. For the sake of fair play, remove whatever bias you may hold and cheer on, Bosnia, Ireland, and Slovenia. The Greece and Ukraine tie holds no real favourite; I'll side with the Ukrainians simply because we had such a good time there.

October 17

Sometimes you wonder why you bother. A day like today reaffirms why you do. Your team play well, and you stay out drinking until silly o'clock, it's even worth getting the silent treatment from the missus the next day.

We've been threatening of late to push on to the fringes of the promotion race, and maybe finally it is going to happen, even though skipper Martin Rowlands has done his cruciate ligament again playing for Ireland and is out for the season.

Meeting Preston Sean for a pre-match pint, I feel it in my Guinness that something is going to click, and let him know as such.

Our Moroccan star in the making, Adel Taarabt, sets the ball rolling into the North End net with a goal of the season contender, and from then on we don't look back, and bang in three more.

Bjorge Lillelien, a name that doesn't ring many bells until the Norwegian krone drops and you remember his crowning moment. Much parodied since 1981, but always worth adapting when the need arises, here is a rough facsimile of the text messages I sent to the relevant Lancastrians:-

Richard Arkwright, Freddie Flintoff, John Inman, Mark Lawrenson, Nick Park, Roy Barraclough, Tom Finney can you hear me? Tom Finney, your boys took a hell of a beating.

No matter how many times you've seen your team's goals, you never seem to tire of watching them again, and the same can be said of the written word, in the form of the Sunday papers. After having my morning constitutional accompanied by 'The Sunday Times' sport section, I'll religiously search out the other editions to verify whether or not I'm in agreement with the comments of the hack assigned to cover our game. This is only the event of a victory, or at the very least a good performance. Many is the time when you feel that the journo wasn't even at the game, and you mark his card for a derogatory sentence, revealing his deep dislike of your club, which you store in the recesses of your memory for the unlikely event you ever meet the heretic in the street.

There is no doubt what is splashed over the sports pages this Sunday, a red inflatable beach ball, with the Liverpool insignia prominent on its curvature. You would have to be an astronaut on a deep space mission to not have witnessed this comedy showcase, Python's 'cheese shop' skit is only just ahead in a poll of humourous moments.

This is one of those hate to say I told you so moments concerning the rules of the game. Rafa Benitez has every right to feel aggrieved about this outrage to the football 'cloob', as he puts it, that he manages. Mike Jones, the man in the middle, must have wished there was a hole in the middle of the pitch to swallow him up. Surely he knew that something was wrong? If that isn't outside influence, then what is? A UFO?

Admittedly this doesn't happen every day, but it highlights the knowledge, or lack of, that many people have of the rules. Steve Bruce certainly didn't have a clue when quizzed about Darren Bent's goal. It always amazes me the amount of 'experts' who are also unclear on law twelve, handball.

Pepe Reina's face was a picture though.

Manchester City are believed to preparing a bid upwards of forty million pounds for the plastic finisher.

October 20

A poor refereeing decision can be very costly as this weekend showed. It can also inspire your team to a great victory. A second home game in three days sees Ben Watson, who has just returned from a ban after his dismissal at Swansea, pick up another yellow card early on for a late challenge. The second booking on the half hour, is one of the most inept I've witnessed in all my football going years. The ginger haired midfielder attempts to take a quick free kick, but the referee, Andy Hall, is not happy, and makes us take it again, issuing another booking to Watson in the process. Incredulous, best describes his and our reaction. There is previous with us and this ref, so perhaps this is a continuation of ill feeling, or he follows Brentford.

Once the furore has died down, Akos Buszaky, our Hungarian play maker, steps up and curls the ball into the Reading net. Rangers are galvanised.

Galvanise, to treat iron or steel with zinc to prevent rust. I always thought that the use of this term, much used in sport, is technically incorrect, and that anneal would be more suitable. So, hoping for an entry in the OED, Rangers are annealed.

The ten men tear into, it must be said, a poor Reading side, and score another beauty before half time. It can often be said that the Rangers crowd, similar to Tottenham, get on the players backs more viciously than others when they are seen to be under performing, but, the enclosed layout of Loftus Road significantly enhances the noise levels when proceedings take a turn for the better. Not quite raising the roof, but, boisterous nonetheless, we run out emphatic 4-1 winners, the Royals supporters who number less than one thousand, see the humour in their plight taking the piss out of us for only scoring four.

Our season is now up and running, the top two have lost, the next eight have won. We are tenth, with a game in hand. The top twelve are separated by only six points.

Middlesbrough, are only one point from first place, this doesn't keep Gareth Southgate in a job. This comes as a surprise only because Steve Gibson has always appeared to be one of better chairmen around, but crowds are falling and pressure is mounting, and therefore, heads, they are a rolling.

Question Time takes centre stage this Thursday, with BNP leader Nick Griffin put under scrutiny, raising the theme of racism, or specifically in football. The 'Kick it out' campaign has attracted widespread publicity for some time now, although I feel that their work is done, certainly in this country. Much of the time racism gets confused with colour prejudice. Is it now not acceptable to have a healthy dislike of the French?

October 24

Roy Castle, I recall, when presenting 'Record Breakers' walked the length of Colchester station, pronouncing it the longest platform in Britain. What he failed to mention was that Layer Road, home of this historic Roman town's team, was only fit for amateur games and, if the truth be told, if ever a club with ambition needed a new ground then this was it. Now they have.

After a couple of Abbot Ales near the station in the Bricklayer's Arms, and then from just by there, a bus, which delivers me to the Weston Homes Stadium, unofficially known as Cuckoo Farm. There's been an accident today, so a five minutes journey takes thirty five, and I miss the kick off.

£18 gets me into the South Stand, going on first impressions; the ground is far better than I had envisaged. Something similar to Northampton Town's Sixfields is what I'd expected, but it is much roomier, with potential to 'fill in the corners'.

Today's opponents, Walsall, were one of the early movers, from Fellows Park to the Bescot Stadium down the road, alongside the M6 in 1990. This is always somewhere I've enjoyed visiting, their fans being a friendly bunch. There are less than one hundred faithful 'Saddlers' scattered around the away end, demoralised after 25 minutes when Kevin Lisbie puts the 'U's' one up. Their reprieve is instantaneous as Darren Byfield finishes well within a minute of the re-start.

During the interval I earwig a conversation the stewards are having about trying to make some youths at the back of the seats to sit down. They are not doing any harm to man or beast, and if ever there was the need for a policy of softly softly this is it. Shaking my head, I wonder if they have nothing better to do. Actually no, they have nothing to do on a day like today when a crowd takes care of it self.

On the hour, another Lisbie goal from the spot, which turns out to be the one that claims the three points for the Essex boys.

That penalty is my cue to be on my toes as my superstars are the early evening BBC TV game at Derby's Pride Park. My timing couldn't have been better planned, arriving back when we are already two nil down, but with confidence now flowing through our collective veins, we hit back with four for the third match in a row. Carry on like this and we'll have to hand out those cricket flyers that are held up every time a boundary is found. We move to third, and I'm feeling good.

A selection of titbits from an eventful week includes, on Sunday, the continuation of the beach ball episode from last week. Stewards threaten to eject anyone found smuggling said item into Anfield.

Predictably, in this instance, this is a red rag to a red devil, and even more certainly, we are transported to the sands of the Costas, which is very babyish and very funny.

Not so funny at Oakwell is the tea bar trashing in the visitors section during the League Cup tie, but the comments are just as inane. About as useful as Boris Johnson's alcohol ban on the London Underground, one tin doesn't make the slightest difference if you've had twelve pints beforehand. Part of the problem was the lack of staffing for the amount of Man United supporters attending. Service is normally by a minimum wage, greasy haired, spotty youth, where a cheeseburger and a bottle of conditioner is the order of the day. Add to this South Yorkshire Police and you have a Molotov cocktail waiting to happen.

Newcastle United are considering renaming their ground under a sponsorship deal, this hasn't been very well received by the Mags. Perhaps a company that produces passion fruit will pump some money in and call St James's Park the Passion Park. This will be totally in line with the media's representation of the Geordies, unlike the rest of us, who obviously exude as much passion as a bunch of librarians.

Swine flu stays in the news, with two Blackburn players suffering the first symptoms of the virus, and then the Health Protection Agency issuing an edict about spitting on the pitch, it includes,' Footballers, like the rest of us, wouldn't spit indoors, so they shouldn't do it on the pitch'. Good grief. Soon all the ball boys will be wearing hygienic masks, spittoons will be every ten yards on the touchline, and the advertising hoardings will be plastered with pictures of Kleenex tissues.

Role model Marlon King gets an eighteen month prison sentence, for being a serial ne'er-do-well. This prompts Wigan Chairman Dave Whelan to comment that he should not be able to continue his football career when the time is up. I'm not quite sure what else he would be expected to do, driving a van is fine, but kicking a ball is not? Like Lee Hughes, Tony Adams or any one else who has been banged up, he'll get stick from the stands, deserved more by some than others, but there is no reason moral or otherwise for him not to play again. No one will expect anyone to warm to him.

October 30

After being featured live on the BBC on Saturday, it is now the turn of Sky to show us off to the nation. My mate Johnny Smith, a Leicester City lad, is down for this.

Our first meeting was in Cascais, Portugal, during Euro 2004, when a few mates and I noticed a big chap slumped in a doorway. When we returned sometime later he was still there, and was tipped into a taxi by friends, who, it transpires, were resident at the same campsite as us.

The next morning at a late breakfast, I recognise a sheepish looking, now fully conscious bloke, and we've been mates ever since!

A few pints in the newly refurbished Queen Adelaide on the Uxbridge Road, and then to a full house at the home of football, for me anyway. The large crowd, inspired by the last three performances, catches many by surprise, including us. I manage to smuggle Jon in with an unused season ticket, and break one of the unwritten rules of spectating, the secret away supporter in the home end. He knows the rules, sit down, shut up.

Rangers are over confident, against Nigel Pearson's well drilled team, and despite taking the lead, suffer a 2-1 reverse, with their winner coming from a dreadful goal keeping error. To be truthful I half expected this to happen, and hope it nothing more than a blip. It's difficult to be reticent when you have to defend your team's performance, and you are writing a book!

Optimism has not yet left me, so I can be gracious in defeat at the post match warm down in several pubs. Jon on the other hand keeps insisting that 'Matty Fryatt is on fire' to the chorus of the Kings of Leon hit, but is complaining of a pulled muscle in his back.

Remember this as I climb into a spacious, warm, comfortable bed with my gorgeous wife, while you sleep in agony on the sofa with the heating turned off, you Baby Squad bastard. I don't bear grudges.

October 31

There is a flight from London City Airport to Dundee. This significantly shortens the travelling time in which Jon can take the piss out of me. Enclosed spaces make this far harder to deflect. Bollocks, only a minor setback for Rangers I keep convincing myself.

The almost every weekend tube engineering works causes us to change underground routes, but thankfully because the check in time is up to twenty minutes before take off, we comfortably make the Cityjet flight.

Bags safely dumped in the hotel room, then a short walk to Dundee station. There's a while until the next train is due, so a quick browse at Captain Scott's ship, the Discovery. There isn't enough money in the world that would get me to sail to Antarctica in a vessel like this.

The train trundles up the coast via the golfing Mecca of Carnoustie, to the small fishing port of Arbroath, home to famous smokie, and the world record score of 36-0.

Randomly picking a smokie vendor, we buy the cured haddock, which is better served warm, and limp, in Jon's case, along the coast eating the white fish as an entree to the main course, a division two fixture against Stenhousemuir.

There is only one option for a pint, the Tutties Neuk Inn directly across the road from the ground, Gayfield Park. A warm welcome is given, along with free stovies, which are a mixture of potato, onion and mince, in an inn that you would not expect near any ground.

£12 lighter, and we are in the closest ground to the sea in Europe. Peering over the wall, it certainly is. At high tide, only five yards or so from the North Sea. Try and picture playing at this place in January.

Nostalgia clouds my judgement, but this is how I like football grounds, distinctive and charming. The permitted attendance here is just over four thousand, yet it is as obvious as the runny nose on my wind smacked face that double that could easily be accommodated. This doesn't seem likely as Stenny, home of Irn-bru, score directly from a corner after a near miss from the same source two minutes before.

Next to one stand is a funfair, O'Brien's Pleasureland (1975), as if vying for trade with the Red Lichties (1878). Their nickname stems for the red lights that used to guide ships to safety, it is unclear if Ajax have ever had a similar moniker for dissimilar reasons.

The final score, 0-3, a result which sees Arbroath switch places with their victors at the foot of the table.

Before the final whistle is blown, we are already back in the warmth of Tutties. The friendly locals present me with a maroon and white scarf which was previously hanging around a stag's head in the middle of the bar, presumably because I'm daft enough to come here, but I'm glad I did.

Halloween in Dundee is a far bigger deal than you would ever have realised, we are the only two at the party that is taking place around the city who haven't turned up in fancy dress. Someone has even put a witches' hat on top of the statue of Desperate Dan.

Trying to enter into the 'spirit' of the night, drinking all the different flavours of 'Aftershock', which tastes more like aftershave, we finally line up in a queue for a nightclub, which is worth the admission fee alone just for the name, Deja Vu. All I will say is, that if you've ever felt old going into a disco, then this is an experience that you are unlikely to have ever lived before. The only deja vu you are likely to feel is being young once again, or more exactly not as old. The downstairs bar/dance floor is full of drunken Dundonians, the majority of whom are fifty plus and 'having it'. This is not a criticism, why the hell shouldn't they, it is funny to see though, and I'm not too far off the half century myself. It's either this or Dizzee Rascal with the younger crowd upstairs.

November 1

Hopefully I was victorious in the hotel snoring stakes, and a new month brings with it new climatic conditions. A 12.45 kick off is never ideal, unless it is arranged by the temperance society. My comments yesterday about the weather that may hit Arbroath in January, have decided to manifest themselves in November. It's raining. In biblical proportions.

We have pint at the Snug Bar as wait for the coach from Glasgow to arrive with the tickets. As Dens Park and Tannadice Park are famous as the two grounds closest to each other, the pub is split into showing memorabilia from both clubs. What is little known is that Dundee is one of only three British cities that have produced two European Cup semi finalists.

One of the more intriguing nicknames of any club is the one adopted by United, the Arabs. These days you could be forgiven in thinking that label has also been given to Manchester City. There are unconfirmed reasons behind this strange handle, but the sobriquet is likely to have stuck from the sixties, when, because of the large amount of sand used to fashion an acceptable playing surface. From then on, all you need is bunch of blokes wearing tangerine keffiyehs and from the beginnings of fiction, fact is born.

Once we have our £22 West Stand tickets in hand, we're happy to get into the ground, if only to keep out of the rain, which is incessant. Rangers have two sides of Tannadice. There are some great sliding tackles, leaving ten yard marks on the pitch. Davis gives the Teddy Bears the lead before half time, which seems to be taking longer than the normal fifteen minutes.

Rumblings without foundation turn into rumours of doom and then statement of fact, match abandoned, unlike cricket, there is no chance of play later today. I wonder if there are many instances of goal scorers or debutants from matches not completed, who never scored, or worse, played again and because of such, their records were expunged from statistical history.

Avoiding the deluge, we decamp to the Dundee F.C Social Club, some of the lads for the second time this week, Rangers having played here in the League Cup a few days before. The coach leaves back to Glasgow, leaving me to face the elements, and have a late breakfast of my favourite fry up, the Scottish variety, square sausage, tatty scones and white pudding. A couple of pints of eighty shilling watching the televised afternoon game then a cab to the airport and back to civilisation as I know it.

Safely home watching the news the next morning, I learn that Sunday's downpour actually managed to cut Arbroath off by road and rail due to landslides and widespread flooding. To a certain extent then, the four hundred hardy souls, excluding Jon and I, present at Gayfield Park the day before, were lucky to have seen anything at all.

As I sit proudly in my new maroon 'Red Lichties' T-shirt, I see that Jim Weir has been appointed the new manager of the very same, good luck to him, he'll need it.

Nine red cards were handed out in the Premiership, a record. Is this because play has suddenly become more physical? Or because the scrutiny referees are now placed under, makes it impossible for them to not give much of a benefit of doubt to decisions any more?

November 3

No rain this time, but after the amount that fell on me in Dundee on Sunday, I still feel wet through. This is the re-arranged fixture from September when it also rained a bit, but not like Scotland.

A spare ticket has been left in my hands, which when my wife overhears me on the blower asking if anyone has nothing better to do with their evening, motions like she wants to accompany me, my blood runs cold. This may seem to be an overreaction on my part but to most geezers an ordeal too far, especially if they want to go all the time. Being one of the lads is fine, as long as it is not your missus who is wearing the Dr Martens. Not forgetting the tug on the shirt afterwards with those nerve shattering words, 'You've had enough, and let's go home now.'

Over the years I've heard comments from young ladies including once when Neville Southall was roundly being booed that it was just like a 'pantomime', and another that the offside rule is when 'he is on his own'. In hindsight, both are partly right in a quaint girly way, that you can't tell your friends.

If the game is on a grand scale the better half will enjoy it for reasons other than what happens on the pitch. Be it at the Stade Chaban-Delmas, Bordeaux; or high up in the Mestalla, Valencia; in Macedonia, letting me getting drunk in Skopje after holidaying in Skiathos; being filmed on the huge screen at the Azteca, Mexico City; or painting her face in the black and white stripes of Botafogo at the Maracana, Rio de Janeiro. When it has an air of romance, football is a candlelight dinner for two, when it involves your mates it's a TV dinner for one.

Thankfully my wife doesn't want to be our household's equivalent of Harry the Dog and it was a convincing leg pull.

Tonight's opponents, Crystal Palace, are a bit like a woman, an anomaly, away win at a top team one week, heavy home defeat to a lesser side the next. They are the Forrest Gump chocolate box of the division.

Julian Speroni, Argentinian keeper of, to use their old nickname, the Glaziers, makes a series of good saves that earn his side a point in a one all draw. Warnock hails him as the best in the country. Not too disheartening for me when you have a release mechanism of five European games coming up starting far too early tomorrow.

November 4

Eighteen months ago, fifty friends and I departed from Bucharest thinking it unlikely that we would ever set foot here again, you wouldn't throw coins in the fountain here to make sure you returned once more. Certainly, if I ever again have the pleasure of selecting where a Stag party should go, then Romania is not going to be top of my list. The original plan was to go to Transylvania, but logistically it is difficult to get to, and more importantly, there is bugger all there.

Bea returns to her homeland, leaving me a three hour purgatory wait at Luton to board a Wizz Air flight, meeting Preston Tony and all sorts of other 'loyal' Rangers lads, and spend a similar time cramped in a Scairbus.

At least last time, for all its shortcomings it was sunny, now landing in the gloom of Baneasa Airport, I'm wishing I was elsewhere.

Once, this city was known as 'Little Paris', I prefer the more accurate recent description, 'the Balkan Moscow'. The highlight, if it can be labelled as such, is the World's second largest building, Ceaucescu's 'Palace of Parliament', there is little else.

Already aware of the currency (the lei) although five Netto's to the Lidl is more apt, and knowing from previous to be sure to be firm with the cabbies, I agree a price of fifty lei, but still he tries it on when we arrive at the hotel, saying the price was each. Fuck off, he doesn't look hard enough to try and get physical, and he accepts what we agreed losing any chance he had of being given a tip. Later, we learn of cabbies trying to charge over one hundred quid to Glaswegians. Let's just say that they didn't get paid, in cash anyway, and are unlikely to try these tricks again.

We are staying out near the airport for accessibility for departure tomorrow, as if you think traffic is bad in London, well it is, but not as bad as this. Two hours to go less than ten miles in the early evening traffic to the bar we used as a base before, the inaptly named Whispers. They've cleaned up since the night of the fire and the riot which coincided with the last night of my bachelor party. BBC3 could have sponsored us for Real Stag Dos/Don'ts. Here, I'm kindly given a match ticket, gratis, by a helpful Scot; they are only a fiver, but not on sale to visiting fans.

Another hell cab later, we arrive at the Ghencea Stadium, home to Steaua, EC winners in '86 in one of the worst finals ever. After being goal less it went to penalties, Barcelona were so bad they didn't even score one then. However, Steaua are not the antagonists tonight, the Romanian champs Unirea Urziceni are, and their ground is too small for purpose.

Since the days of Hagi, Popescu and the Unirea manager with the TV programme surname, Petrescu, Romanian football has gone steadily downhill.

Once again the rain is following me around, making this place appear as bleak as Dickens' house.

With over half an hour to spare until kick off, the police barricades pen in the two thousand 'Gers outside, opening just two turnstiles. On the second body search, I'm forced to discard my biro, clearly a dangerous weapon; the steward must have seen Joe Pesci in 'Casino' and read my plan. Some supporters don't get in until half time, by which time there's trouble down the front with the stewards. Seats are ripped out, which in an open stadium like this seem pointless, when half the season it's freezing and nobody sits anyway. There is no cover, and no toilets, and this is a Champions League match, and at an approved stadium? The stewards use CS gas, there are no police inside the ground, and they have a perspex fence to hide behind. Frankly they deserve a kicking, but we receive reports from home, that the ugly face of hooliganism returns, like the Manchester UEFA Cup Final '08, the usual uninformed bollocks.

If you treat people like shit, then this shit gets flung back in your face. The authorities here deserve only contempt.

Rangers score with ten to go through Lee McCulloch, but concede a first-class leveller late on, to, in all probability, bow out of Europe for this season.

We just escape the clutches of another long wait, by getting out seconds before the fans are locked in. A quicker taxi back to Whispers and a few late bars, and a desire to never return here again, even if I win a luxury trip in a competition. The second prize is two trips. In fact, I won't claim my prize even if the reward is inclusive of a solo bedroom performance of Nadia Comaneci executing floor exercises in her Olympic ten out ten heydays. Time machine and batteries not included.

November 5

If this is Thursday, then this must be Athens. Good riddance to Romania, we fly out from the other airport, Otopeni, warmer climbs beckon if only for a while. T-shirt weather is the order of the day, after finally finding our hotel, we feel obliged to do the tourist thing and visit the Acropolis in the afternoon sunshine. The Parthenon is one of those on a long list that includes the Taj Mahal and the Pyramids at Giza, of the, been there, seen it, had a beer in the nearest bar, monuments. Aesthetically, this is pretty much all that Athens has in its favour, as a tourist destination it's not really up there with the best, or even the mediocre.

AEK, pronounced 'ache', now play at the 2004 Olympic Stadium, which they share with Panathinaikos. An ulterior motive for me to watch tonight is that in '77, QPR lost to AEK 7-6 on pens in the UEFA Cup quarter final second leg, after losing on the night three nil, which drew the tie level after we won the home tie by the same score. (In '84, we go even one better than this, going out to Partizan Belgrade on away goals, after holding a four goal home advantage.)

Irini is the station stop on the Metro, and twenty Euros the entrance fee, but competition rules mean no alcohol is on sale, leaving us with too much time to kill, and have a browse round the site, made infamous over the entry problems for the 2007 CL final. The structure is impressive, but only five years on; the seats already look dilapidated, having turned cream from white.

How were they never given the Olympics in '96? The centenary year of De Coubertin's vision. Apart from money, power and the influence of Coca Cola.

Still this has been 'the' decade for Greek sport, with 2004 being the stand out year, mainly because of the Euro win in Lisbon. To think, there were tickets being given away for free to the semi final in Porto.

Taking our seats just before kick off, which is at the late time of 10.05, we are subjected to a video on the giant stadium monitor of great moments from their football history. In grainy black and white footage that I've never before seen, I pick out hooped shirts from the distant images, then grasp that it is Phil Parkes with his hands on his hips, and our aforementioned defeat that I'm staring at open mouthed. Cheers, you bubbles.

Irony, like most of the hilarity of life, is funnier when you are not in the slightest bit involved, Anthony finds this funny.

My bias now selected, we watch a first half packed full of incidents.

After, I reckon, all of sixteen seconds, Homer and Pythagoras' lot are ahead, cue, flares, smoke and noise from an empty arena, not one fifth full.

More amusement is had watching the newly introduced for the Europa League, goal line officials. They are now, I suppose the fourth and fifth men. When play is up the other end from the relevant goal line man, they saunter into the penalty box, for what one assumes is a better view. Quite why, is beyond our tiny minds, but it is funny. We try and imagine the linesman encroaching in a similar fashion, marking the full back ten yards into the field of play; I hope you get the idea. They do not make a single decision of note between them all match.

The opposition, Bate Borisov from Minsk, Belarus, make a game of it, and by the break it's two each with the White Russians having the edge. They survive a harsh sending off, and the woodwork assists four times to keep the score the same by the final whistle. The locals are cheered by the news that Everton have lost two nil to Benfica at Goodison, giving them half a chance of still qualifying for the knockout phase.

It's a midnight finish, and we are fortunate to get our subway connections back to the Premiere Roof bar in the Intercontinental hotel, which has a great view of the illuminated Parthenon. I painted my nails especially.

November 6

We're up early for the five Euros Metro ride to the easy on the tongue, Eleftherios Venizelos Airport. Yet another Aegean Airbus departure this time to Frankfurt for another weekend feast of Kraut fussball. Armed with a selection of beer and er, crisps, and different beer and crisps, we board a train to Kaiserslautern.

It is known as K- town, due to the large US military base nearby, thankfully there aren't any personnel roaming the streets tonight.

Once accommodation is arranged we gulp a couple of quick beers in a bar near the station. Adorning the walls amongst the regular memorabilia are some scarves from Kilmarnock. One would imagine that this has much to do with empathy for the letter K, rare as the first letter of most town names, except for ones called Kings blank. This reminds me of the silly joke concerning the three fish starting and finishing with aforesaid letter. Like the famous aristocrats gag, it works better with ad-libbing. Do the Germans substitute Kaiserslautern for Kilmarnock as the pla(i)ce in Deutschland/Scotland? Killer shark may translate but Kwik Save boil in the bag haddock however funny will be lost. Aldi may do a range of Kraut filled fish with pork. It could be a popular meal for one here.

Thus, on to the Fritz-Walter Stadium, located high up in the middle of town, for a six pm kick off Bundesliga league two televised game against Oberhausen. A team I've now seen twice in three months, four months ago I couldn't have told you where in Germany it was.

1FCK have a proud tradition, twice Bundesliga champs in the '90s and a ground to be proud of. Just shy of a 50000 capacity, it was used six times during WC 2006, with three enormous single tier stands that interlink. 'You'll never walk alone' sing the fans, but I much prefer it here than to Anfield.

Twelve Euros gets us a seat up in the Gods. One fact that is worth mentioning is the women only entrance, quite why is beyond me, and in this rapidly cooling climate, I've left my skirt back in the hotel room. We move down at the interval to the large terrace behind the goal, not before partaking of the first mulled wine of the season, again bought with the token system, and watch the home team overcome a poor away side 3-1. Without having to stick my neck out too far, the hosts are likely to make a return to the big boys. 26546 saw it, and head into town for Friday nacht. It may not be the best evening's entertainment centre, but there are enough late night bars for us to get suitably wankered.

We're amazed at the concoction popular with the younger crowd, a mixture of local beer and cola, that will leave proper advocates of Reinheitsgebot, the beer purity laws, nearly five hundred years old, coughing in their beer. It is correct of you to assume that Anthony and I showed solidarity with the ancient German charter.

November 7

I squint at my wristwatch and realise that Anthony is an hour late in leaving. Shouting across the room, words to the effect of, 'you wanna get a move on or you're gonna miss your flight.' This is from Stuttgart, quite a distance from here. It is tough trying to suppress a laugh at his expense, attempting to put a shoe on whilst having a slash, safe in the knowledge that I've got another four hours kip. Even though I surface at gone eleven, the landlady moans, but still offers me breakfast, well, cheese and ham rolls, which is marginally better than nothing.

A short walk to the HBF to find I've just missed a train to Heidelberg, leaving me short of time for the afternoon's event. I have to forego checking in at the hotel to head direct to Sinsheim, home to the newest Bundesliga kids on the block, Hoffenheim.

Changing at Heidelberg, you then board the slow train that trundles along the course of the Neckar River. You pass through the actual village of Hoffenheim, population less than 5000; the original ground is perched on a wooded hilltop you can still see from the carriage. They were going nowhere until the intervention of Dietmar Hopp, co-founder of SAP, and Euro rich software entrepreneur. Now established among the elite of German football, they are not liked by other followers, for not being considered a 'proper' club.

Alighting at Sinsheim, a free bus (honest) transports us to the Rhine Neckar Arena, standing alone in the distance.

I'm informed that I might struggle to get in, but I'm here now so there is little else to occupy me until I spot something unusual in the distance, something that no many times I see it, I have to look in greater detail, the ultimate voyeur. A billboard with a naked picture of Dita von Teese, you must be thinking. You'd be wrong, better curves, or angular beauty to be exact, Concorde.

Iconic in the extreme in my eyes, along with the Spitfire and Me262, to the left of the stadium there is not just one but two, well, nearly.

Walking towards them, I pass by the away ticket office who will sell me a 12 Euros ticket for cash only, which I'm short of. The ATM is located in what transpires to be the Auto and Technik Museum, Sinsheim, so a walk down there is essential. Indeed it is an Air France Concorde, and the ill fated Russian 'Concordski', the

Tupolev Tu-144 beside one another. They are set up as if just taking off, and you can go inside then as well, along with many other exhibits including an Imax cinema. Worth a proper look if you had the time. Later, as if driven by a subhuman devil, I point out to the listening passengers the paradox, that the French killed more Germans in the crash of flight 4590 in Gonesse, Paris 2000 than they did in the whole of WWII. One laughs, several don't. There are times when I must learn to keep my big mouth shut.

Moving on, standing with the Wolfsburg followers in a seat cum terrace, it's hard to believe that I'm watching the champions of Germany, especially as by the break they are a goal behind scored by Vedad Ibisevic, one of four Bosnians on the park. His injury last season coincided with the downturn in the fortunes of Hoffenheim, from top to mid-table.

Another, Mimisovic, equalises, and the Volkswagen sponsored team take a 2-1 lead shortly after and ultimately win, buoyed by their 3-0 Champions League midweek victory at Besiktas. There is also a dreadful miss by the highly rated Edin Dzeko, another Bosnian, reminiscent of Chris Iwelumo's for Scotland.

Returning to Heidelberg for the night, I can't help but sense that many people will watch teams as long as they are successful as over 30000 here today will testify. Ultimately history is bunk to the majority in an area when a winning team surfaces, no matter how the prosperity is arrived at.

Unlike MK Dons, Hoffenheim haven't stood on other clubs toes to get where they are, but like Chelsea, and more recently Manchester City, buying your fortune is frowned upon just as much by the have nots.

Tonight in Nuremburg is the WBA boxing heavyweight mismatch freak show of David Haye versus Nikolai Valuev, the freak show that you're drawn to see.

Beforehand, I find a great side street restaurant, 'Schnitzelbank', superb pork dishes, the clue is the title, and my new favourite pilsner, 'Rothaus' from the Black Forest. This and the fact that Rangers have won 2-1 at Hillsborough make for a relaxing evening.

A decent place for a drink is the pretty university town of Heidelberg, albeit on my lonesome. I don't wear a badge that says, 'Talk to me' but people invariably do, I'm potty trained and will always stand my round.

November 8

Yet another expensive taxi to the station for the three quarters of an hour train journey to Karlsruhe, in the Northern Black Forest region. A 1.30 kick off, for my second Union Berlin game of the season. Outside the gathering of scarves direct me to a tram and from then a walk through a park to the appropriately named Wild Park Stadion. Here I meet Bernd and chums drinking in the nearby car park, having driven 400 miles to attend.

Ten Euros and we're in the away end. Many of the young Union followers aren't happy as they are prohibited in putting their flags up on the fencing, only being allowed to lay them out on the running track in front of this old style stadium. Then, in a pincer movement seldom seen since the Battle of the Bulge, the boys leap over the front fence to retrieve their respective banners, much to the displeasure of the stewards, who not for the first time this week are heavy handed without good reason.

The twentieth anniversary of the dismantling of the Berlin Wall is a coincidence not lost on the Union defence, as they are breached three times in the first half, with a back four as square as Sponge Bob's pants.

A half time a feuerwurst, (Friday = Bratwurst, Saturday = Rindwurst) does the trick, and Union carry on their good early season form and battle back, scoring twice and missing two sitters before narrowly losing 3-2. As is usual, the whole team come over to the Berliners even in defeat, and shake hands with anyone who cares to put their hand through the fence.

Union have now slipped to fourth, whereas Karlsruher Sport-Club, relegated last term, aspire to the heady days of the '94, when they lost in the semi of the UEFA Cup on away goals.

A feature of football that is unique to Germany is fan friendship. For example the home side are 'friends' with Hertha, Union's city friendly rivals. Schalke befriend Nuremburg, Hamburg twin with Hannover etcetera. These may be based on shared dislikes, experiences, or just plain old similar wording. At home we all tend have clubs we feel some affinity towards, but nothing to the level it is here, sharing badges scarves and songs. On the face of it this seems like a good idea but can also be counter productive in that it can create rivalries that never previously existed. Interesting concept though, I hate everyone else!

Instead of an awkward journey to Baden Baden Airport, I'm treated to hospitality given by Bernd's friend, Mike, and his family, who live near the airport. They don't speak English, but ply me with drink, feed and probably would have clothed me if that need had arisen. We are much more alike than many seem to, or want to, appreciate.

They drop me at the airport, for my twenty Euros flight home, where I learn that Wealdstone have lost by the same score as Union did in their match at home to Rotherham in the FA Cup first round. Oh well, there is always next year, in which to lose to a team of part time wheel tappers and shunters.

Incidents this week are not of the feel-good variety.

The penalty given at Anfield for the challenge, or nearly, of Lee Carsley on David Ngog (anagram?) where no actual contact was made, creates waves. This highlights the problem of diving, easy enough to ascertain? Or what if it is anticipating a collision?

Sir Alex gets a fine and a ban not for the first or last time, this one was for criticising the referee's fitness.

Rangers get a ludicrous fine for the disturbances in Romania, of which you already know my first hand experiences last week.

Spurs keeper Carlo Cudicini threatens his career by crashing his BMW motorcycle, sustaining serious injuries. Sadly, this is overshadowed by Robert Enke, goalkeeper of Bundesliga, Hannover '96, who takes his own life, poor sod.

November 13/14/15

Much I half fancied the trip, mainly due to the unusual location, I had no intention in travelling to Qatar for the FA's greasing the voting palms for 2018 selection friendly against Brazil, to actually watch the game. Ergo, it's waste of time going. So I wasn't. Some mates are, but I won't be tempted. Even if it is the sixth anniversary of the Al Jazeera Sports Channel, I often watch this station to form a more rounded opinion of world events. Yeah right.

One night, just idling on the laptop, I randomly stray onto the Airmiles site and realise I've still got quite a few of these unused. I have 5021. Return to Doha, leaving Friday morning, returning on the Monday morning, BA, all taxes and fares paid, 5000 miles.

'Honey', I ask my wife, who is busy angle grinding the cutlery,

'Can I go to the England game in the Middle East?' As the sparks fly off her safety goggles, she gives me the answer I was hoping for. 'Just go.'

A few weeks later and I'm sitting on a cramped 747 for the seven hour flight via Bahrain to the Qatari peninsular. One hundred rials for a visa on entry, (about a score,) and then jumping in a people carrier with various other lads also staying at the Intercontinental. Unlike every other airport taxi service we are pleasantly surprised at the low cost, just because we are surrounded by oil, this doesn't naturally equate to cheap cab fares.

Friday night passes without any gossip worth reporting, leading to breakfast and a hasty rush to the pool where it is a disastrous 31 degrees. Leicester Jon, Preston Tony, Fleetwood, Blackburn Ian, Colchester Julian, Gillingham Pugsy, Palace boys Carl and Mark, and moi, all looking about as far removed from an advertisement for Speedo swimwear as it is possible to be. As usual, the media film us, the wacky England followers, in this instance some have dressed as Crusaders and are riding camels along the beach. The locals look reluctant to join in as Saladin and the Saracens, which is re-assuring, as we weren't allowed to bring our scimitars through customs.

Really we should venture out and see whatever sights there are, but the sun is out, and the alcohol is more freely available than I'd expected, so hay is being made. I drape my flag over the swimming pool's walkway, next to another QPR banner from Ruislip. There's no point in taking this to the stadium unless I plan to get in three hours before kick off.

A quantity of large gin and tonics later, we get the last free shuttle bus to the Khalifa Stadium handily running from our hotel. The ground is located by the Aspire Tower, and the British embassy advice is to get to the game by six at the latest, yeah right, there's not likely to be the Doha Arms open nearby to kill two hours.

On entry we're each given a small cardboard package tied with a ribbon, that looks like it may contain sweets, a handy present for the wife, but alas it contains Qatar 2022 car stickers, a lanyard and a key ring. No bloody good to any one, unless you gamble on the outside chance of them becoming collector's items. Their plan is to build an underground stadium to combat the summer heat. There wouldn't be many problems travelling around a nation half the size of Wales, and less than a million inhabitants, but should they really even be given consideration to hold the WC?

Before the national anthems begin, a moment of unintentional inspiration from England fans. The lights are dimmed, and the 50000 crowd are each given a luminous glow stick to hold up. It is a powerful image that soon descends into farce as our lot start to lob them on to the running track, much to the stewards' consternation and glee for everyone else. You Tube has good footage of this, if you care to look.

Robert Enke's minutes silence is well observed.

Brazil, hold a hoodoo over us, we haven't won in the last eleven meetings, though having played footy on Ipanema beach, I can confirm they can't all play like Pele. In fact, more like men with erectile dysfunction problems that he used to advertise. Unfortunately the ones that can, often can quite well and England with the usual 'friendly' withdrawals are relying on the likes of Darren Bent to prove many of us wrong.

The chant, 'If it wasn't for the oil you'd be skint' makes a change from the pathetic ten German bombers, but stating the bleeding obvious is hardly Oscar Wilde. We're playing like him though, and are losing by a goal at the break.

Deciding to grab some rubbish fast food and a 'soda', we queue uncomplainingly until I notice that we are unlikely to get what we are after, as the 'Arabs' are being served in preference to all of us from around the side of the kiosk. 'Us' includes all the other Asians trying to get an overpriced snack. This highlights that the caste/class system is alive and kicking here, but I'm not being treated in such a way, so I create a monumental fuss and they get the message. I'm thanked by fellow bystanders, which is nice, but I'd wager that they get walked over like this all the time.

There's a mass exodus shortly after this, which Anthony and I join, not before getting a photo taken with a replica WC, and head to the Ramada Plaza Hotel, spending a fiver to become a member of Qube, complete with souvenir identity card. It later feels as if the whole drinking population of Doha is in here, watching

Ireland lose to France, followed by the hate game between Egypt and Algeria.

Only next morning, nursing a hangover, and reading 'The Peninsula', a Qatari newspaper, do I realise that Brazil also missed a penalty. Between five of us, the hotel bill comes to over two grand. Money squandered in pursuit of happiness or just imbibing somewhere new? The latter, tick this off a very long list, and if you plan to venture here, don't do it under the premise of watching any football, go to Dubai instead, there is a much wider selection available there.

After a Wales 'B' team beat the Scots by three, George Burley is shown the drawbridge. They simply haven't got the players at present. Turd polishing is not as yet recognised as a replacement sport.

Robin van Persie is allegedly having treatment on his injury with placenta. Quite how this is any different to wiping chopped liver or half a pound lean beef mince down your leg, God only knows.

Thierry Henry is as popular as Oliver Cromwell in Ireland right now. His handball that leads to William Gallas nudging home the equaliser has already seen the FAI call for a replay. Knee jerk reactions continue all week, Martin Hansson and his linesman are berated, but were both unsighted. The only difference would have been to actually ask Henry if he handled it.

Four key questions must be answered. Will France keep wearing a kit that looks like it has parachute strapping? Will Gillette keep him on as a sponsor, especially after shagger Tiger Woods revelations? Did anyone laugh at Maradona's first goal against England in '86, not laugh now? Video evidence, will it finally be used?

Rugby League has not suffered as a result of tries being replayed, if anything it adds to the drama. The fourth official rather than telling mangers to sit down, checking substitutes studs, and holding up a digi-board would have a more active role. Then there is the new goal line officials, call me stupid, but they would probably have a clearer viewpoint than most. The money at stake means this will run and run and at then end of it all, FIFA won't change a thing.

Terry Henry, to give him his correct English name, usually celebrates with the 'aeroplane' which is not sufficient to gain an entry into the referee's notebook, although removing your shirt is.

This yellow card offence I find ridiculous, and if it is a booking on the grounds of taste then the swapping of shirts should be outlawed also.

In recent years, hitting the back of the net has led to more and more elaborate routines often involving half of the scorer's team mates. Not content with the homo erotic run and leap into the winger's arms, we now see 'the new born baby', 'the shoeshine' and 'the golf putt and caddy'. Surely this can be extended to 'twenty two yards' by the England team in honour of their cricketing associates, with bowler, batsman, wicket keeper, slip cordon and umpire with index finger raised skywards after the air catch taken on the long on boundary by the goalkeeper. Then, for any player cleared of a conviction, 'the twelve angry men' who can involve the substitutes along with the manager in a JP's wig and imaginary gavel. Ian Holloway would probably be agreeable to such high jinx.

Nope, a firm shake of the hand it is, which does at least allow for solo merrymaking, which sounds like a euphemism which would get you a life ban. Alan Shearer adopted the traditional one arm in the air befitting a forward of his stature, none of this shadow boxing the corner flag nonsense or worse, the cupped ear. If that isn't bad enough, the index finger to the lips is just plain irritating; anyone can score a tap in son. Quite what Andrei Arshavin is on about when he finishes God only knows.

Robbie Fowler's famous touchline of coke, could be further expanded to include a crack pipe, hidden in the physio's medical bag or further still, miming a needle entry in the vein and imaginary tourniquet pulled with teeth for hard core revelry.

Other honorary mentions should include the Mick Channon 'propeller', and my best-loved leap of joy, Bob Latchford, scaling the fence at Elland Road, after equalising against West Ham in the FA Cup semi final replay in 1980. Nowadays this would mean a booking.

What many would like to see, is the craze of writing on T-shirts worn under your kit. Old hat I hear you say, but there's whole new untapped revenue stream in undershirt sponsorship. I'll get the ball rolling with reference to the events in Paris and the inevitable outcome; world class players throughout the globe bearing the legends, handwritten or otherwise, BLATTER AND FIFA ARE (fill in your own expletive/s here.)

From a selfish standpoint, Ireland not making it to SA, means there are more flights from London for the rest of us; the French won't travel in the same numbers, and depart from Paris as well.

At least, of the less fancied nations, Slovenia managed to defeat Russia, depriving Blatter and Co of the no questions asked rouble.

November 21

I should have known better. Last season I left after 28 minutes, when we were already two down, and looking likely to concede more, only lasting that long because it took a while to convince someone to go for a pint with me. My only previous visit to Doncaster was in the FA Cup in 1985 at the old Belle Vue ground, when we lost inevitably one nil in the third round as we always seem to.

Yet previous defeats couldn't be further from my mind, as I board the coach at the Target Roundabout, Northolt, not for once organised by myself, but the incapable hands of two of my regulars. For arguments sake, let's just call them Corky and Frank. The good thing about not being in charge, is that you don't have to have your sensible head on, and generally act in a way that you did when you went on school trip to Madame Tussauds aged ten, substituting milk for alcohol. Sticking your spotty, naked bum against the window doesn't seem the same when you reach your forties.

Well oiled, we park up just outside Donnie in a pre-arranged stop at the 'The Styrrup' in Rossington. They do a roaring trade in steak lunches and shandies.

More lubricated than an F1 engine, the short journey to the uninspiring Keepmoat is enlivened by a singalong to Johnnie Cash. At this stage you could play Abba's 'Dancing Queen' and fifty geezers would howl along to it. In my experience, blokes at football like, what I term, 'yob music'. This would be The Jam, The Specials, Madness (urgh) or from a more modern era, Oasis tapped into the hooligan ear nicely, as perhaps Kasabian now have. Most of this isn't really to my taste, but the more discerning musical palate is not likely to have the superb arrangements of Steely Dan or the brilliance of Jimmy Page's Gibson be given the time of day on any fifty seater. In fact, 'turn that shit off, Mel' is a phrase I'm often used to hearing from the back of the coach. I can't believe that Frank Zappa is not to everybody's taste though! Today I'll grin and bear it; at least it's not roots reggae.

It's windy, and raining at this plastic ground, we have two debutants playing today, unnecessarily so in my opinion. Rovers play exactly how I would suggest that the opposition tackle us. Close us down early, never let us get a rhythm, and hit our flair players hard. They do, and deserve their two nil win.

In a filthy mood on the way back down the M1, alcohol only masks over the fact that the cracks are beginning to show in our promotion push.

Special mention should be made to the Wigan Athletic goalie, Chris Kirkland whose trip to the bookies surely cannot go unnoticed. However, for him no huge payout, he backed Spurs to get ten instead of nine, and Defoe to hit six instead of five.

November 24

Gareth Ainsworth could be fairly described as a journeyman's journeyman. Growing up in Blackburn, he made his League debut for Preston and has since had a career spanning ten different clubs. The highlights of his calling have included one magnificent season for Lincoln City, where a plethora of goals persuaded Port Vale to part with £500,000. Multiply this figure by four and you have the amount paid by Wimbledon for his talents. This is both of these clubs record transfer fees, paid out and received. The most appearances he's made for one side are in the blue and white hoops of W12s finest. Here, he also had two brief spells as caretaker manager, but this season he is just registered as a player.

Although in the twilight of his playing career, he is still as fit as a butcher's dog, and wants to play on as long as possible. With first team opportunities now limited at Rangers, he has opted to take a month's loan up the M40 at Wycombe Wanderers, now managed by former player and manager at QPR, Gary Waddock.

This is an area I know well, having once worked here, at a manufacturing facility, like much of Britain, no longer in use. The Chairboys, as they are known, the area was once home to many furniture makers, were non league until making the grade in '93 under the guidance of Martin O'Neill. This was achieved only three years after moving from the sloping Loakes Park to the current Adams Park, which is located at the end of the Sands Industrial Estate. The original gates are now used at the entrance to the car park outside the new ground.

Rumours abound of another ground move, along with co-hosts London Wasps rugby club, and part of the reason for this is access, or the lack of it. The Hourglass, where I'm having a pre-match pint or two, sits at the entrance to Hillbottom Lane, the only way in and out of the ground, which is a right royal pain in the arse if the capacity of over ten thousand is any where near reached.

Gaz, who I know well enough for him to sort me out a complimentary ticket, has a great game, typical head down, no nonsense mindless boogie which earns him the man of the match champagne. If he stays injury free, he'll play until he's forty. The only goal of the game comes from Matt Harrold, ex Brentford player, and the opponents tonight, from the penalty spot. He also misses one.

No doubt I'll see the Bees again before the season is out. Wycombe will have their work cut out to stave off relegation. It seems they are the lesser partner of the football and rugby ground share alliance and because of such they are unlikely to achieve anything greater than the level that they are currently striving to remain playing in.

With Liverpool out of the Champions League, you would assume that the blue side of the city would be smiling, but this is not the case as Everton's new ground application is turned down. Doing the rounds is the theory that their shirt sponsor, Chang, stands for, 'Can't have a new ground.'

I'm here all night, try the fish......................

November 28

It is not often that a team gets applauded off the pitch when they haven't won, especially my team, today is the exception. Unfortunately our two all home draw against Coventry only goes to highlight our soft underbelly. Chris Coleman, the City manager is very complimentary about our performance, but this only masks the truth, that this is more points dropped, if you dominate a match so comprehensively, it feels like a defeat.

The comradeship of your fellow sufferers is one of the chief benefits of being a regular at whomever it is you follow, whether you realise it or not. After a nomadic life watching Rangers from all four sides of the ground, in all guises, be it terracing and enforced seating, finally, over fifteen years ago, settling on an area in the Loftus Road Upper tier. The faces generally have stayed the same in this time even if our fortunes haven't. Most of us have stayed loyal season ticket holders, and these days they even put your name on the seat front, spelt wrongly in my case. In acknowledging the people around me on match days, it strikes me that bar one or two, I would not know any of these people otherwise. Many good mates sit in other parts of the ground, but selfishly, a big up for all these friends around me on match day:-

Danny, Mick and saucepans, Ian, Clive, Steve, Kingo, Tom, Lil Dave, Martin and sons, Ken, Neil and sons, our bird Paula, and Chris. Up to my right, are Bruce, Ken and Rick, behind me Craig, Scott, Daren, brothers Nigel and Trevor with their kids. On the left, Aussie James, Mark, Mick with Ivor, Michael, Harry, Polish Paul, Del, Gary, John Shaw further across, and a special mention to George Gristwood and his elder brother Bill, home and away with Rangers and England for the best part of eighty years.

To anyone I've missed, or upset they've been included, sorry. I'll reiterate, that we and all people like us are the essence of football. The sooner the powers that be stop taking us all for granted, the better it will be.

That was a party political broadcast on behalf of the football spectator let's have a party party. One tends to get like this when feeling all melancholic after the hangover kicks in, and it dawns on you that your aspirations for the season may not be fulfilled. As per fucking usual.

An entertaining game on Sunday, where I forego the Mersey derby for the delights of Rockingham Road, and Kettering Town drawing with Leeds. This is followed by the key date of the football calendar, the third round draw for the FA Cup. More of which in January.

The ridiculous notion that Ireland could enter the WC playing as the thirty third team is muted, but will get about as far Liam Brady kicking a ball with his right foot. He joins in the Blatter bashing, calling him an embarrassment to FIFA, a bit of a law unto himself. You can't say he's wrong; in fact he should have called him a fucking eejit. Jules Rimet would be turning in his grave if he foresaw the way that his vision is now being exploited. Along with IOC they are unanswerable to no one but themselves, and the world does what it is told for fear of losing what little influence it has within the Swiss based money printing factories. It is a shame that there is no alternative as in boxing, but no single entity would dare to break away for what would likely to be years in the wilderness.

December 3

Fulham finished seventh last season, and somehow managed to qualify for the new Europa League by legitimate means, not via the Intertoto rubbish as they had done so before.

It can be a bit galling for some these days, once upon a time qualification was much tougher, and for a while at least, impossible.

Rangers missed out in '88 and '93, top London club in fifth position both times, but no UEFA Cup place because of what I call the 'Thatcher ban'. This, of course, applies to many teams from that era. Ones that were to miss out on their day in the sun include FA Cup winners Coventry and Wimbledon. It would have been worth seeing a poncy Italian side going to Plough Lane on a rotten December evening and seeing them kicked all over SW17 by Jones, Fashanu et al.

Still, one shouldn't begrudge the Cottagers their European adventure, they have a decent side, and even Mohammed Al Fayed, the Harrod's camel jockey as he is unofficially known, has kept a relatively low profile of late.

I meet Dave Brown, a supporter from the days when they were shit, and his wife Steph, in a Hammersmith pub, and walk the back way beside the Thames, past the River Cafe, to Craven Cottage.

It's busy outside in Stevenage Road, the statue of Johnny Haynes looking over proceedings.

Admission prices have been reduced, working on the theory that it is better to have some money for a seat than no money at all. At first, it looks like membership only, as loads of Bulgars and me struggle to gain entry. Being from these parts, ie, West London, I manage to get a box office ticket for £15, I later learn that they were on offer for a fiver at lastminute.com.

Eventually, I take my seat in the Putney End, the only goal of the game already having been scored by Zoltan Gera. There is a nice incline to this stand, once a large open terrace, and as a whole, the ground still keeps an old fashioned feel which I like. It has one of the oldest stands in the world, built over a century ago, and there is still a tree within the ground's confines. For how much longer remains to be seen?

Where I'm lounging is normally designated a neutral section, quite why is beyond me. Tonight many noisy CSKA Sofia supporters, no doubt London based builders, doormen or au pairs, have smuggled themselves in here, with many locked out. Under normal match conditions, the idea of a mixed bag of fans is asking for trouble. The bigger clubs will take liberties with this, and unsuspecting football tourists will find themselves cheering for the wrong team at the wrong time, the demographic may have changed but human nature has not.

Other liberty takers are the stewards, obviously bullied at school, catching some Bulgarians smoking behind the back of the bike sheds, I mean stands, manhandling them as if they were terrorists, causing a chain reaction of resentment among their friends as they are ejected. Surely, a quiet word would be sufficient?

Leaving early, for a quick pint in The Crabtree before the long walk up the Fulham Palace Road, I say goodbye to the mono browed Emil, a Levski Sofia supporter here to watch his rivals lose, and shake his hand.

This is more than Arsene Wenger could muster last night after his team's League Cup defeat to Mark Hughes' Manchester City. This will cause major repercussions throughout the world. Kim Jong-Il, and Iranian leader Ahmadinejad have both blamed the West, and conspiracy theories are rife on the internet. 'Handshakegate' will shake the walls of the very foundations on which our civilisation is built. I blame the French.

The circus comes to town, Cape Town.

From two hundred entrants, we are now down to the last thirty two.

Charlize Theron, Haile Gebreselassie, Makhaya Ntini, amongst others give us what looks like a decent enough draw. David Beckham is the only non African involved, surely this will help our 2018 bid no end, or just confirming its likelihood?

England will play against the country with the largest population left in the competition, USA, and the least, Slovenia. We'll also compete against the one with the most Algerians.

One million tickets go on sale to those who can afford them.

December 5

The omens look bad for this one. Ranger's opponents today, Middlesbrough, have never previously been victorious in any meetings at Loftus Road. An extra twist being that new manager Gordon Strachan has yet to record a victory since taking over the reigns from Gareth Southgate. I'm not very superstitious, but the writing is on the wall. Records are there to be broken, and with just a tiny amount of hindsight I can't believe I didn't put all of Jake's piggy bank money on a 'Boro win. It's not as if they have a team full of duds, and most of their mercenaries are now flying another flag of financial footballing convenience.

They don't just snatch it, they defeat us 5-1. The wheels are starting to come off. Confidence is starting to wane.

I wonder what my old friend Steve Edwards would have thought of it all. 'Magilton out' or words to that effect I would suggest. Sadly he died more than three years ago of motor neurone disease. Not a good way to shuffle off this mortal coil. To the last he still attended as many fixtures as possible, losing first his voice, and then his ability to walk as his muscles wasted away.

Ever since his premature departure, I've had good intentions about raising money for the motor neurone charity, especially as with an illness such as this, along with Parkinson's and Multiple Sclerosis, you get the impression that somehow a breakthrough and cure should be possible in the foreseeable future.

Naïve and optimistic as that may be, there are two reasons why, as of yet, I haven't put your money where my mouth is. Being bone idle, is one, which is not a valid excuse, the other puts me on the horns of a dilemma.

The preferred choice of fund raiser for me is the ascent of Mount Kilimanjaro, which I would quite like to do, and there's the rub. I get to achieve the not inconsiderable feat of climbing Africa's highest peak, and get 'you' to pay for doing it. This is an over simplification, but the whole sponsorship for accomplishing tasks which you are keen on undertaking anyhow, sits heavy on me.

No doubt many celebrities mean well when accepting these assignments, but I'm buggered if I'm going to pay for them and a film crew to fulfil them.

This is by no means a criticism of the fund raising machine, it can be viewed as means to an end, but surely there are ethically better methods of achieving their targets.

At least Niall Quinn helped to start a trend, that when the already super rich players receive testimonials, some, if not all of the receipts are donated to their chosen charity. Quite why you would want to pay millionaires pension funds otherwise is beyond me.

December 7

Another televised game this time on a Monday night, a derby against Watford, but one without too much animosity. The main object of their hatred is of course Luton Town, however QPR have a longstanding dislike of the Hatters too, and one with a much more violent history.

My old strike partner, Paul Murray, meets me early enough for a few beers, not sure why he is a 'Hornet', for the same reason that I'm not sure why they adopted that particular insect as a mascot from the late '50s when they used to play in blue and white. Yet they do still have a 'hart', as in white, on their badge. At least if they had stuck with gold before changing to yellow it wouldn't look so bad.

With the threat of administration hanging over them all season they've done reasonably well, although the old East stand, I assume, remains condemned, awaiting redevelopment, which could very well be a long way away.

After a couple more beers in the aptly named Oddfellows Arms then to the match, another Sky special, where it is instantly noticeable that we've changed our formation and players and started four, four, two.

Despite taking a first half lead, their body language is not right, and this lack of conviction sees us beaten three one. We, as supporters, make our feelings clear from the stand, and we do not deserve the flak we receive from the club for this.

Disillusioned by the change in our fortunes, there are whispers of player disgruntlement, and the internet message boards are rife with rumour and counter rumour. On Wednesday, these turn out to be more than just hearsay.

When undertaking this self assignment, my intention was not to write solely about the experiences surrounding my team, although it is undoubtedly the case that I'll watch them more than any other. This is unavoidable, but my hope is that you absorb my thoughts as if I was following your club and the similarities encompassing all aspects of football culture.

Now it has got to the stage where I feel impelled to talk about the fiasco, the soap opera that is Queen's Park Rangers Football Club.

In my lifetime, ie, the Sixties onwards, we've been relatively successful, certainly when it comes to winning plaudits if not much silverware.

Here is a potted history since then, whether you like it or not.

After years of mediocrity, the club sprang to life when car dealer Jim Gregory bought the club in the mid '60s, he could be considered a bit of a wide boy, but nonetheless he took Rangers to level the hadn't attained since before World War I.

The unique double of Division III winners and the first Wembley League Cup Winners in 1967, followed by another promotion to Division I the year after with Rodney Marsh to the fore, put us in the big time for the first time. An immediate relegation, but followed four years later a glorious return. This time they meant business, Gordon Jago, then Dave Sexton, fashioned the greatest QPR side ever, pipped to the title by Liverpool in '76 by just a point. A side containing England internationals, Parkes, Clement, Gillard, Francis, Thomas and Bowles as well as Mclintock, Masson, Hollins and Givens, and the unsung Leach and Webb.

The break up of this team saw relegation in '79, but Terry Venables managed a side that reached the FA Cup Final in '82, Division II Champions in '83, and top London club in '84 with our second UEFA qualification. Effective team players such as Fenwick, Gregory, Stainrod and Waddock saw Rangers often give the top teams a run for their money. This continued on and off for the next twelve years, with the '88 and '93 sides being particularly useful with players the calibre of Paul Parker and Les Ferdinand grabbing headlines and England caps.

This often over achievement stopped being the norm after relegation in '96, a bad time to not be in the Premiership suddenly awash with money.

A succession of bad or badly advised chairmen, and a further demotion, but Ian Holloway's spirited side aided by spirited support returned to the second tier in

2004. From here on we have hardly pulled up any trees, until it seemed a light at the end of the tunnel appeared two years ago in the shape of Formula One impresarios Flavio Briatore and Bernie Ecclestone. Allied to this was the 20% stake purchased by the uber wealthy Mittal family. On the face of it, trophies would be ours in a matter of days, so to speak. The volpe argentata, or silver fox to us, wanted to create boutique football, a term coined by broadcaster and big 'R's fan Robert Elms when interviewing his majesty. Quite what this entails is beyond most mere mortals, or anyone else. Supermodels in the directors box, Cipriani's restaurant behind the executive boxes, Krug in the ice bucket, uncertainty on the pitch.

Briatore's constant interference has seen a revolving door policy of managers, leaving the supporters as baffled as Gregory, Di Canio, Dowie, Sousa and Magilton have probably all been.

This year it appeared that something had finally gone right. Not so. After a poor run, Madge is alleged to have head butted Buszaky following the Watford defeat, which he denies, but is suspended pending further investigation. His assistants stand by him, and will not work again until he is cleared.

Temporary charge is given to youth team coach Steve Gallen, brother of 'R's hero Kevin, and blue haired ex-star Mark Bircham, as Rangers as you get, but with very limited first team coaching experience. It is rumoured that Ipswich were paying some, if not all of Magilton's salary, as they had dismissed him earlier in the year.

This hooped roller-coaster plunges us into another nadir, without ever seeming to reach its zenith. Wankers. My wankers.

December 12

Saturday morning, I get away from Rangers problems. These cannot get worse until Monday night, which is when we are next taking the field.

Flying from Gatwick at a reasonable time, for a more than reasonable cost (just over £30) with of all people, Aer Lingus, to The Netherlands, and the team run by the electronics giant Philips, Eindhoven.

Whether I'll see total football today remains to be seen, but there is no doubting that as whole, the nation have over achieved on the pitch. This refers to both the national team and club sides. The brilliance of Van Basten and company in '88 being the only reward they have to show in the international stakes. They have had a production line of players from Cruyff and Neeskens, to Gullit and Bergkamp, that all can be considered great.

Feyenoord was my preferred destination, as I'm friendly with a few QPR Dutch fans from Rotterdam, unfortunately they are away this weekend, and having already been to the Ajax Arena, and more specifically Amsterdam too many times, the novelty has worn off. Walking around the narrow streets, stoned off your tits, whistling the theme to Van Der Valk, and taking your life in your own hands jay walking in front of trams, has lost its once magical appeal.

On the 401 bus into town, it is revealed that Philips town is no longer what it was, derelict buildings, part futuristic, part practical, not aesthetic, strangely reminding me of the end scenes of 'Full Metal Jacket' (which was filmed at Beckton Gas Works). Much of the production has now been moved to the Amsterdam area, and, no doubt, the Far East.

PSV continue to flourish, arguably the most successful Dutch side of modern times, European Cup winners in '88. Twice managed by the late Sir Bobby Robson, with Romario and Ronaldo having cut their teeth here, in a place that was little more than a village a century ago.

Last seasons surprise Eredivisie winners AZ Alkmaar are tonight's opponents, minus manager Louis Van Gaal who left in the summer for Bayern Munich, and this week his replacement, Ronald Koeman, was sacked and succeeded by the wily old Dick Advocaat.

The amazingly named Philips Stadion is located bang in the centre of town next to the Bavaria brewery, and thus is easy to get to by foot.

Not so easy to get is entrance. A membership is required to buy a ticket, or you are forced into paying through the nose for a gold or silver package. As this is classed as a top category match, a silver package is going to set me back seventy Euros. To book this in advance, you had to inconveniently pay by bank transfer. The package comprises of ticket (21Euros), tokens or munts of ten Euros, and forty to spend in their fan shop.

The girl in the ticket office won't budge from this, at this price I expect her to be part of the deal. Even though I plead that I've got a 32" LCD TV, a kettle, a toaster all manufactured by Philips, that help keep her in a job.

Later, I enjoy a great supper in an all you can eat tapas bar (16.50Euros) named La Gitana. Always eat food unique to the area! At least I managed to avoid a burger or pizza.

A kick off time of 8.45pm, gives me time to offload my voucher to a genuine local in the Fan shop. This is an awkward task, but I really don't want a PSV shirt, but the man who does, saves himself ten Euros and hands me thirty.

Inside, the ground is as near as damn it full, very similar to Anderlecht, not a hundred miles away.

Heaters in the roof make the experience bearable at this time of year. I'm struggling to spend all of my tokens, so in the spirit of Xmas I donate the remainder to a disabled child making me feel good until I notice the kid next to him with a 'you could have given that to me instead' face, swinging my mood in a second. You can't win 'em all.

PSV can though, blond supersub Swede, Ola Toivenen heads an 86th minute winner, keeping their unbeaten record, which they share with Steve Maclaren's Twente Enschende. Then bizarrely breaking into 'Happy Together', sixties hit by The Turtles, I had always thought it was a Beatles song.

34,000 devotees it seems, head into the town, only a ten minute walk away.

Outside an ice skating rink, the Queen Hotel advertises gluhwine enticing me in, like, er, an alcoholic in need of a drink on a frosty night. This one comes complete with a cinnamon stick, a nice touch, but I'm left clueless as to how you are expected to utilise this with your warm beverage. It doesn't dissolve like a digestive, and as I'm the sole consumer of this on the premises, I can't look to anyone else to give me tips. I assume it should be nibbled. Then I try and picture this catching on, like alcoholic lemonade in years gone by, with a pub full of say, Millwall, all standing with their little fingers cocked, discussing whether or not to dip. 'No one likes us, we don't dunk.' Good stuff this hot vino!

Watching the pre-Christmas festivities, it hits me that the Dutch or Germans do this sort of thing so much better than we do. Patently the colder the climate enhances the feel of what we envisage the holiday season to be about. Piped music accompanies the skaters outside, which I'm oblivious to until I hear a familiar tune, 'Stop the Cavalry' by Jona Lewie. Not unusual at this time of year, but funny for me, as it's my dad playing cornet on the song. Even out of the country, it is often hard to escape from the clutches of your family!

Speaking better English than an inner city kid, the waiter points me in the direction of Stratumseind, where he says there are a lot of bars. He's not joking; suddenly I've walked into a street in Ibiza. This place is kicking. Over forty bars and clubs, open until four, stacked up next to each other, techno at full blast, shots on offer with lagers, the odd brawl, I feel right at home.

At the very end of parade is the obligatory coffee shop, where as a cure for imaginary insomnia, I grab a ready rolled as a nightcap. The walk back to the hotel that should take about fifteen minutes takes me two hours, at least it seems to, and talking to your self as a substitute for company is quite natural. Perhaps though, not out loud as I explain to Harvey the rabbit. I'll wager that he didn't have to pay seventy Euros to watch the match.

December 13/14

Approximately thirty miles from Eindhoven to the north, also in the region of Brabant, lies Tilburg. Here lies the home of another lesser known Eredivisie side, Willem II.

If you venture here in the middle of July, you could stumble across the biggest fair in the whole of Benelux.

A little travel tip here, that when you get the train in The Netherlands, machines don't take credit cards or notes, only coins, which can be as frustrating as it is odd.

Far smaller than PSV, but much less impersonal, my pre-arranged 17 Euros ticket for entry to the King Willem II stadium is sorted within thirty seconds. The club colours are the same as the flag of the Netherlands, and the club is named after the King who died here in 1849.

Speaking as someone who doesn't much feel the cold, I'm cold, or more accurately under dressed. An investment in a Willem II ski hat is essential.

This will get me quizzical looks wearing this at home. What team is that? Blokes edging nearer to me to get a better look at the emblem will wonder.

Apart from the titfer, Arbroath T shirt, Union Berlin badge, Celta Vigo scarf (bought at a game there three years ago) and a Fuck Me It's The Faroe Islands jacket, these aficionados will think that this chap knows his football onions, and looks like a proper ground hopping window licking retard.

Grey woollen headgear aside, thankfully the rest is not true, today anyway, anything to distract the chill from my bones.

The score is level 1-1 at the break, where the entertainment is supplied care of Belgium's largest beer producer Jupiler, who fire a few hundred red T-shirts (Large) into the crowd by means of a compressed air mortar device. I now possess said item, mainly because my line out skills were far superior to the pre-teen Dutch kids who were vying for this glittering prize, and are left strewn all over the stand.

Roda JC run out comfortable winners, 3-1, and leap frog Willem II near the foot of the table. The standard seemed poor to me, but this won't bother the 800 or so away followers of a 12500 attendance. Often, there is an airport type walkway direct to the away pen. There has been a big hooligan problem in The Netherlands for some time. Roda hail from Kerkrade, not five miles from Aachen, with whom, given the more recent Dutch/German history, they are actually friends not enemies, even sharing the same club colours.

My Smurf like hat becomes the best investment I've made since I paid a bargain ten pounds for the Vermeer original painting at Oxfam. 'Girl with a pearl necklace', is a lesser known portrait, from his pornographic period. This is especially the case now, as I have to walk back to Tilburg station, the number 450 bus runs hourly and I've just missed it.

I toy with the idea of helping myself to a bicycle which are available everywhere. This would not be right I reconsider, as just after seeing your team lose, all you need is to have your bike nicked by an English bastard too lazy to walk. Besides, the fact that I didn't bring my QPR mittens to stop my fingers from freezing to the handlebars.

Back to Eindhoven for my bag left at the hotel, then home, with the self satisfaction that not paying on the Stansted Express brings you. For sure.

Maynor Figueroa, whose shot from 67 yards for Wigan past Stoke keeper Thomas Sorensen can only be described as brilliant. Try and kick a ball like that. Probably or possibly, you can flight the ball into the net from that distance, but the goalie will watch the flight and comfortably collect. To take a shot, which it certainly was, and score is some feat. Take a bow Manny.

Ryan Giggs also takes the plaudits after being named BBC Sports Personality of the Year. Why? Much in the same way that Barack Obama won the Nobel Peace Prize. If they had presented him with a lifetime achievement award, fair enough, but there was no way 2009 was 'his' year. Questions should also be asked on the change of format, as now the nominees are selected in advance, not giving the general public the opportunity to decide for themselves. Once again I'm drawn to Paul Weller's wise words about the public wanting what the public gets.

Back in the ordinary world, a Monday night fixture at West Brom, live on Sky. I'm not a lover of watching my team on TV, and unbelievably get offered corporate hospitality tickets and a lift but my wife threatens to move out if I go.

'You'll be rubbish as usual.' I know this of course, but blind faith and optimism drive me on.

The twenty or so of us in my local are open mouthed as manager less we take a two goal lead with half an hour to go. Ha, what does my wife know? More than me, as the Baggies pull one back, and then equalise three minutes into stoppage time with the last kick of the match. Bollocks.

We all shout and swear at the plasma in front of us, I'm probably the worst offender. It's not is if anyone at the Hawthorns can hear you, but you do it all the same.

Being honest, most would've settled for this result beforehand, but it feels like a defeat. Thankfully, I've been drinking here for nearly thirty years; otherwise I'd probably be barred.

In Scotland, news that Rangers fans are planning on boycotting the re-arranged game at Dundee United abandoned, you may recall, on November 1. The Arabs have decided to charge half price again for the ticket holders. Would they have tried this if it was the Accies game that was forsaken?

Being a man of high moral fortitude, I will stand alongside my blue brothers and will not pay the extra admission fee on a Tuesday night on Tayside in December.

Will the half used ticket now become a collector's item I wonder?

An under strength Wolves team go to Old Trafford and inevitably are defeated. You can't really blame Mick McCarthy for making ten changes from the team that won at Spurs, he's a realist if nothing else. As always it's the fans who get the thin end of the wedge, '£42 to see the reserves' sing the Wanderers faithful, who have to buy well in advance and have no say in the matter, it's not as if they'll receive a refund. We're all mugs.

Jim Magilton and John Gorman 'go mutually', whatever that means, replaced, surprisingly, by Paul Hart along with our former coach Mick Harford.

Inadvertently, Hart has already helped Rangers reach promotion, when playing for Leeds at Loftus Road in April '83. He scored the own goal that won the game. This is the only straw I can clutch to, one of fate.

If he knows what it is like to work with one hand tied behind his back at Portsmouth, he may now find out what it is like to work with handcuffs on, and not the pink fluffy variety supplied by Ann Summers. I've been reliably informed that they can chaff a bit.

December 19

Snow. Bloody cold. Being honest I would have rather gone on an all day pre Xmas bender without the football disruption in the middle. This is exactly what some of the lads did, even though they had match tickets, the warmth of open hearth fire being too tempting to leave. Actually just a shitty three bar heater, but you know where I'm coming from.

A dour one all draw against a dour side. I'm not being particularly unfair here. Even with half an hour to go they were time wasting.

The highlight of the afternoon was a message to our supporters from the scoreboard which is located high above the away 'school' end. We are encouraged to text in anyone consistently using foul and abusive language. This will be completely discrete; in doing so you are advised to attempt to give the seat number and row of the foul mouth you are grassing up.

Text 'QPR ABUSE', I kid you not.

Many of us are swearing today just to keep the blood flowing. Whilst I concede that much of the crowd, at all games, myself included, go over the top sometimes, there is a time and place for cursing, and watching football live, is that time and place. Admittedly if you sit regularly in the family section and have a potty mouth, you deserve having your collar felt. Being brought up in an age before 'Baa baa black sheep' became 'woolly sheep', my old school of thought being from the 'never did me any harm' era. It would be less shocking if insurance companies started advertising on the hoardings concerning 'no win, no fee' compensation claims for back pains from cramped stands seating or deep vein thrombosis from being unable to move your legs for ninety minutes during a crowded cup tie. A bit like some of the forwards we've had over the years.

Some of the lads start to text, to dob in each other and themselves, which is fair enough after having to watch this shit.

After a few pints, realising that sometimes you do have to be a dad on a Saturday and call it a day as my son has a fever. Boxing Day will be the alcoholocaust.

Referee Mike Dean deserves credit for making Frank Lampard take a penalty three times at Upton Park due to encroachment. The comical reactions of Ballack, Drogba and company indicate to me that they don't know the rules. Funnier still, is, if you watch closely, the third penalty, technically, should also not have been allowed, as a Chelsea player still encroaches. All that money, yet no clue.

In true Christmas spirit, Mark Hughes is given the boot by Manchester City for failing to deliver the league title yet. Time is not a quality the new owners are prepared to negotiate on.

December 26

The Metropolitan Police decide (I assume) that our Boxing Day game will kick off at 1pm. Normally you would expect a bumper crowd, but with the Met seemingly wanting to put their feet up early, added to this the closure of the main line to Paddington, thereby discouraging the normally decent turnout by Bristol City. Then couple this with the general disgruntlement within our ranks, thus making the whole experience somewhat dispiriting.

Two games in three days moan the put upon managers, oooooh, the horror. Just to think they used to play on Christmas Day with the reverse fixture the very next day, they wouldn't moan about that much now would they?

Much of Europe are in the midst of their winter break. Every year the idea is muted here, mainly by foreign managers with no sense of tradition, or love of cricket, or, as is more likely, the thought of spending two weeks back in their homelands over Christmas and the New Year.

Apart from the fact that we still get warmer weather from the North Atlantic Drift, it is also difficult to predict exactly when the cold snap will hit, if at all. Leave it as it is.

Bernd with three other Germans, Karsten, Oliver and Tilo are glad that as of yet we don't have a break as they do, and are over for a few days to inject a shot of football. Perhaps this where the expression cold turkey has evolved from?

They are as nonplussed as us when finally, we win two one. A lot of our crowd still boo anyway; we would have probably smashed our own ground up if we'd lost. Special mention must be given to Bristol City's scorer Nicky Maynard, three touches without a bounce and the ball is in the net before our defence has blinked. A fantastic goal.

By three, we are all in the pub and a long days drinking begins in earnest, enjoyed by bachelors and football dads nationwide. Happy Christmas.

December 28

Portman Road, Ipswich does not appeal today. The body language of the players two days ago, doesn't auger well, allied to this I join the stay aways due to the cost of the tickets. £33 and £39 plus booking fee, too much for this division. (QPR are also guilty of high prices.) Even the kerb crawlers near the ground are staying away at those prices. My high principals mask my gut feeling that we are going to lose. (We do, by three. Wankers.)

Instead, with the Germans still in town, a League One encounter at the old capital of Middlesex, Brentford. The opponents at Griffin Park are Charlton Athletic, whom the Union boys and I will meet up with, Tony and friends, Valiant Supporters.

It is a good area for imbibing, with a pub on every corner of the ground, and even with the amount of recent closures, there are still plenty of choices.

Brentford are our original derby foe, and they hate us. However, in much the same way Chelsea's Surrey based support will view us, we're now nonplussed by The Bees. In fact they haven't beaten us in a meaningful game since 1965, pretty much a turning point in the fortunes of both clubs.

Leaving the Addicts and Germans to the all ticket away end in Brook Road, once a fine terraced stand, I bump into Mick O'Connell, fellow 'R's season ticket holder, escaping his horde of kids for the afternoon, and we spend a score for the privilege of standing in the Ealing Road end. It's a shame that the Bees have let their ground fall into a shadow of its former self, as always money issues have dictated their fate.

'Hey Jude' is still their unofficial anthem, it's re-assuring to know some things remain the same. 1-1 is the final score, Charlton get a point they scarcely deserve, Brentford have two valid appeals for penalties turned down. Sitting in second, it is still a valuable point for the South Londoners, with an in form Norwich breathing down their necks.

Until their recent downturn, Charlton had been a real success story. Returning to the Valley after their enforced hiatus at both Selhurst and Upton Parks, mostly going about the right way in attracting support back to the area. Once the parachute payments from the Premiership dry up, like most teams, it can become a struggle, with your big earners failing to put in big performances, and before you know it you're in the third division with a mounting mountain of debt to deal with.

To their credit, the directors have kept faith in manager Phil Parkinson, when many boards would have sacked him and at least one other by now. (Well mine would.)

A few more beers up near Kew Bridge, then homewards unless I want my knackers detached from the rest of my body by my wife.

The end of an unremarkable decade in football, speaking personally, I'm hoping the tens will deliver much more locally and internationally, starting with the second half of this season and the months of June and July in the summer.

January 2

Strangely, the top three divisions in the non league world are playing on New Years Day, Possibly to attract the floating football fan. This doesn't cut the mustard with me, as a mixture of being hung over, the cold, lethargy, and just the thought of wifey staring daggers at me, put me off venturing out all day apart from to put the rubbish out. Even that takes an age these days, plastics, bottles and cans, food waste, papers, human remains you name it. You could build a new stadium with just the detritus from my street over the Christmas period. It would doubtless be an improvement on some of the newer arenas fabricated recently.

On Saturday, realising it is as such, I'm undaunted by the weather, and piss about in the morning, trying to fathom which game is going to be given the go ahead, and if I can still get there in time for kick off. My early selections are postponed, and panicking, I eventually find myself heading to not so leafy at this time of year Surrey, for the Ryman Premier League fixture between Carshalton Athletic and Sutton United, a very local derby, for local people usually. In addition to the warmest coat of my collection, I also pack my oxygen mask as I venture south of the river, a Middlesex boy can get panic attacks coming here.

The weather enforced choice of game is a bit of an anti climax, as today used to be my favourite day of the football calendar year, the FAC third round.

This is the weekend when, unofficially, you are allowed to go mental. When normally placid adults become Jake La Motta for the day. When teams with the usual away following of a man and a dog, bring thousands of Broadmoor outpatients and rabid bull terriers. When the big boys get spanked on and off the pitch. When the most ordinary professional or otherwise footballer in the country scores with a forty yard diving header and is a hero for life.

Certainly the aura seems to be lost, Ronnie Radford and the like look to have had their heyday. The FA now run Premier League, and that takes pride of place, the cup is now secondary.

Jeff Stelling and cast try and accentuate what exceptions there still are, with records now only dating back to 1992, the year Sky invented football.

Whilst it is tempting to vegetate in front of the telly on a day such as today, I brave the elements and walk out of Carshalton station for a Guinness in a little boozer named 'The Hope'.

A short stroll to the War Memorial Ground, which is located, charmingly, between numbers 33 and 35 Colston Avenue, you'd never know unless there was a game on, and even then only if a car happens to turn into the alley.

A decent crowd (1014) looks likely with the long queues at the turnstiles to relieve you of your nine quid. There is a distinctive slope to the pitch, evoking memories of celebrated cup matches from long ago.

The match ebbs and flows but is hardly gripping, and I'm glad to retire to the warmth of the clubhouse to focus on events elsewhere. Once I find a decent observation point from which I can see both the field of play and the score updates, I don't have to go outside again until the goalless ninety minutes are up.

There are no major happenings today, non league Barrow take 8000 fans to Sunderland, whilst top division Wigan Athletic only achieve a home attendance of 5335.

Up early tomorrow, QPR are unbeaten in this year's competition, mainly due to the fact that they haven't yet played.

January 3

The apathy continues on Sunday, when my coach to Bramall Lane is not much more than half full.

Most 'R's fans glasses are currently half empty. I'm not in the slightest bit shocked, using the weather as an excuse not to go is pathetic, more understandable, is to admit the glaring truth that QPR are fucking useless in the FA Cup.

Being the nearest, geographically, league team to the former twin towers, or punnet of strawberries as it is now known, doesn't count for much. Our cup record in recent seasons has included defeat to a pub side, sorry, works team Vauxhall Motors, my nadir in following Rangers. It has now got to the stage that when the draw is made it will be announced something like,

'Number 53, Sheffield United, will beat Number 33, Queen's Park Rangers.'

No victory since 2001, on course to better the record of Leeds United, who surprisingly, were win less from '52 to '63. They have rectified this on several occasions since, including today, as West London boy Jermaine Beckford helps provide the first real upset of the round in their triumph at Old Trafford.

In the mean time, we've made good time motoring up the M1, even the threat of postponement has not materialised, and turn off at Junction 30 for Worksop and head for 'The Cannon'. This is down the road from our previous stopping off point, 'The Three Legged Stool'. My mate, 'Northern' Craig Thorpe, a Wednesdayite, has changed locals, and greets us with a volley of snow balls.

A good humoured couple of hours later and we're off to Sheffield, where you are conveniently allowed to park directly outside the away end.

Rangers start positively, and even better get an FA Cup goal. Is it too good to be true? Yes. The Blades level before the interval.

Yet the second half sees us in good spirits, time for a sing song, and to put my plan into action.

One of the things that makes me laugh, is the sight and sound of a bunch of blokes singing, or at least attempting to sing a song completely inappropriate for the tuneless, mainly baritone, out of key yobbish voices that would be suitable for 'Britain's Got Talent'.

With this firmly in mind, I want to select a tune that will enhance the special aptitude that the voice on the terrace has, allowing a chorus with lines encompassing harmonies, vital to an adopted anthem. The perfect air, in my opinion, is the Burt Bacharach/Hal David standard, (They long to be) Close to you. The definitive version is of course, the arrangement and performance by The Carpenters. There is also the added advantage of the allegorical nature of the songs theme, switching from Karen Carpenter musing about a man, to the 'R's Male Voice Choir bellowing about a football team. If you get my snow drift.

A couple of dry runs at Loftus Road, have met with little success and indifference. My bigger picture hasn't yet captured the imagination of the friends who sit near me, but familiarity will breed competence, and contempt from the poor souls that will have to endure it.

Today just feels right for a more co-ordinated version, with just enough alcohol to perform.

In the key of G, 'Why do birds suddenly appear? Every time, you are near'.

Not a total success, but not a complete disaster either. Quite a few join in, to the extent that we are mentioned on internet despatches.

Big Frank and little Steve turn around mouthing, 'What a racket', excellent, the noisier the better.

The seeds have been sewn; a future time and place will see and hear this in all its glory.

We're still in the cup for at least another week as well, settling for a money spinning, full house televised replay. Not.

January 9

Everywhere is frozen, and to the best of my knowledge, only two contests took place during this week, at the Britannia Stadium on Monday and The Hawthorns on Friday.

Our home game with Plymouth is called off on Friday lunchtime. This is bollocks.

That morning, I was in the vicinity of Loftus Road before the postponement, and speaking to people at the club, the pitch was in reasonable nick. Plainly the South Africa and Bloemfontein Roads adjoining the ground were clear, there's no way that this should be off.

The blame here lies with two agencies. The United States of America, and the Health and Safety Executive.

Compensation culture brought to Europe by Yank insurance companies now invades our lives everywhere, and as a consequence of this the local council make a decision on our behalf, predicting that we may fall over and injure ourselves. Whilst just down Wood Lane, the relatively new Westfield shopping centre can cope with thousands of shopper bastards. Of course this isn't the official reason for deferment, but you feel that it lies at the very core of the decision making process.

These tribulations pail into insignificance when compared to the events in Angola, at the African Cup of Nations.

By all accounts the Togo team were lucky to survive, as most of the bullets fired by the Cabinda separatists hit the first coach, killing three, whereas the players were all travelling in the second. The way of the world dictates that the fate of the celebrities such as Adebayor is of far more concern than the poor old driver and the two other unfortunate individuals whose luck ran out crossing the border.

Strangely, during the 2006 WC, I actually saw Togo play Switzerland.

This tenuous link brings me to the venue that afternoon, my favourite football stadium on the planet, the Westfalenstadion, home of Borussia Dortmund. I don't say this lightly, having seen games at the Azteca, the Maracana as well as the majority of significant European stadia. As an out and out football ground it takes some beating, with a home terrace that when full, as it usually is, holds 26000 bright yellow shirted Ruhrlanders. Try and see a match there when they play rivals Schalke.

With nothing much else to do, it now gives me the chance to sit down and apply for WC tickets. The prices are not cheap; a top category ticket for the final itself is nearly a cool one thousand US dollars.

The general feeling is that, bar the big games, tickets will be easy to come by when you are out there. Return flights are already the best part of a grand if you want to fly direct and not sit in a Middle Eastern airport for six hours while you change planes.

The application I submit will, when I receive a successful notification of ticket allocation, come from the percentage FIFA give our FA throughout the competition. Unlike previous tournaments, all the tickets can only be collected in South Africa. If I seem blasé about the fact that I'm positive my request will be fruitful, there is a reason.

To get entry to England matches both home and away legitimately, you must join the supporters club known as 'Englandfans'. This sets you back about seventy notes every two years, or for each qualifying campaign. Each game you attend gets the award of one cap for a home match, and two for an away. Being high up in the pecking order after frequenting most games over the past few years, means that, going on figures given when logging in to your account, I know the tickets are going to be in my greasy hands.

If you are going to go to all this trouble to obtain entrance six thousand miles from home, you would expect that this puts you in the prime position in respect of ticket allocation. It does. However, there is always an however, money talks, and Thomson are offering official packages for all potential England games, flights, hotels, the whole affair. No caps required only pounds, dollars or rand. This leaves a bitter taste in the mouths of followers like me, who understand that you can always pay through the nose for everything, but to be invited to do so on the same terms as those of us who bothered to build up our points, is a complete and utter piss take.

Having got these unscrupulous ticketing arrangement details of my chest, gives me time to browse the internet, and scan Ebay for QPR memorabilia. Old programmes in fact.

I'm not quite sure why, but I pick them up now and then, flick through them and give them to my dad to put with the rest of the collection, which is now fairly substantial, and worth a pretty penny to a collector. (We still require Norwich at home, 26 December 1970, a postponed game, never officially issued, if you would care to check in your lofts).

There's no character to modern day offerings which are similar to coffee table glossies, consequently I rarely buy them, unless I've a lot of time to kill. Like today.

January 12

The replay, competing for the privilege of a fourth round tie away to Bolton Wanderers. Another game, free of glamour. For everyone concerned.

It's cold, but the game is on, an hour into it, most were wishing that it wasn't.

The majority of club's season tickets don't cover cup ties as they once did, this being the one of the main reasons that crowds are lower than they used to be. Fans just aren't prepared to splash the cash, even at reduced admission prices, which is the case tonight.

Nearly two decades ago, a few of us were daft enough to agree to all get a QPR tattoo in the event that we were to win the FA Cup. We may as well have agreed to get Jimi Hendrix playing a flaming Fender Stratocaster etched across our backs, in case of the likelihood of him rising from the grave.

No need to book an appointment at the local tattooist parlour, at three down with about half an hour to go, loads leave, booing profusely, we're playing like a team already relegated, apart from one going out of the cup.

Back in the warmth of the British Queen, word gets back that we've pulled two goals back; I'm so nonplussed I don't even ask who the scorers are. Surely they can't force extra time? No, they can't.

So then, no coach to the Reebok, to face the Trotters now managed by Owen Coyle, who has jumped barge from Burnley.

Still, at least we made it to the fourth round draw this year. This is all that Liverpool can muster, as they too lose a replay, at home to Reading.

Twenty eight days later, not the film by Danny Boyle, but the time it took Paul Hart to realise that being the first team manager of Queens' Park Rangers is not for him. The win against Bristol City was merely Pyrrhic, as he knew from then on that the crowd were against him as well. He leaves by 'mutual consent', and was 'unhappy with aspects of the job.' It must be said that he wasn't the most comfortable in front of a camera, an old nickname 'Horlicks' seems an accurate tag, as his chat has the same effect as the bedtime potion.

The complete alienation of our fan base continues, I don't need to draw you a picture of who we all feel is to blame. It's rumoured that the new 2010 club calendar features twelve different managers instead of players.

On a more distasteful level, that Ian Huntley even turned down the caretaker's position.

January 16

The big thaw sets in, and my lot are up at Bloomfield Road, Blackpool.

The North West Riviera, like Amsterdam, appeals only if you haven't been there umpteen times, and in January it is distinctly unappealing. Today, Siberia feels more tempting.

A lot of games are still touch and go, but cabin fever propels me out before the wife commandeers me to look after Jake while she goes to doctors to get her black eyes seen to.

Not being a seasoned ground hopper, I end up in North West Kent or South East London if you prefer, at a Blue Square South fixture, Bromley versus Maidenhead United.

My selection of this fixture is of interest because the manager of the Kent side is one Mark Goldberg, he of Crystal Palace bankruptcy infamy. Seemingly taken to the cleaners by some hard nosed business men including Ron Noades. This is the politest description I am legally allowed to give. It does strike me as weird that he is actually the team manager given that he was previously the owner, bossing a club at any level isn't the piece of cake black cab drivers would have you believe.

A tenner ends up giving me a perfect view from the window of the bar, level with the halfway line that I'm reluctant to relinquish, like a non league executive box. The ground, which Cray Wanderers are currently sharing, has some unusual features, the stands behind both goals resembling golf driving ranges, and a strange configuration of wooden benches behind one goal, looking half installed or half removed.

My pint glass is less than a third full of Guinness, fetching the refill turns my head to watch SSN, as the fare in front of me is of paint drying proportions. Some former QPR fringe players are now plying their trade out there for both clubs; their former club are drawing 2-2 at Blackpool. 399 Arctic clad idiots like me have viewed this game, which finishes 2-1 to the away team.

Given a choice, most here would have preferred to have seen the Northern Irish League Cup tie between Newry City and Larne, which was abandoned after 82 minutes. Viewing the photographs, there was no video footage; it looks more akin to watching the great Paul Newman '70s comedy 'Slapshot', the ice-hockey/punch up movie. Mystic Mel can see lengthy bans for those involved, or will it be community service whitewash?

January 19

When researching for the previous match I browsed the Maidenhead website and noticed two important items.

Firstly, that they are at home on Tuesday in a re-arranged FA Trophy game against Barrow. This is handy as it is fairly local to me, a ground I've seen and passed many times from speeding trains, and it gives me an excuse to meet a mate for a pint.

Secondly, the bold statement, 'the oldest continuously used senior football ground in the world', makes York Road definitely worth a look.

The competition has had to come a long way for a Tuesday night, any night in fact, I guess at thirty hardy souls making the effort.

Drinking with an old work colleague, Conor, in 'The Bell', means I arrive late, well, later than usual, with Barrow already one up. Being a latecomer, I nearly get away with sidling in without paying, but an eagle eyed steward relieves me of my Ayrton Senna. Feeling guilty, I stay and chat with the gatekeeper and the bloke who announces the result of golden goal who both enlighten me with the club's historic background, playing here unbroken since 1870.

Now as Mr Crow flies (not Bob), I live only fifteen miles from here, and as a self confessed clever cunt and football nut, I was unaware of this fact about York Road, their long time home, and I doubt that most of my mates would know either. My point is that this 140 year tenure should be shouted from the rooftops, the oldest ground, along with the oldest clubs, Sheffield FC or Notts County, sold as a living antique. With better marketing, every weekend that they're at home, they could be inundated, or at least get a few more on the gate from Scandinavia or Holland or anywhere, eager to see this ancient, in football terms, treasure.

Further refreshment is required by the break, so I dart into the clubhouse, the Black and White bar, and get a Guinness. You are allowed to take this back outside with you, albeit that your hand may freeze solid to the glass. Here, as I had suspected, I find John Little, Barrow maniac, who I met on flight to Moscow, a two day stop off before a further flight to see England win in Azerbaijan in 2004. I haven't seen him since, but just knew he'd be here tonight.

In case you are unaware, Barrow was a FL club until '72, when they lost a re-election vote that went in favour of Hereford United. The same fate also happened to rivals Workington Town in '77, replaced by Wimbledon. Call me cynical, but isn't this mainly due to the geographical location of both towns? Sod going to the Irish Sea coast in mid-winter.

The coach load that that travelled here to deepest Bucks, are rewarded with a home tie against Gateshead for their 550 mile round trip. These are proper supporters. Insane to a degree, but nonetheless, are amongst the people who help keep football alive.

Saturation coverage has made everyone a football expert, but most can't tell you the whereabouts of York Road, tonight's venue, or for that matter Loftus Road, but most of these 'experts' would know Anfield Road. Stirling Albion also used to play at Annfield, but would the modern day football consumer care?

Carlos Tevez is unhappy with comments made by his old team-mate Gary Neville, and when scoring against his old club in the LC semi final first leg, his gestures for 'all mouth' looked more like he was mimicking the song 'Happy Talk' from 'South Pacific'.

It has not been revealed whether Neville saw his hand movements, or whether he was too busy licking some boots at the time.

FIFA notify me that my application is successful, and that a vast amount of money will shortly depart from my credit card. In a moment of supreme optimism, and world beating straw clutching, I notice that this is only the second time the WC has been played in an (ex) Commonwealth country, this must be an omen, as sure as the numbers on my scalp start with a six.

January 23

The only good thing about Rangers not doing cups is that it frees up a Saturday to go shopping. Not being of the Victoria Beckham or Gok Wan persuasion, this also means one of these things, depending on your age.

1/. Play Footie

2/. Watch Footie

3/. Pub & TV Footie

4/. Home TV Footie

Luckily shops are open on Sunday now.

With the changeable weather lately, option two only gets the go ahead in the morning, and a new ground for me it is, if not a new team.

My only previous visit to Shrewsbury was in February '83, a goalless draw with Venables' Rangers at the now defunct Gay Meadow. Those were still in the days of the football special, when the only priority once arriving was to give the Police escort the slip, and head for the nearest tavern.

Thus, my knowledge of this historic border town is limited to the fact that there was a battle here, in 1403, during the War of the Roses. Simon Schama I am not.

With regards to the football club, the stand out details for me is that a coracle was used to get the balls kicked into the River Severn. (I'm later informed that this was stopped due to Health & Safety reasons.)

The other is Harry Shearer, whom when playing bassist Derek Smalls in 'This Is Spinal Tap' wears a Shrews shirt during the famous airport security cucumber tinfoil down the trousers sketch. A minor detail perhaps, but you can be certain that every Town supporter who has ever watched that scene spotted it.

The 'New Meadow' is out of town, so a £3 return bus journey is required. £18 procures me a seat in the West Side, and my first impressions are that the ground is a template of Colchester's one, both constructed around the same time.

A committed game against Dagenham & Redbridge, with both teams currently occupying play off positions, is quite enjoyable. Maybe, in part, this is due to watching a better standard than I have over the last couple of games, though not quite Brazil circa 1970.

The bloke near me is a noisy bugger. He wears his mobile phone in a pouch, and has one of those claps that echoes, and he continues to applaud when every one else has finished. There's a large amount of empty seats around him, and me. I should have known better.

4812 is the attendance, and most leave happy, as the Salopians win 2-1. Crowds have generally improved here since the Shrewsbury chairman, Roland Wycherley, decided on a switch from Gay Meadow, even if the new ground is soulless. How though do you make them soulful?

Again, however, the FA Cup fourth rounds crowds are poor, though the final may be less predictable than recent seasons.

Apart from a few Daggers fans, the train journey home sees lots of Brighton boys on their way back from defeat at Villa, with a large British Transport Police presence. I just manage to get a couple of expensive tinnies before the buffet car is shut because of unruly behaviour. The Seagull's fans I talk to seem to be happy with their lot, finally due to move into real ground for the 2011/12 season.

The train slows and eventually grinds to a halt; primarily we think that this is down to a fracas further down the back coaches. For once I wish I was right, it turns out a passenger has had a suspected heart attack. The silver lining here surrounds me; we make an unscheduled stop at Wembley Central to allow a medical team access, and a quiet word with plod who decides against being a jobsworth and lets me out. A 92 bus ride and I'm in my local, easily a good hour quicker than the journey would have taken via Euston.

Whoever was taken ill, I hope you have recovered, and if, by chance, you are reading this, it denotes one of two points,

I. You are still with us, and/or

II. There is a hell!

January 26

'Never won at Forest.' The title of a compilation CD put together by my brother for last season's drive up the M1. We should have won then, but drew 2-2. Forest were poor, this time around not so. Twenty seven matches in all competitions we've played at the City Ground without a win. I've attended roughly half of these, the most memorable being a League Cup defeat in '89 played at a time when bringing inflatables into the ground was in vogue, and Cloughie gave a Forest fan a clip round the ear. In addition, our relegation party in '96, when the previous night we ended up playing football against the hotel staff at about five in the morning. Nottingham is a good place for a night out, he says stating the bleeding obvious.

Now they unbeaten in eighteen league games, an unfathomable force drives me to attend, if we were to upset the odds and win, I MUST be there.

With this in mind, this morning, I decide to go. Jake is safely offloaded with the lads in the public bar of my local, not really, but it would be nice if it was as easy as that.

I turn up near our ground unannounced and comfortably get a seat on one of the unofficial coaches that have plenty of space. The journey is tempered by the sale of speedy winger Wayne Routledge to Newcastle for an undisclosed fee.

Why are clubs so keen to announce they've spent the GDP of a Pacific island on your new star, but are loath to do so when a sale is likely to fund an outstanding debt or make a decent profit?

You can't blame him for leaving, he must have been wondering along with the rest of us what the hell is going on? Especially as he'll almost certainly be playing in the top tier next season.

Moaning about this loss of a decent player over the phone to Bea, she asks if ' They haven't sold that Hungarian have they? The one punched by the last manager.' It shows that at least some of what I speak does actually register!

Armed with four tins of Lowenbrau, they just about last me until our pre-match stop at the Red Lion in Kegworth. This reminds of the British Midland air crash here that took place the month before the aforementioned Clough pitch invasion incident.

Arriving at the turnstiles earlier than is strictly necessary, we probably could have necked another pint, I hang about trying to get a cheap ticket to no avail, and I pay full whack for the Bridgford Lower Stand. Unless my memory is deceiving me, the Trent End has had a makeover since last season, and if England's 2018 bid is successful it may well need a further upgrade as the venue for the East Midlands is the City Ground.

Shortly after, another player we shouldn't have sold, Dexter Blackstock, scores Forest's third from the penalty spot with just half an hour gone. Unable to convince anyone else to leave early, I make my way to the Trent Bridge Inn, the first pub I find on my ramble.

Some may question my frequent decisions to leave matches early, as you have seen this is not always a wise move. However, these are far from the norm. Why put yourself through this agony any longer than is strictly necessary? Do yourself a favour; keep your blood pressure down but not through drinking any less. Have you never walked out of a bad film before the end? For every one great comeback you miss, there one hundred annihilations you don't. England games are particularly easy to depart early from, Copenhagen, Madrid, Paris, and Vienna, in recent years, good examples of the end only needing to be bitter if it involves a pint. Poetic alcoholic licence is in use here.

The pub is reasonably busy, a lot of females, one of whom is over excitable, well endowed, and under dressed. The only thing that makes me smile all day is when word comes through that Forest have scored and she jumps up and down near me saying 'It's great isn't it?' With hindsight I should have said 'its five now.' just to see her and her friends bounce around again. We don't have to wait too long until it is, but by this time I've had a dark rum for the road.

Back to the coach, coat over my head for the journey home, wishing I had a Tardis, or a gun. Wankers.

Robinho decides that the Manchester Ship Canal is inferior to the beaches of Brazil, and goes home, on loan to Santos. You can guarantee that his miniscule salary is still, in part at least, being funded by Citeh's more money than sense owners.

Simon Jordan decides that Crystal Palace aren't worth wasting his complete fortune on, as he allows them to slip into the void that is administration. From being reasonably well placed, they now face a potential fight against relegation; as per usual the suffering is borne by the fans.

January 30

In a weekend when the captain of the England football team is unmasked as a serial killer or worse still, an adulterer, our home game against Scunthorpe is about as important as advert for hair replacement. It's difficult to not sound sanctimonious here, but JT (even that abbreviation is annoying) does not deserve any sympathy.

Justice Tugendhot, it seems, overturned the edict to prevent publication of his affair details, because Terry was more concerned with the likelihood of losing lucrative sponsorship deals than the actual misdemeanour itself. He might be a good player, but he doesn't sound like much of a good friend. Does he? The very same thing happened to Michel Platini I recall, in France they will just give a Gallic shrug, or maybe have a duel with muskets at ten paces.

One has to feel sorry for Wayne Bridge, not commonly known as WB, and I'll wager there aren't many amongst the majority of red blooded non Chelsea males who would be keen to see him plant a two footed tackle above John Terry's knee. Then hit him with a torque wrench.

It's reassuring to note that his ex, the mother of his daughter, has run straight into the arms of the well known marriage guidance counsellor, Max Clifford.

Back in the world of us mere mortals, I'm duty bound to check in at Loftus Road, though today with Marco Bettini, the Cesena supporter who I met earlier on in the season. He did, it turns out, have a sense of humour. He'll need one today. Is it possible to get him a ticket? He asks. Bloody hell, you can lie across the complete row if you like, Scunthorpe don't really get the juices flowing.

Meeting at White City tube, he presents me with his team's shirt as a present, along with a bar of chocolate from his wife that contains salt! A local delicacy, no less. I reciprocate, and get him a scarf, which I insist he wears in the style of Roberto Mancini and his Manchester City throat warmer.

Approaching the turnstile, I say hello to Stan Bowles as he passes, and then Mick Jones from The Clash, who poses for a photo with my new Italian friend. He is made up. This is quite usual, I explain, George Clooney, Johnny Depp, and Ban Ki-moon, the United Nations Secretary General, are all regulars, but are probably away filming at the moment, or in the case of the latter, not much at all. Comedian Bill Bailey, who does sometimes watch Rangers, has included a sketch about this in his live shows, concerning The Queen, and her Park Rangers, on his Tinselworm tour.

Celebrity fans are much higher profile nowadays, you like to hope that your favourite musician or actor turns out to be a long time supporter, but in reality, they either have no interest or worse still, have no clue. Unless you are one of the bigger clubs, you are more than likely to end up with the B listers, or your personal nightmare scenario, I'm dreading the day Boris Johnson professes his lifelong passion for QPR.

The game passes by without any real incidents of note, except Gareth Ainsworth waves goodbye at half time after reaching an agreement to leave, (we miss this as we are inevitably in the bar) and Scunnie get a second half winner against a dispirited side with dispirited supporters.

There is a planned demonstration outside the South Africa Road stand, with a handful of fans dressed in clown outfits to indicate that we are a laughing stock.

Much as I agree that something has to be done, shouting at double glazing doesn't really achieve much, especially when the target of the abuse is not even there.

After a brief spell of voyeurism, we retire to the back bar of the British Queen on the Uxbridge Road. This is one of several taverns that we frequent in the Bush area. From season to season we adopt an unintentionally nomadic drinking policy due to changes in pub management and décor.

Gastropubs and football in general don't mix, both from the viewpoint of the clientele and the management, perhaps the 'new' fan will disagree, but the majority like to binge when given the chance, and do not eat lobster thermidor, unless it is served with chips. I'm sure Hartlepool fans regularly relax on a chaise longue in 'The Swinging Primate' to discuss whether Stockport will play with a libero. I hope they never do as on one trip there, we saw the most memorable strippers ever, and this only ten minutes before kick off. If they didn't finish then, nobody would ever go to the game; it was bad enough having to walk down the road with a newspaper covering your vitals. A broadsheet in my case. The Lilliput Times.

A lively evening ensues in the face of adversity, with Marco seeming to forget he had to meet his wife, and I do likewise, and get home at five in the morning. The sofa for me for a couple of days. In anticipation of these instances, I purchased an extremely comfortable one a year or so ago.

Midnight on Monday sees the last transfer window of the season close, Sky cover this milestone with the fervour of a general election, even the chimes of Big Ben are used to signify the finish.

It passes without any major transfers, only loan deals, most of this seasons silly money has already been spent. These are the days when what I would consider to be average professional players are all millionaires. The better and wealthier ones are termed legend before they have started to shave.

They are not legends.

Dixie Dean, Tom Finney, Bobby Moore, George Best are, and with true bias, Evelyn Lintott is. He was QPR's first full England international, later killed in the early days of The Battle of the Somme in 1916. His name is one of over seventy thousand soldiers without a grave, whom are remembered on Sir Edwin Lutyens' memorial at nearby Thiepval. That, good people, is legendary.

February 7

My wife's birthday, so a short break is in order, somewhere new for us, Cyprus. At random, I pick Limassol (Lemesos) and our initial impressions are not favourable.

Although out of season it's expensive, the Euro change over has not helped the consumer here. There is wall to wall football coverage, which at the moment means wall to wall John, Ex England Captain, Terry.

Mainly because of laziness, I've grown a beard; there are a few more worrying grey hairs on my Jimmy Hill, although sporting a growth here in the Eastern Med is just the ticket if you want to fit in. Apparently, my new look reminds friends of a fat Dave Grohl.

This place has, in recent years, become virtually a Russian enclave. The world miserable git champions in my book. Not just this one. Moscow is on a very small list of cities that I don't care to go back to. There and Lagos.

Rangers are at London Road, Peterborough, a pleasing old style ground, whose team are struggling. They will defeat us as they have just appointed a new manager, and my fortune cookie opened for the Chinese year of the tiger predicted it. It's not wrong, a one nil defeat for free fall Rangers. Glad I didn't witness it. Useless wankers.

Cypriot footy has improved greatly in recent years, earlier this season Omonoia competed in the Champions League group stage. They share the main ground on the island in Nicosia with APOEL and the national side. My only real recollection of Cyprus as a football entity, is the five goals they conceded at Wembley in 1975, all scored by Malcolm Macdonald, some from pinpoint crosses from my hero as a child, a shin pad less Dave Thomas.

The irony would be complete if England were to meet them on Sunday in the draw for Euro 2012.

Danny texts me, we have avoided a Cypriot holiday game, but interestingly have, in the qualifying group of five, drawn Montenegro. A new destination for most.

No break, my wife understands, would be complete without yours truly, under the pretext of popping out for a pint of milk and a paper, sneaking to a game.

In this case, a Sunday five pm kick off between Apollon from Limassol, against another resort team, Paphos.

A taxi to the Tsirion Stadium, there's not much in the way of bars around, so I buy a tin of tasteless Keo lager from a grocer and hang about like a tout. Four local teams use this stadium, and the national team have previously played here in the early '90s. 17 Euros to get in, which seems a bit steep like most prices here. As you enter and walk up the ramp, it's a ticket collectors dream, with hundreds discarded on the concourse. Keeping your stubs has not become important here as elsewhere. Yet.

The ground reminds me of White City, for those of you old enough to recollect it. The two tiered stands that curve around the athletics track give cause for me to reminisce about the home of the 1908 Olympics, of QPR in two different seasons in the Thirties and Sixties, one game (France v Uruguay) of the 1966 WC, and speedway as well as greyhound racing. I only ever saw the dogs myself. It's a travesty that it was allowed to be swallowed up by the BBC in the mid Eighties, the only former Olympic Stadium in the world no longer in existence.

Capacity wise, the palindromic number 13,331 does not compare with the old London venue, neither do the open ends behind each goal, one with a motorway and Orthodox Church being renovated, and the other with concrete blocks topped by solar water heaters along with the Mediterranean Sea in the distance.

A noisy home crowd around Gate 1, bely the low attendance of just over two thousand, the poor away support numbering only one hundred, yet only forty miles up the coast from here, giving them the complete whole adjacent side to themselves.

Junior Agogo, I notice, playing for the hosts, he played for several clubs at home with varying success, and I wonder if he ever gets nicknamed 'Einstein'?

A thoroughly tedious goalless draw, which was also shown on TV, and on screens in bars and betting shops (of which there are many) all over the island, a good one for us all to pick.

Rio Ferdinand is named as the latest England captain. In the past he missed drug tests and got banned as a result. Other contenders for the role included Stevie G the DJ basher, young Rooney and his prostitute preferences, the affairs of A. Cole, Lampard, and Beckham. I know I'm throwing stones at the windows, but none of this lot seem like they could take on the responsibility of anything more taxing than a word search.

The previous incumbent, enjoys a huge reception from the Chelsea crowd, I'm not sure quite why, did he do something deserving? After allegedly paying off a vast sum for the silence of his partner in grime, and then being allowed to jet to Dubai for a Valentine's marriage reconciliation break, to then receive sympathy?

Again, I'm sounding too judgmental, don't get me wrong, most red blooded males would love to bang a lingerie model up the wrong 'un, but to then get applause? Perhaps that is it, I'm reading all the signals wrongly, and this is why he got the reception he did. An appreciation of a job well done.

February 9

Cyprus is nearly five hours on a plane, sort of a long short haul flight. Hard work with a riotous baby on your lap. Worse still when your booked taxi doesn't appear, and he has the car seat for Jake.

Then an hour's wait at the carousel for the buggy, tests even the most patient of parents, of which I am not. An airport employee informs me as my temperature rises that they usually leave the baby stuff until last. Great.

A none to happy wife sees me alight at White City, just before eight o'clock, and sit down in my seat just in time to see Ipswich score.

A completely spiritless side trudge to the tunnel at half time two down (it could have been five) to a chorus of boos. 'Sack the board,' and the like, are yelled from all parts of the ground, with Briatore being singled out for special criticism, he slopes off then as well, as do many of the crowd.

Strangely for me I stick it out, a couple of substitutions and more determination nearly salvages an unlikely point. A two one reverse does not seem as bad after what was earlier witnessed.

Our fate is now becoming serious, for the first time this season the fatal word, relegation, is now on all our lips. Only two wins since October when we were sitting pretty in third, Old Trafford is now looking more like the old third division.

The support is now completely alienated from the people running the club. It is not ours anymore, in truth it never really has been, but at least it felt as if it was.

February 10

Bea takes Jake to her parents for a few days, leaving me free to run wild. Or at least jog deliriously.

Ringing around for crime partners, I meet up with Dave Haseldine, bar owner and Hammer, whom I met on a return flight from Krakow after an England victory in Chorzow, 2004. It has been a while since we have had a drink together, and he offers me a spare season ticket for West Ham v Birmingham, my first trip to Upton Park in roughly five years.

After a rendezvous in a Green Park bar of all places, we tube it to Upton Park. It's just as well that I didn't have to pay, as my seat in the large East Stand would have set me back £51. A great view, it bloody well should be at this price.

Gold and Sullivan the new owners have certainly been making headlines since their takeover, upsetting manager Zola in the process by requesting that all the players take a 25% pay cut in the summer, almost as if goading him into resignation. At least he hasn't been asked to star in one of his employer's upmarket top shelf publications.

The other overtures they have been making concern the possible move to the Stratford Olympic Park after 2012, truthfully, if they redeveloped the East Stand, the one that used to house the infamous 'chicken run', the Boleyn Ground would become a top notch stadium.

Normally I have an aversion to players wearing gloves; however, tonight I turn a blind eye as it is freezing. Last night a T-shirt and light leather jacket was sufficient clobber, but tonight wrapped up, but more importantly not getting worked up at my team's ineptitude, I'm chilled to the bone. Luckily I haven't had a problem with my Chalfonts for some years; otherwise tonight would really be the time to inflame the grapes of wrath.

Against the run of play, the Irons score, this is while my frozen bladder is attempting to take a leak, but is blowing bubbles instead.

Brum's away support is disappointing, as it often is, especially with them having one of their best seasons for years. Perhaps they know from experience that their travels do not normally result in much Premiership success.

A nervy West Ham run out two nil winners, but I'm already on the District Line by the final whistle, trying to reverse the cryogenic procedure that has just taken place for about eighty minutes.

Back to Green Park, where thanks to my sparkling wit and repartee, I'm treated to a meal at Langan's Brasserie, the usual end to an evening match in the East End. Which is nice.

Thanks then Dave and his mate Johnny for the hospitality, but I've never been a lover of claret and blue shirts, they just don't seem to colour co-ordinate with any of the items in my wardrobe.

Back in court, Portsmouth gains a reprieve of a week over the unpaid eleven million pounds tax bill.

Chester City aren't looking so good though, as they receive a seven day suspension, after it emerges their unpaid players refused to board the coach to Forest Green. The local derby against Wrexham is also called off as the police haven't been paid. Already starting the season with a fifteen point deduction, to borrow from Enid Blyton, they look fucked to me.

Bizarrely, in '90, four of us on our way to Blackpool for a Sunday FA Cup tie, stopped off the day before at Sealand Road, their previous home ground. Here, we were offered out by Shrewsbury supporters as we entered the turnstile, then on the terrace, a large space opened up around us, so the coppers try to move us on as we are obviously Shrews firm. When I explain that 'we are QPR', the answer is, 'well just don't cause any trouble'. In the meantime fighting breaks out in the main stand amongst a crowd of only about 2500. Have you ever been to a game such as this, when you feel you have entered surreal world? Just like watching Major League Soccer in the US.

At Meadow Lane, Sven Goran Eriksson has gone, and Notts County have new owners, but who were the outgoing parties involved? Why are we not told? Sol Campbell wasn't so daft after all.

Ashley Cole breaks his ankle, which is ironic as this would more than likely make Wayne Bridge the first choice England left back if he was so inclined.

February 12

Fuck going to Coventry's Ricoh Arena this weekend. To quite possibly getting arrested for fighting with our own supporters, failing to see eye to eye over who should be playing and where. Or hospital admission for a burst blood vessel from screaming at my team's incompetence.

Bundesliga for me, BA to Dusseldorf, not making the same mistake as in I had August, by checking in online, which is just as well. The Piccadilly line ruins my relaxation, by making me sweat for 25 minutes to go the last two stops to T5, forcing my profuse apologies on all and sundry as I'm smuggled to the gate.

Dusseldorf, along with Cologne and Mainz, are known as the three party towns, and are gearing up for their annual festivals, which take place mainly on Monday, but start earlier.

When I return I'll have to check again with my mum whether we used to have a postman called Wolfgang or Gerhardt, such is the draw for me of this area, and I can't explain, fully, why?

With time to kill, I wanted to go and visit the Kling Klang studio as used by music pioneers Kraftwerk, luckily I checked and it has since moved. Walking around the shops, I see if I can add to my no logic collectables, T-shirts, matchbooks and sexual diseases. My penchant for cotton torso wear stems in part from the days in the early eighties of casual wear. Fila and Tacchini have now given way to Giorgio Armani and Yohji Yamamoto, much in the same way that a Club 18-30 holiday will eventually be superseded by Saga in years to come. A cheery thought for the day.

'Give me a B', is the start of the famous joke concerning the singing the name of mein hosts this evening, Borussia Monchengladbach. If the gag is taken to extremes, would it be said on the second word, second letter, 'Give me an 'O', with an umlaut? Two eggs or three?

Incidentally, Borussia is the Latin word for Prussia.

Only ten miles or so from Dusseldorf, BoMo are one of the German 'cult' teams, like Schalke 04, with a large loyal following. Their great sides of the 70s, contained Gunther Netzer and Berti Vogts, their more recent stars have included Lothar Matthaus, recently spotted in the South Africa Road stand at QPR, is he the next on our merry-go-round?

On the local iron horse to Gladbach, in my own irreverent way I ask two BoMo fans, 'What's the apple, Fritz?'

As usual, they say they can't speak English, and then proceed to do so. To a German, speaking a language means you have to be fluent. Two better blokes I could not have chanced upon. Daniel and Steffen, both season ticket holders from near Offenbach over 200km away.

They take me to the fan's bar, where we start the evening off, then procure me a 13 Euros terrace ticket, ply me with alcohol, and we skate to the stadium in the middle of a snowstorm for the game. No chance of a postponement here. Borussia Park is bathed in green light, and is very similar to Fortuna Dusseldorf's stadium, with a 54000 capacity, built at a similar time. There appears to be a template for modern German grounds. Standing in the home section, (12000 here) and all seater for the rest of the ground, with the exception of the visiting area, set in one corner, a triangle of terracing next to an allocation of seating. It may not be ideal, but they are a whole lot better than the newer ones that have gone up at home. The Taylor Report was only a set of recommendations, and not all of these were implemented, but it suited the government of the time to introduce all seater stadia measures for appeasement purposes. Please take note, planners, police and relevant authorities. As if the supporters are ever likely to be consulted on important issues that effect them, and the South Yorkshire Police remain blameless for all the events that led to the adoption of these gifts from the plastic factory. Or seats as they are usually known.

Gluhwine is again selling well, perfect; you can stick your cup of tea, Johnny Englander.

Final score, BoMo 2 Nurnberg 1. The Bavarians are in big relegation trouble, less so now for mein hosts.

Back to Dusseldorf and a binge in the Aldstadt. There's a great buzz, and some of the strangest fancy dress costumes you are likely to see. Wearing one of these is comedienne Alan Carr, mincing about in a pink and white outfit, but not feeling particularly chatty tonight. Sod you then. Not literally. Doubt if he has much of a view on Kraut football anyway, unlike his dad.

A thoroughly enjoyable night finishes between four and five, the two lads wish me good luck to which I'm careful to not to fall into the trap that Gordon Jackson did nearly seventy years before!

I try to get a cab back to my hotel, but the Mercedes driver, in a gesture of goodwill, turns down the chance of easy money and points out to me that it is fact only a one minute stagger away.

February 13

At midday I wake up, fully clothed on the top of the hotel bed. At least they are my clothes, and in my hotel, I had at least managed to get my Timberlands off. I'm somewhat limited now as to what game I can get to in time for kick off, so it's going to be Vfl Bochum v Hoffenheim. The home sides badge says 1848, which would make them the oldest club in the world, though closer investigation reveals that they were then just a gymnastics club, the football side didn't materialise until 1911.

The Ruhrstadion as was, now the sponsored, Rewir Stadion, is about a fifteen/twenty minutes walk from the station.

A bratwurst and a gluhwine (with rum) later, and half in a daze, with both sets of supporters wearing blue and white, I pay 11 Euros, and walk into the away end by mistake. Let me put it this way, the riot police will be underemployed today. The plus side is that I get a good view of the home terrace for any photographic opportunities.

Sobering up, the cold starts to bite; my Willem II winter hat is paying its way. I jump up and down a bit with the barely two hundred TSG Hoffenheim fans to an air from 'Aida' just to keep myself warm.

They do like a sticker here in Germany. Walk into any toilet at a game and it is like a modern art installation. Every team it seems is represented here. Ultras in every shape or form. However, I would recommend that you do not loiter in gazing at the walls, craning your neck in reading them for too long. As you are likely to get some funny looks, or an offer you can certainly refuse. Especially if you are standing with your lad still out, hoping to find the visiting card from a Freddie Mercury loving pink service crew.

With the score poised at one a piece, the away side looking the more assured, I slope off to ensure that I don't miss my flight home. It's a pity I don't have more time to explore, as Bochum is meant to be good for a evening's entertainment.

The machine at the station doesn't take my bankcard, so I expect to be charged at least 10.90 Euros by the approaching female ticket inspector. Out of the blue, the passenger sitting opposite to me, having noticed the match ticket in my hand, quietly informs the lady that because of this, my journey should be free. She examines it and concurs. Cheers. I'm not totally sure this is right on the national network, but I'm not going to complain. If you do get collared on a match day and have a ticket to hand, just say that you are going to/from a game. Alternatively just say you are English, this is another valid excuse. (Do not try this on Trenitalia, you will get a hefty fine.)

At the airport I learn that Bochum have snatched a vital winner after all, so not for the first time I miss a crucial goal.

The edge is taken off my weekend when I also discover that I was correct to give Coventry a miss, a single goal defeat means they are now in trouble. Hopeless wankers.

My wife returns in time for the legalised extortion racket that is Valentine's Day.

Another racket, the Premier League, talk of play offs for the clinching of fourth place. If you finish seventh, you could end up playing in the Champions League. When will this stupidity end?

February 16

Rangers are at home to Watford. Well, at least they are meant to be. Only minutes after exchanging baton Jake in the relay with Bea, I get to the Tube and discover the game is off, because it is as wet as the shadow cabinet. Undeterred we go for a pint down an old haunt, the backstreet Crown and Sceptre, famously known in QPR folklore, though relatively recently changed to a gastro pub. Recently, finally understanding the history of the area, it has become more adaptable to the fan's requirements.

Here we watch AC Milan versus Manchester United, and with South Africa coming up, it is good to see Wayne Rooney looking like an unselfish version of Alan Shearer, having only now seemingly discovered how to head a ball.

Steve Gallen, brother of former R's player and hero Kevin, a proper Ranger, and, by the way, our youth team coach, joins in the conversation, soon matters turn to our common ground.

On our books, we have a young man named Raheem Sterling, of whom, everybody who has seen him play, pros and all, have said he is the biggest thing since powdered milk. However, it seems that despite financially and socially offering him and his family as much as any other club, we are destined to lose our wunderkind. If he stays with us the agent receives little, but if he moves, the agent benefits a great deal, simply because of the fee involved.

As with all agents, they are only acting in the player's best interest. My ass.

Have you noticed how the Champions League at this stage has surreptitiously moved the ties to over the course of three weeks, instead of two? Almost no one has seemed to notice, or at least comment, on the extra week during a WC year. Great for the armchair viewer, and for the maximisation of television revenue. UEFA will not want be left behind by FIFA in the financial and profile stakes.

Well after midnight, I climb into bed, my wife, ever concerned, asks how we got on?

We drew honey.

February 18

Bribery is illegal in the business world, but fine in the context of a relationship. So armed with promises of perfume, holidays, and orgasms, Bea lets me elope to Hamburg on Thursday morning. My mum agrees to look after pocket battleship Jake and I head to Heathrow.

Germany's second biggest city is a first for me, but the trip is spoiled by a heavy cold, no doubt not helped by the previous weekend's excesses, I feel like I'm walking around wearing headphones all day. The woman next to me on the flight keeps tut tutting every time I sneeze. It's sorely tempting to let one go at the speed of snot all over her cereal bar, but live and let live, so I further gain her displeasure by making a disgusting phlegmy throat clearing noise after finishing my Bloody Mary. On disembarking a businessman is pushing his way past the other passengers up the aisle causing a commotion. Being in belligerent mood, and knowing the unwritten airline etiquette rules of allowing the passengers in front to exit first, I block his path. He then tries to explain, 'I haf to get off!' We all do mate, and we've landed early. The tut tut woman now changes her tune, and utters 'Well done' and gives me a smile. Bastard one minute, St George the next.

Hamburg is a winter wonderland. Next to my hotel, the lake known as the Alster, is frozen over, so I literally step into the unknown, and walk from one side to the other, careful not to stray from the beaten track, recalling the scene from 'The Omen II', even though the barman informed me the ice is 18cm thick.

This may not rank in your top one hundred things to do before you die, but for me it is a novel experience.

Most people, when you mention Hamburg, immediately think of being sunk to the nuts down at the Reeperbahn. I don't think I could raise so much as a smile tonight.

This place has already won me over even with a fuzzy head; it suits a winter environment perfectly. Note to self, apply to German tourist board for head of marketing position.

To ensure that I don't miss out on a ticket, I get the metro to Stellingen, alighting for the HSH Nordbank Arena. There is a bus service later on for the game, but for now it's about a mile making snow tracks, beginning with subways leading from the station that make the infamous Wolverhampton one look like a mouse hole.

The helpful staff sells me a 21 Euros ticket for tonight's main event, HSV v PSV. The man behind the counter tries to explain to me the differences between the Hamburg emblem, a blue and black diamond in city colours with naval connotations and the red and white club hues. He's not exactly sure either, and asks in passing if I know of anybody that can get him tickets for the League Cup Final as he also follows Aston Villa.

On the way out, I pop into their museum to look at various stages of Kevin Keegan's perm, and the last thing they won, the European Cup in '83.

Now many supporters talk about having their ashes scattered over the playing surface of their home ground, but here you can go that one metaphorical step further, as there is a dedicated cemetery covered in turf from the original pitch nearby. Dead ball specialists?

Fast forward to kick off and using Jagermeister as cough medicine. Outside the stadium, there are the usual vendors selling club merchandise, along with junk food and beer. Every fixture in Germany attracts a fair number of bottle and can collectors, unlikely to win best dressed men of the year awards, but they do serve a purpose, and it is another example of things that work when a small reward is available. They have shopping trolleys full to the brim of empties, so will eat well this week you hope.

Another Seventies throwback is the common practice of wearing scarves on wrists, popular here still, although it must be said that the haircut of the gods, the mullet, is rarely seen to the same extent as it once was.

An added incentive for the home side is that their stadium is the venue for the Europa League Final. 57000 capacity in a roomy yet somehow, close knit ground.

Contemptible UEFA regulations mean that it's only alcohol free lager on sale inside the arena, but not missing a trick, they keep the restaurant doors open, meaning that Holstein is available to the masses, with a queue that goes back to Bremen.

HSV win a poor game with a first half penalty, only enlivened by the second half introduction of Ruud van Nistelrooy against the side where he made his initial impact. The second leg should be tight.

Not feeling one hundred per cent, and bearing in mind the kick off wasn't until 9.05, I give the Reeperbahn a swerve. No night of dominance and submission for me, the working girls will be inconsolable.

February 19

As per usual, the 10am ICE train to Berlin is bang on time. Ice is very apt, hurtling through the snow covered land, deers frolicking in the distance like a Barbara Cartland novel. With panzers.

It strikes me that before the fall of the wall in '89, much of this train journey would have been have been in East Germany, as was my destination tonight, the Stadion an der Alten Forsterei (Stadium near the old forester's house) as if you didn't know, home of Union Berlin.

Pulling in to the impressive Berlin HBF (main station) a gun shot away from the Reichstag and Brandenburg Gate, I decide to have another look around this atmospheric area, and meet Bernd in Potsdamer Platz just after sneaking a peak at the famous Hansa Studios nearby. David Bowie, Iggy Pop, Supergrass, U2 amongst many have recorded in this hidden goldmine, and I learnt that Lou Reed did not in fact lay down his classic 'Berlin' album within these walls, ruining my assumptions. Better double check on 'Abbey Road' when I get back.

From what was once Checkpoint Charlie we travel to what was the other side of the wall to East Berlin, and Kopenick to be precise. A six o'clock start against struggling Koblenz, now minus unlikely Finn, Shefki Kuqi, who has been transferred to Swansea.

My first visit for a couple of years, their championship winning season was spent using the rival stadium of head cases BFC Dynamo whilst their ground was covered from the elements on three sides like never before. Later I learn from one of Bernd's mates Fred, an electrician that he, amongst many others, had helped out for free for two weeks in the summer, in exchange for gratis entry to two high profile friendlies before the start of the season. It is estimated that the involvement of the supporters has saved the club in the region of two million Euros in costs to assemble these roofs and all associated costs.

Drinking near the Old Foresters isn't as pleasant an experience as I would hope to say it is, no beer cellars as you would like, but you can't have it all, and good company is a better substitute. I'm an honorary Union man now, and am greeted by the Ludwigsfelde (their town on the Berlin outskirts) regulars, that include the fine German names of Christian and George, as an old friend.

Ten Euros for a ticket gives entrance to three quarters of the ground. Their mascot is a knight complete with chain mail with ball and chain. The Health and Safety Executive would probably ban this as potentially dangerous at home.

Now I'm accepted by my fellow Berliners as a fully fledged follower, I'm confident and drunk enough to try and endear myself by showing my knowledge of German football history by shouting out 'Sparwasser' to the Koblenz travelling support. He was the scorer when, during the 1974 WC, East defeated West, even though the West went on to lift the trophy. This goes down well with the older folk, whereas the younger lot have got about as much clue of what I'm on about as the readers of Hello! Magazine has. It must be stressed that to a man that they are all happier since those dark days, although much of what was the lesser known parts of East Germany have become virtually ghost towns.

Thirty minutes in, with Union 2-1 ahead, Bernd divulges that the referee is not all that he seems, because he's a woman. My camera viewfinder cannot discern how curvy her figure is, concealed beneath her orange luminous blouse/shirt, so sexism is postponed for footballing matters. From here on in I over analyse her performance, and being over critical, find that she is satisfactory until a passage of play occurs that requires firm decision making. Then she is a rabbit in the headlights, which is understandable, all the more when twenty two Teutonic machines are bearing down on you.

Here's the comments of Joe Royle from ten years ago, summing up my thoughts still now.

'I am not sexist, but how can they make accurate decisions if they have never been tackled from behind by a fourteen stone centre half, or elbowed in the ribs or even caught offside?'

Mind you, this would apply to the majority of male referees as well, unable to use their instep to knock the ball back into play, and falling like Kenneth Williams when pushed by Paolo di Canio.

Final score, 3-2 to the Eiserne (Iron), consolidating their safety, and pushing the West Germans nearer to the trap door.

There is a late flight back tonight, and on the way to Schonefeld, Danny rings me to give me good news. A good friend has been released from prison early, and the control freak Briatore, has relinquished overall control of the 'R's. Ryanair aren't going to spoil my passage back to the motherland.

She's got her own website has Bibiana Steinhaus, the only female referee in high level Deutsche fussball. I research this in the early hours upon my return, laughing to myself that she is a policewoman and single. You could have written the script.

My mind brainstorms to the finish of Steve Martin's 'Dead Men Don't Wear Plaid'. The scene when the poor girl played by the chesty Rachel Ward invokes Martin's character Rigby, into a deliberate rage by creating a situation where the Field Marshall utters 'Reinemachefrau', or the 'cleaning lady'. I envisage her cast in this role as she points to the penalty spot, failing to notice the clear dive by the forward. It is so convincing that 5.9 is being uniformly held up by the fans behind the goal, along with a solitary 6 held up by a tourist from Uzbekistan. Then there is a vast REINEMACHEFRAU banner held aloft by the local kop. Well done for understanding my four in the morning conjecture.

February 20

Now it seems that Mussolini has been deposed, a black dog has been lifted from our collective shoulders. Whether or not he'll be hung from a meat hook remains to be seen.

In a game free of quick free kicks assisted by Swedish referees (ala Porto v Arsenal) and ably helped by a full debutant Antonio German we beat Doncaster two – one. He cannot fail in my eyes, as you are now well aware, I have a soft spot for Germans!

This is our first win after five straight defeats, the first of this year, and of this decade even.

Another loss would have been more embarrassing than the Tiger Woods press conference apology.

Wayne Bridge, cuckold, announces his withdrawal from any future England squads. Personally I think he's being brave. Do you honestly think that he would pass up the chance to play at the World Cup Finals? John Terry should be the one who is crawling more than my son Jake.

Portsmouth, it is revealed, are actually 60 million pounds in debt. The FA should not have allowed this to get so far out of control. If they were actually monitoring the clubs it is meant to oversee, it wouldn't have.

Chester City are banished from the Conference, you cannot imagine a return to the ninety two, as they have already once managed, against the odds, in 2004.

One should feel sorry for the followers of both clubs, just do not shed any tears for the owners.

February 27

With a kiss for my wife, and a thousand for Jake, I head to Heathrow for a BMI flight to Caledonia.

A few more miles to the tally I've accumulated under the British Midland/Star Alliance reward scheme, untouched for five years, so that one day we fly around the world first class, only paying taxes and 'charges', still about a grand, but well worth it. I still nearly miss the plane. Prick.

Early enough to not have to waste money on a sherbet, I grab the bus 500 to the city centre, £4.50, not so easy to bunk the fare here, as the terrorists found out nearly three years ago.

The bus drops me at Queen Street, where a short train journey to the Exhibition Centre and our hotel, the high rise Crowne Plaza on the banks of the Clyde. I run to check in, hoping to not be late for the main event of the day, which I make with a couple of minutes to spare, rushing to turn on the television and find the correct channel.

More significant than Paisley and Adams, Arafat and Rabin, welcome to the Golden Handshake. I've got to admit that even I'm holding my breath for the will he, won't he moment. SSN have helped build up the tension, and thankfully let us view, live, the split second that John Terry has to stand face to face with Wayne Bridge. Craig Bellamy shows his solidarity by not making eye contact, but the man himself passes by his protagonist and moves his hand straight on to the mascot.

After all that excitement I need a drink, so with Preston boys Tony and Sean, we get a £5 taxi to the Star and Garter in Maryhill, and catch the boring bit, the actual game. Perhaps there is some kind of karma at work, as Man City run out with an impressive 4-2 triumph, Bellamy looking especially on form.

We're here to watch one of the forgotten teams of Glasgow, Partick Thistle. Crossing the road to Firhill, you are reminded by the dereliction that you are in what once was a proper working class area, which has seen better days. Much of the regeneration of Strathclyde hasn't caught up with this neighbourhood as of yet.

£16 gets us into the Jackie Husband Stand, 6000 plus capacity, but the only side open today. Somehow we have managed to end up sitting in padded directors seats, a padded cell might be more appropriate. It seems a shame the ground is only one quarter open, the once terrace stand to my left, now overgrown with grass, and known as 'The Bing', is likely to be redeveloped but not to watch fitba.

The Jags, great nickname, beat Ross County 2-1, but the Highlanders look the better side. The highlight is the half time 'Pie of the week', which I'm compelled to indulge, the Ragu, and very nice it is too.

Only 2192 have ventured out here to see it, and at least three of them are

Sassenachs, but they live in the shadow of the Old Firm, as does the rest of Scotland. It's a shame.

My Rangers have lost two nil at Celtic reserves, or Middlesbrough as they are known on Teesside. English wankers.

Back at base camp, we remember that eating is essential for life on earth to continue, and enjoy a microwaved lasagne from the kitchen, whilst Arsenal's Aaron Ramsay's leg is nearly detached from his body by Stoke's Ryan Shawcross.

The night out isn't the best planned, as we end up drinking down the Paisley Road, including the football tourist pub the Louden Tavern, bedecked in Rangers blue. We should have gone into the heart of the city, as it is much improved.

Later, back in the all night bar in our hotel we drink with Welsh Falklands hero, Simon Weston. He can put them away, as we realise by four in the morning, when the draw of the duvet has become inevitable. You get a choice of pillows; I'll opt for all three.

February 28

When I was a child, the same as now really, but not as big. Every May Cup final day I'd sit and watch the main event and always take in the half time and full time highlights of the Scottish version played the same afternoon. Invariably in the Seventies it felt like a permanent Celtic v Rangers tie. For some reason which I have never quite understood, you were meant to pick either one of these two as your team from north of the border. Not understanding the political implications at such a young age, my judgement therefore was not clouded when making my selection. My decision was reached by a simple plus and minus system. Rangers, have the same name as the third part of my team. Easy, 1-0.

Celtic play in hoops, as do my lot. 1-1.

Rangers play in blue and white, and win 2-1.

There you have the thought processes of a football mad lad. The outcome could have been very different had QPR not changed their kit in the 1920's from green to blue hoops. Green it was decided was unlucky. The Irish were not consulted.

This is before I understood sectarianism, and being an atheist protestant, I made the right choice.

1987 was the first time I saw this fixture of fixtures, at Parkhead, three-one to the hosts, Brian McClair even scored, as inevitably did Ally McCoist. It altered my perception of Glasgow, and Scotland as well, and I've enjoyed every visit since. I have as many Celtic supporting mates, all from Irish descent, as I have from the blue side. Both will criticise my fraternisation, but it so much easier for me to be open minded when your bias is in your head and not really in your heart. They can be both as bad as each other.

I'm QPR loyal though, especially today.

This is 'the' derby; it encompasses far more aspects away from football than any other worldwide. Teheran v Tel Aviv hasn't yet become a regular fixture on the calendar. You have to laugh when after years of hatred; people are shocked by the songs and language. Get real, do you want it as timid as a crown green bowling match?

Kick off at 12.30 is the norm these days, but it doesn't dampen the fervour. Although with at least four per season, it does make getting tickets much easier to come by. Today mine is Club Deck.

Thirty six Scottish Pounds.

The Glasgow Metro is a novel experience, handily it stops at Ibrox. After a full Scottish brekkie and last nights fluid still lying heavy on my stomach, the beer I've been attempting to guzzle, tastes as appetising as WD40.

A poor game is played out by two poor teams, when compared to the great sides of years gone by. It is enlivened by the harsh sending off of Celtic's Scott Brown. To my left, is an old boy with crutches, who for the life of me, straining my ears as much as is physically possible; I can't understand a word he says. This matters little when Edu scores for Rangers in the last minute, to send Ibrox wild, and virtually guarantee the Billy Boys title number 53. This is as opposed to 42 for the Bhoys.

They say that every dog has its day, but north of the border, there are two great Danes and the rest are a bunch of chihuahuas.

Cheerio is waved at the Tims through a police operation on a par with D-Day, as I rush back to the centre on the mini metro just in time for the League Cup Final, and the next saga of the Wayne Rooney show. He can play a bit this kid, even when substitute.

At Glasgow Airport, passing through security, I sidestep Rangers defender Madjid Bougherra on his way to play for Algeria against Serbia. I'm the only person who has managed this feat all day. I hope he doesn't play as well against England in the summer.

As predicted, our wunderkind Raheem Sterling does join Liverpool, it will make the club a significant amount, but that is not the point.

Whether Neil Warnock could have persuaded him to stay given a bit of time is unlikely, but I hope he is given more time than the others were in his new capacity as our manager.

In a strange twist of fate, Crystal Palace appoint Paul Hart as his replacement. Either of these positions could be said to be out of the frying pan and into the fire.

March 2

Under the premise of meeting my friend Jon Gordon, or Wiggy as he is known, to discuss our plans for the World Cup, the missus not knowing or caring that I'll see him at Wembley tomorrow, I make for Thames Ditton. Then a short walk to convene in the bar of Imber Court, sports ground of the Metropolitan Police. Evening all.

Tonight, their opponents are the team who are meant to epitomise the spirit of amateur football, Corinthian Casuals. A meeting of two of the more unconventional clubs in the lower leagues.

This is Ryman League One South, so it seems strange in this day and age that the Casuals players still don't get paid for their toils, whereas all the others at this standard will at least receive at least a small amount of folding. The Casuals most unique feature is the pink and chocolate shirts, which stand out against the boys in royal blue.

In no rush, we are given a discount by a helpful chap on the gate for turning up late. He also informs us that there are only four coppers playing tonight. Nowadays it is not necessary to work for the police to play for them, in the past, some weeks that would mean they were only be able to field a half strength team, as they were too busy nicking people like me for wearing a woolly hat in a public place.

There is a distinct lack of sponsorship around the pitch, and there isn't much of a Corinthian spirit on show, with a large amount of industrial language being audible from the stands. I've often thought that the loneliness of the long distance runner could be replaced by the strange life of a non league follower. Tonight would be a prime example.

Another rare moment that takes me back to my youth is when the ball is knocked out of play near to where you are standing, and you get to return it. With a non league game space is usually available to at least kick it back to the cheers of your mates. If you can catch it on the back of your neck and flick it to perform a scissor kick miles past the full back waiting to take a throw in, all well and good, but this rare. Tonight an opportunity presents itself for the first time in years when the ball is skewed towards me at playing height, but I fail to seize the chance and shin it. Red faced I turn to Jon and say, 'you don't lose it do you?'

You would be wrong if you thought that a sense of humour is absent amongst the bill. As we walk round to the tea bar at half time, Billy Joel tells the meagre crowd that he is an innocent man over the Tannoy. This makes me smile in an ironic way, and the thought of a 'Spartacus' moment amongst us, all proclaiming to be not guilty in front of constabulary team crosses my mind until the next song trumps the first, The Clash's version of 'I fought the law'. This is laugh out loud funny. They do as well, winning by the only goal that we missed, scored by Sir Robert Peel, no, Sir Ian Blair, deflected in off Jean De Menezes at point blank range. I can't be sure, as I was busy stealing Curlywurlys from the tuck shop at the time. A career of evil is far more lucrative despite what the song says.

March 3

A bit of a bonus today, an afternoon friendly at Loftus Road between two teams destined to appear in South Africa. Ironically, only the largest stand, in South Africa Road is open, so WC fever isn't exactly gripping this part of London yet. The top tier is meant to be split fifty/fifty between the dog eaters and the elephant killers as the Sun would no doubt say. In actuality, the South Koreans have all turned out as if under penalty of death from Seoul, with as many women as men. Whereas the Ivory Coast following is a handful of Africans keen to get an eyeful of Didier Drogba and his natural hairstyle.

The Asians have got the lot with them today. To start with, a giant 'passover' flag of their national shirt. For some warped reason I've always thought that you could commit a murder during this process, like the Georghi Markov umbrella tip variety, and am surprised it hasn't been the script in a TV show like 'Spooks' or something equally outrageous. Murder is also the word at the forefront of my thoughts, when the next gadget is uttered, hot stix. These are like giant red inflatable dildos, when whacked together in a large quantity they make quite a racket. The novelty is gone after five minutes, and you begin to wish smoking was still allowed; as well directed fag ends would puncture their fun. The Koreans are so polite they probably would let you, thinking it was all part of the football experience.

I'm handed two different reasonable quality T-shirts as a souvenir. One has the motto, 'The Shouts of Reds United Korea'. It is difficult not to fall into stereotype here, and adopt a Benny Hill 'sirry iriot' voice, and ask for 'extra rarge'. Even the kick off time begs for the Chinese dentist joke, two thirty. I know this is wrong but they are so fucking nice, and such a defenceless target, that the oriental racist jokes seem to slip through the net unquestioned. This is until the Korean equivalent of the Yakuzu get hold me.

Sun Ji Park drives them on to a two nil victory, the Ivory Coast meanwhile search for a new manager to lead them during the summer, half of perspective candidates are in the crowd this afternoon, including Sven Goran Ericsson, who seems to be up for every position that is available these days.

Drogba is booed by some, including me, just out of habit, and practising for later tonight.

My vocal exercise is in vain, as I get to my seat at Wembley slightly after eight o'clock, thus missing out on John Terry heckling. You pay your money and you take your choice when it comes to the decision to boo or not to boo, it is not as if you are questioning his sexuality.

No prizes for guessing that our tardiness was alcohol related, in some measure due to using a pub at least a twenty minute walk away. Like with most major sporting venues, drinking in the area around them is a less than enjoyable experience, unless you are a fan of over priced industrial lager served in a barely strong enough plastic beaker and waiting fifteen minutes to get it. Our current selection 'The Fusilier', at the Sudbury end of Wembley on the Harrow Road is not the best, but a whole lot better than anything near the stadium. At least they are far enough from the throng to not increase prices, serve beer in glass, and in true English tradition do great Indian food. If that doesn't get me a free curry, I'm not sure what will?

Mr Capello, I'm sure, won't view this friendly as meaningless, but most of the rest of us do. The team where black armbands in honour of Keith Alexander, a genuine pro. My abiding memory of him is scoring Grimsby's only goal in an FA Cup tie at Plough Lane, Wimbledon, with the inflatable Harry the Haddocks filling the away terrace.

Peter Crouch is taking it seriously enough, now twenty international goals, better than one in two games. The gloss is taken off with the news that Michael Owen's seemingly innocuous injury is not so harmless after all, and he'll be out until next season. Not good in a WC year when he seemed to be hitting form once more, a thirty year old with forty goals worth of experience, and having featured in three previous World Cups, will be sorely missed.

March 6

It's a pity that West Brom lost their cup replay, as this would have meant our game against them was off, and it would be all down to Church Road, home of Conference Hayes and Yeading for a bit of Luton baiting.

New manager syndrome will hopefully come good, or the Colin effect as it can now be termed.

Mr Warnock, we're not yet on first name terms, must hate the epithet he was given by Sheffield Wednesday fans. If you have nothing better to do, as someone obviously didn't, and you re-arrange the letters of his forename and surname, the anagram is Colin Wanker. Funny if it's not you.

The embryonic referee Stuart Attwell is in charge today, which gives me doubts about any sort of outcome, favourable or otherwise, best give it a miss on the fixed odds coupon. Whilst appreciating that everybody has to start somewhere, I am of the opinion that in your twenties you should be playing not refereeing. If you haven't played they game, you really shouldn't be taking charge of it. Understanding of the rules is not understanding of the game. This didn't stop the FA fast tracking him, even with the monumental cock ups he has already made.

Energised, or simply trying harder under a new manager, we score three to the Baggies one. The relief this brings encourages even more copious binging than usual, as Jimmy and I meet up with some Tottenham friends in Hammersmith, after their cup draw down the road at the Cottage.

This is the one that lets down me down in my wager. Spurs had a few key players out, and with Fulham decent at home, a one was placed in the box next to this fixture. The remainder all complied with my choices, but what do I know? Quite a bit actually, in betting this equates to bugger all.

Regular gamblers will be aware of the old adage of not putting your own team in, a bit like not changing your mind when backing a horse. This, I would agree with only if you expect them to win, backing them to lose is perfectly acceptable, logical and only marginally lacking morals. Whichever way you look at it, the blow is softened whatever the outcome. I've lost count of the times that I've felt good or won money simply by being realistic.

The FA Cup semis are drawn to be played for the foreseeable future at Wembley, reigniting the debate of whether or not they should be played there. Personally, I think not, it devalues the final as a spectacle, even though more of the spectating public are able to see their teams, the aura has gone. The new stadium has to be paid for regardless, so whether you like it or not, it will happen for the next twenty years.

Some results from the weekend that interest me if hardly any one else, are that in Germany and Holland, Bayer Leverkusen and PSV both suffer their first league defeats, and this is March, yet are only third and second in their respective divisions. Not surprised? Well you should be.

March 9

A re-arranged fixture from early January against England's most westerly League club, Plymouth Argyle. Unfortunately, they look destined for the third tier.

It is largely uneventful once Rangers score a second for an easy victory.

Tamas Priskin, our Hungarian loanee from Ipswich, is a bit of a tart. Apart from playing like one, he also looks like one as he wears yellow boots. Call me old fashioned, but would you use yellow dubbing? Allied to that, when you are in a sports shop selecting what style and colour to wear, would you choose yellow? I've never been a fan of Nike sportswear, no history, always wore Puma myself, Kings, ones with long tongues, which meant you were automatically marked out as a good player, or a girl.

These banana boots sell for £225.00, which means to me that when you are not kicking a ball with them, you can also wear them to a wedding reception. Patrick Cox, Oliver Sweeney and other high class cobblers are all missing a trick here, in not branching out into sports wear, especially with the money that players earn now. Your Christian Dior moulded (pour homme) can be kept in a Louis Vuitton boot bag for the best part of a couple of grand.

Slagging off somebody for wearing such rainbow coloured footwear can also backfire.

Chelsea mate Pete Wheatley and I were watching Yeading (pre Hayes merger) about six years ago in an FA Cup tie at Slough. We were there because a mate, Steve Daly, was playing, he's one of those that we all know, should have been a pro, he just didn't get the breaks. One who later did was a certain DJ Campbell, who was wearing what looked like gold blocks on his feet. We heckle him until the bullion boy scores twice, and his career has since blossomed into the higher divisions of the professional ranks. The joke was on us.

Whilst the Manchester United supporter's group 'The Red Knights' campaign has been gathering pace, voicing its concerns over the debts being amassed by the current owners. Another however, has stalled indefinitely. Spare a thought for Chester City who no longer exist in their current capacity, having been wound up in the High Court.

They will survive in some shape or form, probably in the Cheshire League, whereas the gold and green 'Newton Heath' scarf wearers will moan that they haven't won three trophies this year. That's a real heartache.

On the same day the Pompey administrators lay off 85 staff, yet Peter Storrie is still there with a 40% pay cut. That's very noble of him.

Later this week, it turns out that he has actually left, but will be employed as a consultancy figure.

Is he doing this for free? I doubt it. You can almost picture him meekly saying 'I was only following orders.'

March 13

It has got to the stage now where Bea just asks on a Saturday if we are at home or away. Not that I necessarily get in any sooner if we are at home.

I am happy for some time and space away from the nine month dynamo named Jake. Fatherhood is probably easier when you are younger and more energetic, and your recovery period from a day out is not yet equal to the length of time you were away.

Rangers are at Bramall Lane, which is Warnock's childhood 'team', but instead I plump for an FA Trophy semi final first leg. A few mates were initially going to accompany me, but develop excuses such as influenza, beri-beri and techno sickness, where your message, oddly, doesn't get received due to problems with their mobile phone.

Salisbury, a place I've never previously been to, mainly because they've never been in the football league, all I know is it has the tallest spire in Britain. Not being from theological stock this was never going to inspire an earlier visit.

It makes a change to hear an accent other than similar to my own; the Londonisation of Southern England is now widespread. Ironically, the capital is now becoming absent of the salt of the earth who originally hail from there. Contrary to popular opinion, moving to the capital city doesn't make you a Londoner. This is applicable to people such as Madonna or Boris Johnson.

Bussing it from the station to the Raymond McEnhill Stadium, located in Old Sarum, the ancient fort close by, I'm fully expecting a large crowd, into what must be Salisbury's biggest ever game. The kick off is delayed to 3.15 not, as predicted because of a ground swell in numbers, but because there are hardly any turnstiles open. £13 later on, the gate is announced over the intercom as 1782, with 274 from Cumbria, low you have to admit.

The Barrow fans left at six in the morning, John Little informs me, it is a semi final after all, yet looking on all sides of this uninspiring ground, you wouldn't think it.

Their trip home is made more comfortable by scoring the winner with their only meaningful attack of the game.

The Bluebirds, a nickname shared with Cardiff, will start slight favourites for the second leg at Holker Street. It's a shame that we have to use names like this, and lions and tigers, none of these creatures are indigenous to Britain. Surely Barrow should be the Submariners, after the Vickers factory, and Cardiff the Taffs, after the river. This is not meant to sound patronising, that would be calling them the sheep shaggers, and whilst admitting the names are not as romantic, it just alludes to where we are, or should be proud to be from.

Rangers have drawn at Sheffield United, so today they are not the useless so and so's you've probably now come to expect.

Newport County have romped to the Conference South title, bringing up the question of the Welsh club's eligibility to play in the English leagues. Previously, the winners of the Welsh Cup were guaranteed entry to European Cup Winners Cup, now that trophy is no more I can't see that there is a problem. Historically the biggest five clubs, Cardiff, Merthyr, Newport, Swansea and Wrexham, have performed across the border for many years, so change would not be for the good, and would create a situation similar to the one already in Scotland. That's that sorted, if only the Middle East was as easy.

Becks is out of contention for South Africa, this is a blow more on the commercial front than the playing side. There is no truth that Victoria is trying to sue Achilles tendon for causing the injury.

March 16

Following on neatly from discussing relevant nicknames, I make an evening trip to Berkshire, where we will play the identity thieves. My reasoning for this is not the kit Reading wear, but their recent adoption of the chant, 'Come on you 'R's.' I have no axe to grind with 'em, but for some reason this gets under my skin. You can understand that once the old Huntley and Palmers factory closed, that using the 'Biscuitmen' as a label was soon going to crumble, into your tea. Luckily enough, hailing from a royal county they had a ready made replacement, the 'Saxe-Coburgs' didn't catch on, so 'Royals' it is. In fact, I would go as far to say that most clubs would be more than happy with this being applied to their team. Nothing untoward here, but if I had a goat I'd get it when 'R's is uttered. We are QPR, unrivalled in being the only team known for its initials in the country, and hence the 'R' for Rangers is celebrated with a sustain to diminuendo when we get a corner or the like. Rochdale or Rotherham have not borrowed this for their own purposes, so neither should anyone else with unsuitable names. So Thames Valley choir, please refrain from persisting in the use of our tune, it sticks in our craw like one of your local custard creams used to.

Brian McDermott has done very well to turn things around, early on in the season they looked certainties for relegation. Elm Park also seems a long time ago, but since their move to Legoland, they've finally become established in the top two divisions, even though they now share the stadium with ruggers London Oirish.

After downing us much as is possible in an hour, at Wetherspoons in the town centre, we jump in a cab as the ground is by the M4, a right royal pain to get to.

Pay on the day is no longer a wise move, as most clubs now charge you a couple of nicker more for the privilege, £28 here.

The biggest cheer of the night is reserved for the news that Inter have scored at Chelsea. Mourinho has got into their heads.

On a list of things that I thought I would never hear, 'Neil Warnock's blue and white army' is right up there. The honeymoon period is over, the fake 'R's grab a late penalty against our ten men, foolishly given away in one of those I'm going to go to ground if you challenge me moments.

See you next season, and try and introduce a new song by then. How about resurrecting one of the old ones? 'We're Reading, we're Reading, we'll kick your fucking 'ead in'? Sounds like a winner to me, a catchy and retro mnemonic, with a hint of pathos.

March 20

Today's the day the teddy bears have their picnic. Not quite, but the day when my son has his life changed forever. No, we haven't converted to Islam, but something with far greater implications. Jake is briefly taken to QPR, just like his dad was, with the words 'This is your team' forever emblazoned on his memory. Heaven help if he ever decides, once reaching his teenage years that another club has stolen his heart. You're no son of mine, and its chimney sweeping for you unless you come to your senses, or at least lie to me about it, until you are old enough to fend for yourself.

Regrettably, my own initiation is not documented. Mainly because my dad can't remember what my first outing to Loftus Road was, and photography with a Box Brownie was not as simple as the point and smile technology now. Therefore, I'm reliant on my own memory for the first game not that I attended, but can recall. It was away, setting a precedent for my future life, at Brisbane Road, Orient, junior ground hopping. It was over the Christmas holiday period, late 1971. Believe it or not I was handed down to the front of the terracing over the heads of helpful spectators. My vague recollections are that both sets of supporters mingled, and that Rodney Marsh missed a penalty. We lost 2-0. Idiots. I wasn't aware of the term wankers at the age of seven, and would have got a clip round the ear if I had. Never did me any harm though.

Bea brings Jake to the ground at half time, for the photo opportunity, but forgets the camera, twenty lashes later, for me. Digital mobile phones make an adequate replacement; mine has eight mega pixels, whatever that means. Posterity ain't what it used to be.

What can I tell my stinky son about the events of his debut match? Even if he is only there for five minutes, much like his daddy sometimes. Well, I'll say opening a packet of Werther's Originals, proving that advertising works, as I had never heard of them until I was an adult.

Rangers' season was going nowhere, though the next one may be better now the evil Italian dictator has been imprisoned, in an iron mask or luxury yacht. The Portuguese man used to be friends with Italian man, but they argued so now he manages the Welsh side, who are hard to be beat, and take the lead in the second half with a flukey goal, but the nice men in blue and white hoops get one back before the end, so 15502 people go home all a bit happy. Some mouthy Swans causing trouble, are given a squeeze on the Uxbridge Road, lucky for them, but we won't talk about that bit, as the media will have you believe that this sort of thing doesn't happen anymore.

FA Chief Executive Ian Watmore resigns. He must have been doing a good job, because he kept his head down and got on with it, and barely anybody knew his name.

Is it worth updating my CV? Or does knowing what is right from wrong on football matters, mean I'm overqualified?

March 23

Dismal. A one all draw with Derby County. Thom Yorke from Radiohead had the right words in 'Creep' with, 'what the hell am I doing here?' There is normally at least one of these games per season, when you question your will to live.

The Rams are content with a point, which is obvious when manager Nigel Clough, once possessing of a decent touch, deliberately takes about five to get the ball back into play. Just what his father would have made of it all, would have been worth a listen.

Four seasons back, kicking and screaming, my then girlfriend dragged me to the very same fixture, but had the brilliant idea of bringing a novel in case of a downturn in proceedings. Ha ha, you'll be glued to your seat with the non stop action I said. Even I read two chapters, which was written in Spanish, and wish I had a copy of 'War and Peace' tonight.

The half time refreshments don't measure up to much either. Like a McDonald's sausage and egg McMuffin, you are tempted from time to time, then you bite into one and remember how awful they are, but this selective amnesia still remains. This is the rule of thumb concerning pies and burgers sold at Rangers, tepid and hardly any meat, like the fare on offer pitch side tonight.

When, it's said that the supporters don't deserve the treatment they receive from their clubs, here are prime examples. Shit food, shit football.

Without a fanfare, it is announced that the qualifying ties for the UEFA 2012 competition in Poland and Ukraine will take place on Tuesdays and Fridays to allow players time to recover before their club matches the next weekend. Switching from Wednesday to the day before really doesn't make too much difference for the majority of football watchers, but moving from Saturday has far bigger repercussions for the spectating public.

Taking the example of England, with all home games at Wembley, eight o'clock kick off. The rush hour in London on Friday starts just before four, and finishes about midnight. Add to the mix, football traffic approaching from every angle, and chances are you will end up with gridlock.

Then there is the element of time. Home games, will mean leaving probably more than just a little bit early, and away games? An extra day off work, at least, for anybody attempting to travel further afield than the off licence.

It is reassuring to know that UEFA have taken us into consideration, and as my wife says, you can always watch it on the telly. There is no suggestion that Platini and co has kowtowed to club pressure, and can guarantee Europe's influential super clubs held absolutely no sway in this decision whatsoever. None at all. Not one iota. Not a jot.

Under the radar also, are the fines imposed on QPR and Bradford City for repeated failure to provide accurate information to sampling officers trying to locate players that they want to test. Rangers punishment, £6000, dates back from December, when there was even more turmoil at the club than usual. Makes you wonder if any of the squad were bang on it over the Christmas break. Bloody played like it. The Bantam's penalty was lesser, a grand, no doubt their fans feel the same.

If, over the course of eighteen months, three tests are missed, then a lengthy suspension is likely. Rio Ferdinand must have wished he could have blamed the club officials when he lapsed six years ago.

One gets the impression that performance enhancing drug use, is nowhere near the level that athletics or cycling have to deal with. Recreational use however, is probably at another level.

Modest Tony Mowbray, whose sides style of play are completely at odds with what one would expect from a tough tackling centre half, says cheerio to Celtic, after a four goal loss at Paisley's finest, mighty St Mirren.

March 25

'This is a man's world' sang James Brown, 'but it wouldn't be nothing, without a woman or a girl.'

Does this apply in football? No.

All that springs to my sexist mind is the tea lady or kit washer.

You must have heard 'Get your tits out for the lads' all over the country a thousand times, yet I smile to myself at the thought of hearing it tonight as I walk down South Africa Road just before England v Austria (Ladies.)

I've never before watched a female football match live. You half watch on TV the women's FA Cup Final and the Olympic games, with the female equivalent of Fatty Foulkes in goal, and high pitched squealing when a ball goes in. Somehow this gives me visions of sitting in the WaG section at an England match with the girls staring at the sky, trying their level best to outdo each other with the latest look, not really having a clue about what is happening on the pitch.

Doing my best to keep an open mind, and not to use many clichés, especially the one about swapping shirts at the end, and the one in the post match shower, 'Where's the soap?' 'It does doesn't it'.

At least they will play for forty five minutes each way and not less than the men, as the women tennis players do. Mind you who wants to watch five sets of female tennis? Not even if it is Kournikova v Ivanovic. Perhaps you would watch a bit if forced at gunpoint.

The bookmakers are open in the ground leaving a lot of us scratching our heads as for whom to waste our money on. Correct score is always your best bet here, 4-1 it is then, at the skinny price of 14's.

Comedians in the stand notice that in the Austrian squad is Susanna Koch, a popular Germanic surname, but gold if you are watching from the terraces. We have a player with a far funnier name and not in the least bit sexist, full back Rachel Unitt. Austria once gave us the only player whose name has ever rhymed with ankle, that's Hans Krankl.

An early positive is that the referee doesn't receive any backchat; there are many of us wishing that our other halves would act like the centre halves here.

No long ball game is likely in the woman's game, genuinely, as they are not prone to be able to boot a ball seventy yards. Passing, certainly amongst a lot of the defenders on show, is very deliberate, almost as if coached time after time, pass with your instep, manufactured not natural. This isn't the case with every player out there, Eniola Aluko, scorer of the second of the three England goals, plays like she was born with a football. Until most of the girls become as comfortable in possession as Eni, it is unlikely that the general public are going to take that much of an interest. It is noticeable that four of our squad play in America, where the standard is improving all the time, not to mention the lure of Yankee dollar. This will be for generations ahead to decide, men of my era have already made their minds up.

March 27

It is unlikely that Crawley will ever be twinned with the likes of Prague or even Bath. A post war 'New town', it is not noted for its tourism. This is being kind here. You will go to Gatwick, down the road, with the reason of flying from the airport, you will not find much of a reason to come here. Unless you are researching the latest edition of crap towns. It's kind of an overspill's overspill.

Cancelling my planned 'How to win friends and influence people in overspill towns' guide, more to the matter in question. A ten minutes bus ride gets you to the modern Broadfield Stadium. Not seeing a public house on the horizon, instead I enter the Crawley clubhouse bar, Redz.

The home side have aspirations of league status, whereas today's antagonists, Stevenage Borough look likely to achieve that feat in the very near future. They won the Conference in '96 but their ground was deemed not fit for the fourth division, much to Torquay United's pleasure. This time around they have no such worries, and the rest is all in their own hands.

As Stevenage are table toppers, it has been decided to make this game a Category 'A' fixture, and prices rise accordingly, £15 today.

The council owned ground, built in '97, can be best described as functional, what looks like a floodlight in one corner of the ground is actually a mobile phone pylon.

Two first half goals from Yemi Odubade, show why they are top.

Blue skies turn to grey, then charcoal, and then we get first rain, sleet and then hail. I'm actually glad I'm not playing, apart from being out of my depth, aged forty five with a dodgy Bertie Mee.

1229 people stop being attentive to the action and talk about the weather, or as is often the case at non league, are consulting phones to discover how your other, professional team are getting on.

Mine have fought back to draw 2-2 at Deepdale. Only first half wankers today.

Moment of the afternoon has to go to substitute Joel Byrom, who seals victory with a third goal, a superb strike from the halfway line. Seeing the keeper off his line, bang, his shot dips just under the bar. It is unfortunate that there are no cameras here to record it, as it is the best goal I've seen live this season. If Ronaldo or the like had done something similar, it would make the top five one of those of great football moments programmes presented by a RADA educated Mockney.

Assuming they bring their deserved promotion to Broadhall Way, and keep the nucleus of this side together, Stevenage certainly won't be the whipping boys of League Two.

Wayne Rooney hobbles off in Munich and the nation holds its breath. There is no doubt he has been in exceptional form over the last six months, and is key to any success England may have in the summer which is drawing ever closer. Parallels with a certain D.Beckham and the metatarsal bone break before the 2002 WC will be made, but for me, Wayne's fitness is far more important.

Cesc Fabregas also breaks his leg against his hometown club and suitors Barcelona, the injury looks far more serious than Rooney's, this is fine, as he plays for Spain.

It's not the taking part; it's the winning that counts!

April 2

Easter, the long weekend that often decides the fates of our heroes.

Under pain of death from the missus, we have to 'do something' this weekend. Of course, I have an ulterior motive as we hurtle towards Preston, our weekend base.

Virgin Trains now do Euston to Preston in just over two hours, pretty quick, on a par with Japan's 'Shinkansen' or bullet train as we know it. However, with half of the carriages designated first class, the majority of us have to squeeze into aisles and roof racks, by the time we alight at Preston, I've already won three games of twister. Good value for £70.20 return.

As we arrive at the station, Anthony and his friend Russ are there, almost as if to greet us, which they are not, they're ground hopping, Leigh Genesis v Lancaster City.

Bea, of course, does not believe this is a coincidence, Crying Wolf, my Cherokee name, does not aid me in pleas of innocence.

Crisis narrowly averted, I stress the importance of getting to Morecambe before the tide has receded, not having the slightest inkling on lunar movements and their effect on this part of the Lancashire coast.

After the obligatory photo by the Eric Bartholomew statue in 'Bring me sunshine' pose, I settle my family in the warm confines of 'The Palantine'. The menu looks fine, so they will be happy, as I explain to the manager that I'm a selfish bastard abandoning his kin, and here is my credit card to be used sparingly, only in event of malnutrition and extreme dehydration.

Quarter of an hour after the desertion, I'm in the York Hotel. The barman informs me that this is the nearest pub to the ground, and also to the new version ready for next season.

Whilst nurturing a pint of Bank Tops 'Flat Cap' in the back bar, which is loosely decorated with scarves from lesser known clubs. I am sent, for the umpteenth time, a nudge to make a mental note to always take some form of QPR memorabilia away with me, to donate on such occasions. I never do. I'm never likely to.

Now, a cautionary tale of unfailingly ensuring to stand under cover and keeping the old adage of it ain't over till it's over, firmly in mind.

£12 sees me into the Car Wash stand that runs pitch length, and affords me a good view of the action. Despite the fact that I'm standing in the worst of the four stands, the one without a roof, it is by no means the worst ground I've visited. It has the unusual feature of a police control room set back in the middle of the away end. Why with a small bank holiday attendance of only 2347, they are bothering to get a new ground at all, is beyond me.

Crewe, managed once more by Dario Gradi, take a two goal lead into the break. No big deal. The second period begins with more adventure from Sammy McIlroy's men who grab a goal back, but it quickly gets worse. The Railwaymen re-establish a two goal margin, followed by the dismissal of Morecambe's Andy Parrish, and then miss a penalty for good measure. They've won.

Five minutes to go, Bea texts me to see when I'm coming back to pick her and Jake up, as tap water can get tedious after two hours, and it starts to rain. No head wear about me, not even so much as a baseball cap let alone a fedora, so I decide to call it a day.

Being quite tall, means that I have a long stride, and can walk for England, or so I've been told. The rain has not got heavier, and two minutes up the road I hear a roar, probably another Alex goal and I don't give it a second thought. I quicken my pace to avoid a potential deluge, and arrive back at the bar ten minutes later.

There are only a handful of league fixtures today, but one result stands out as I watch the results service on the pub TV.

Morecambe 4, Crewe Alexandra 3.

The Shrimps have fucking done it, with only ten players and less than five minutes left. This must be the best result in their short league status, and they did it all without my bloodshot eyes to take it in.

There is only one thing worse than not being there, it is not being there, when you were there but left.

I can't turn round to a stranger in years to come and say I was there. Well I was, for a while. I blame the wife.

Bea smiles, in a sympathetic way at my misfortune, and loosens the reins on my harness for the evening.

Meeting up in Preston town centre, first Hartleys, then The Fox and Grapes, and several others until Anthony falls asleep in the Dog and Partridge allowing me to take a photo to include on my Facebook page, photos of friends who have fallen asleep in pubs. This is next to another group, snaps of matches that were memorable but I missed the best bits because I went down the pub.

April 3/4

A twenty minute train journey from Preston gets you to Horwich, straight to the Reebok Stadium, newish home of Bolton Wanderers. To be frank, even though my lot have played and lost here on a couple of occasions, I've never bothered going since the days of Burnden Park. Over the last few years the Trotters have become what I would term 'established' in the top echelon of the English hierarchy.

On first impressions, it's of a similar design to Huddersfield's multi named stadium, but with a larger capacity.

Reluctant to pay full Premiership price, I hang about near the ticket office, to see if I can blag a cheap spare. David Moyes, Everton boss, collects his complimentary, rebuking my request to 'get me in', wisely, I would have chewed his ear off.

My diligence bears fruit, £15 for a 'Help for Heroes' freebie in the Lofthouse Stand, or beer for a squaddie as it transpires. No complaints from me.

This is an opportunity for me to take a good look at England's potential future stars. Amongst them are Agbonlahor, Cahill, Delph, Wilshire, and Ashley Young who curls in a sweet opener after only ten minutes.

My guess is there's roughly 2500 away supporters, I expect more, for a team in the ascendancy, but, they are at Wembley again next week, so that must take precedence on the wallet.

21,111 is the official attendance, for a game settled by that early goal. Bolton look poor, and are very one dimensional. Owen Coyle has his work cut out, replacing the popular Sam Allardyce, now looking more like Les Dawson every day, via the disliked Gary Megson. Villa, marginally better, but to my critical eye, always look like they have a soft underbelly, play them right, and they are prone to implode. This is what I would've written had the Sunday papers asked for my opinion. Is the national job mine do you think?

Even leaving five minutes before time doesn't get me back to Preston for my promised schedule, not wise after yesterday's events, but lightning will not strike twice today.

Trains zoom past, and nearly an hour later, one finally alights, forcing me to murder two queue jumpers hoping for a seat. Like Stalin, hard but fair.

A deal is a deal, so I bust a gut to get back for an evening meal and repay my wife's leniency when she says as I go out to meet Anthony and watch the boxing in Preston town centre, 'Make sure you're in by four!. 'What a girl! No time to check the horses dentures, I'm off, but get back to the hotel early, after seeing David

Haye retain his title in a bar called 'The Angel'. Which my wife is, if three can be considered early, and there's me criticising her in the past. What a wanker, similar to my team, who can't even hold onto a lead to beat Sheffield Wednesday at home.

On Sunday, we spend enjoyable family time in the Lake District. If Windermere had a league side, I would no doubt have been here before; the same goes for towns in Cornwall. The truth is it's easier for me to get to say, Spain, than here, and travel inconvenience makes often makes a Philistine of me. In saying this, I would like to pay a visit to Philistinia when I get the chance. The rumour is that they have a fantastic terraced stand.

April 5

In the morning I take Jake off Bea's hands for a couple of hours, and on his insistence, together we head for the National Football Museum, which at present, is to be found at PNE's Deepdale ground. Not for much longer, as it will soon be relocated in Manchester. Surely Wembley would be the logical choice.

There is no charge to enter, and even though not all the attractions are open, the main exhibition is a pleasant enough way to spend an hour. Here, is the perfect excuse to search out new trivia and reaffirming facts that you already knew, but would like to bore others with. Such as the first Charity Shield being played in 1908 between Manchester United and what was then a big club in the South, Queen's Park Rangers. Was the centenary of this event celebrated two years ago by a community re match at Stamford Bridge, the original venue? Of course not.

Another little did you know, is that in the first ever WC Final, Uruguay 1930, they used two different types of balls.

The Argentinian ball was used in the first half, and after forty five they were two-one up.

In the second, the Uruguayan ball was used and saw them run out four-two winners.

No you didn't did you? Liar.

Back where they belong? Probably. The club that wouldn't die? Definitely.

A thirty minutes locomotive journey to the smallest of all the towns of the current ninety two, but with one of the most famous names, Accrington Stanley. An uphill walk past the impressive viaduct and after ten minutes I find the Grey Horse near to the ground. This is a milestone for me, the last of current teams of the four divisions. If you want to be picky, I'm four short of the 'current' grounds, but in my eyes, I've done the lot. The 92 as they stand, at their home grounds or where they once played.

The ones I'm missing are, the Emirates, Arsenal, which I have been saving for a visit by QPR, having passed through Highbury's gates umpteen times; Yeovil's new Huish, I saw us win at their old sloping pitch in '88; Rotherham's temporary Don Valley, sadly replacing Millmoor; and Darlington's white elephant, which will be non league next season, pointlessly ousting Feethams.

Somehow it feels right to finish here. The original Accrington FC were founder members of the Football League, not that that counts for much, just a sense of history, and 'Ripping Yarns' deja vu when thinking about vintage matches in places with names such as Oswaldtwistle. Northern exotic to coin a phrase.

Stanley now compete at the Crown Ground previously sponsored by Fraser Eagle before they went to the wall. The club first went to the wall in March '62, and ceased to be in '66 along with the original ground, which is where I'm now headed, a fifteen minutes stroll away from their current one. This is my homage, like Lourdes or Mecca, but more noteworthy.

A school has taken the old grounds place, and as I walk around the streets an ironic sign declares 'No ball games.'

The only reminder is the original changing rooms beside the school playing field, with the Peel Park Hotel adjacent to this brick built block.

Inside the pub, which I would recommend, even if it is a little off the beaten track, there are black and white photo's of yesteryear, all that remains of the original club and there brief 1950s heyday.

A friendly group of locals give me a lift to the ground, where I part with £13, and stand with them behind the goal, which because of ridiculous league regulations, is partly fitted out with seats. The roof of the main stand has the appearance of one much larger, but has hardly any height at all. It is probably the poorest ground of the ninety two, and the bank holiday crowd of 1839 would probably say exactly, if the Milk Marketing Board hadn't said it before and I hadn't said it earlier this season.

After being outplayed for most of the half, the home side find themselves two up at the break, with the Grimsby followers resigned to Conference football next season. Their luck changes ten minutes after the re-start with three goals in five minutes to seal a deserved victory. Whether or not the Mariners can reprieve their relegation plight is unlikely, but they are giving it a go.

Back to Preston, where, en route, I learn of Rangers defeat at Leicester's Cheese and Onion Stadium by only four to nil. Useless wankers.

Paul Simon, apparently, wrote 'Homeward Bound' sitting on a railway station not too far from here, his sentiments mirror mine. London for all the bad publicity it receives is still my home, and the greatest city in the world. Maybe it's because I'm a Londoner, that I love London so ....etc ad nauseum.

Two cracking games in Europe this week that sees the demise of England's representation in this season's Champions League.

Arsenal, as expected, lose in Barcelona, but they were powerless to resist Lionel Messi, who gave what can best be described as a masterclass in finishing. His ability to fire in a shot with little or no space is phenomenal. He could become a legend, in the true sense of the word.

At Old Trafford it can genuinely be said that Manchester United were unlucky, in a game they were controlling, the harsh dismissal of Rafael swung the balance in favour of Bayern. The finishes of both Nani and Robben were top draw.

On the plus side, less matches for our England players to have to worry about in advance of the World Cup, bless their tired legs.

April 10

Crystal Palace, which burnt down in November 1936. Have the embers finally gone out this season?

The accent below the Thames boundary, always strikes many of us from over the bridges as a parody of our own.

Most of us from West London have never liked going here. Certainly if travelling by car, it can be easier to get to Birmingham than South East London, or France as we refer to it.

However, with the opening of the Westfield shopping centre in Shepherds Bush, a new over ground station has been opened, tapping into a line which can now transport us to Sarf London in half an hour.

Before midday there are already plenty of us in the Flora Sandes opposite Thornton Heath station. A lot of old faces are out today, of which I suppose, I am now one of.

Rangers could still be relegated, though it is more likely to be Palace. There is more of an edge to this game than usual with the switching of clubs by the managers, and accident specialist lawyers Hart and Warnock.

Twenty five pounds entry into the dilapidated Arthur Wait Stand, wooden seats where you hurt your legs far more than the modern plastic variety, which is the case less than ten minutes in, when Akos Buzsaky opens the scoring with a gem, highlighting not the state of the seats, but the need for the reintroducing terracing. This stand was built in 1969, named after the former chairman, but has the feel of pre-war at earliest; such have been the changes in design, and also in the size of Homo sapiens. It is almost as if no one was over six feet tall then. All 3000 of our following are standing, in a totally seated area.

The warmest day of the year so far, with The Grand National due off around half time, Rangers playing well, every other supporter in our end wants a drink, and the kiosks run out of beer.

Now I understand the club is in administration, but surely they could put some sort of sale or return policy in place, at least on bottled beer. Any old piss would do, let's face it, this is what you get, and have to be happy with. An estimate with no factual basis made by myself, reckons that this short sightedness has cost Palace up to five grand in profit. Money sorely needed. I'm not too bothered, it's my round.

We continue to dictate the play, and as we discover that Tony McCoy has finally won the big one, the celebration of several is expanded to the majority as we get a second, by another Englishman, Kaspars Gorkss.

Even the most cool or reserved of us join in the singing. As the home supporters leave early, the chant, 'Is there a fire drill?' emanates from our smiling section. Neil Warnock is the consummate professional and refuses to acknowledge our calls for him to wave. He's right. I do feel for their plight. From tomorrow onwards, the moment is ours. We weren't wankers today.

All the pubs in the area are shut afterwards, this never used to be the case. As all trains head to Britain's busiest station, Clapham Junction, this is where many of us go. We swamp the Slug and Lettuce, and the Falcon next door.

The FA Cup semi final kicks off, and when Chelsea score a couple of fellas jump up unaware there are loads of us at the back of the pub. They get bullied, which I am not comfortable with, but much more palatable is seeing the doormen squirm when half the pub burst into song, and much to their chagrin (if it's possible for a bouncer to feel chagrin?) it continues for an hour without abating, with their futile efforts to eject over zealous singers, being greeted by angry looks from the dozens of 'R's still there.

What is surprising is the amount of people who want to watch the El Classico game between Real Madrid and Barcelona later on. Only a few years back, many of these pundits couldn't have pointed out Madrid in an atlas. Such is the coverage now afforded to world football. This is not a bad thing, but, it shows that the top level is all that seems to matter to the majority. Talk to any teenager, they will likely be able to tell you the one to eleven for Barcelona, but not say, Birmingham City.

Two shocks in the Cup semis this weekend.

At Hampden Park, Ross County from Dingwall, dump Celtic out of the Scottish variety, following in the footsteps of Queen of the South in recent seasons as unfancied sides in reaching the final.

Harry Redknapp is not the first person to moan about the state of the Wembley pitch, though in all fairness if Dawson hadn't slipped, you still feel Pompey would have won anyway. At least they are taking something from what has been a nightmarish season for them.

In addition to the two encounters played here on consecutive days, next week our national stadium will host rugby union, all this plus car racing, and American football (one of my Room 101 choices), gigs in the summer, and a roof that doesn't fully cover the playing surface. What on earth is that all about?

Despite another away win, Darlington bow out of the FL, not for the first time, but now they are saddled with what is now the biggest ground in the Conference. In all truth, they would have been better off still playing at Feethams.

The Premier League decides to increase parachute payments for sides who are demoted from two to four years with a total sum of £48 million. This will further increase the disparity between the haves and the have nots, and make it even more difficult for a smaller club to break into the promised land of the money league. Whoever grabs the third place from the Championship next month, will, literally, be laughing all the way to the bank.

April 17

Eyjafjallajoekull. It looks as though Jake has decided to type this for me. What this translates literally to, or should, is volcanic bastard ash. Iceland, who suffered badly during the economic downturn, and owe a substantial sum to our Government prompting the comment that we wanted cash not ash. They do a good 'buy one get one free' on chicken Kievs though.

Much as I would like to vent my spleen about the rights, wrongs and frustrations of the flight ban, there is bugger all that you can do. It is better to not be able to travel than to not be able to travel back. So say the wise words of Marco Polo. This was after he got stranded at Hong Kong Airport, and before they charged him for overweight luggage. Silk pyjamas are heavier than you might think when you carry four score and ten pairs of small, medium, and large.

The plan was to watch Braga, currently lying second in the Portuguese Liga, theirs is the unusual ground next to the cliff face that you may recall from Euro 2004. Another ground used during that tournament was that of Boavista, the other Porto side, whose kit resembles a chess board, now languishing in the third tier due to mismanagement and financial irregularities. They broke the monopoly in 2001 and won the title, and I once saw them play in the hills of Madeira at Nacional, Cristiano Ronaldo's old club, which is well worth a visit should you take a break there, for the vista if nothing else, actually nothing else. This was due to be my Sunday match and then home in time for MOTD2.

My only previous visit to Porto was during the aforementioned competition, I got the train up from Lisbon after I was left with twelve Category One tickets with a face value of 120 Euros each for the quarter final clash between Denmark and the Czech Republic at the Dragao. It would not be inaccurate to say that I couldn't give them away, in fact, near kick off I try to barter an exchange for one paltry tin of beer, no dice said the street kid. Obrigado very much.

If you ever fancy a free days drinking and you aren't friends with Gazza, try the port tasting on the side of river Douro here. I managed to visit nine 'houses', which set me up nicely for an evening of staggering later on. Quite right that it should be free for us, as we share certainly, one of, if not the oldest treaty in the world. You would think the next time it comes to penalties they'd deliberately sky a couple, or just roll over because of the 1386 Treaty of Windsor. Just remember that next time you wink, pretty boy.

Lounging about Saturday morning, my wife, cleaning the blood off her apron after her morning shift at the abattoir, foolishly falls into the trap that I haven't even had to prime.

'So you are not going to football now are you?'

'Of course I am honey; it's our annual punch up against Cardiff City.'

True to form it is. Much gesturing, swearing and a large police presence. Fighting before and after. Many of their supporters cry foul, yet they have been bullying teams for years.

The situation is not helped after The Bluebirds sneak a late one nil, (they'll need to better than this if they are to get promoted) when both sets of fans are let out onto South Africa Road together, rather than keeping the away section in for ten minutes to let the home crowd disperse.

I ask Jacko, one of the Met's coppers who regularly police Rangers why this is? He explains that the decision, to keep Cardiff in, which would suit them, is not theirs to make. A committee, which includes the council, decides that the inevitable health and safety implications should not keep supporters in against their will. The safety of the stewards also has to be taken into consideration, we're told. Good grief. This is also to do with the fact that the home team has to pay for any extra police present inside the stadium. It is all a blame game nowadays.

Norwich come back up, with Paul Lambert in contention for manager of the year, after overseeing their heavy defeat on the season's opening day.

Notts County and Rochdale leave the fourth tier behind; the latter is more remarkable in that they have been in the bottom division for the last 36 years. Everyone but their most bitter rivals should be pleased for Keith Hill's men, a small step for mankind, a giant leap for Spotland. That would have worked better if his surname was Armstrong or Aldrin.

April 20

Now it is mathematically impossible for QPR to get relegated, we can relax and take pleasure in the misfortunes of others, which is the type of people most of us are. It's odd that as the nation that is the master of this phenomenon, we have to use a German word to describe it, schadenfraude. This confirms the myth that we have nothing in common.

Watford aren't in such a fortunate position as Rangers, so when a first half penalty gives us the lead, texts ensue such as, 'Have you ever been to Spotland?'

Being the nice blokes that we are, we also leave sing a long messages on answer phones, 'That's why you're going down' to the tune of La Donna e Mobile from Rigoletto by Verdi. You knew that already, being the opera lovers that most football geezers are. Doesn't it strike you as funny that arias from centuries previous are still commonplace behind the goals? Wouldn't Verdi feel honoured if he knew that a piece from Aida is also in usage? It is a shame that the composer of one of the most famous Gregorian chants is unknown. 'You're gonna get your fuckin' 'ed kicked in,' rarely heard these days, could have been worth a fortune in royalties.

The biggest cheer of the night was reserved for the sight of aircraft lights in the dark coming into land at Heathrow.

That solitary goal is enough to keep the pressure on Hertfordshire's finest, who along with Barnet, have now been joined by Stevenage as the county's representatives.

Pitches are in the news, or the amount of H2O present on them. Wembley have put too much on theirs, causing many players to lose their footing, and Mourinho refused to water the San Siro to hinder the passing game of Barca. Shades of John

Beck's Cambridge United? His justification could be that Hose A wasn't working. I'm proud of the fact that I managed to include this with legitimate reason!

Because of the ash in the air, transport to the UEFA ties is not to be taken for granted, but you'd think the staff had to hide in the back of forty feet containers next to frozen meat, they way it's portrayed to be a hardship, like Napoleon's retreat from Moscow.

Lucky old Portsmouth discover they won't be allowed into the Europa League next season as they didn't fill in the form on time, and more good news their debt is now a whopping £119 million. Surely the Serious Fraud Office will now smell a rat and become slightly interested?

When travelling by train, if finishing with a newspaper, I always leave it on the seat for the next passenger to read when I alight. So when on the tube a like minded soul leaves a copy of 'The Independent', this makes me happy enough for half an hour until I come across an article written by Alex James, bassist with Blur. In what is one would imagine being a weekly column, the only piece I happen to read would be the one that he gives his view on watching the game. He goes on to explain how he was invited, from the comfort of a box, to watch a game which although not mentioned by name in the article, is QPR v Cardiff, I'm sure.

After the excellent food and facilities his day takes a turn for the worse when the away lot appear next to his viewing area. 'What a horrible sight that crowd was. Nothing like the rapturous faces of big crowds at a music festival.' His synopsis being that it is better to play than to watch any level of footie, and if 'the men on the terrace' did the same ' they wouldn't be so angry, or so fat.'

Jeremy Clarkson, I recall, wrote an article similar in its naivety in The Sunday Times a while back.

Now, I'll give you my opinion of the aroma of a four week old gorgonzola, along with the handling capabilities of the latest Lamborghini. Second thoughts I won't bother as I wouldn't have the faintest clue what I was babbling on about. This doesn't seem to stop virtually anybody who is asked, more than any other topic, talking about football, as is shown by these experts.

One gets the impression that if you compared Noel Gallagher and Alex James on matters football, rather like Danny Baker and David Mellor on radio that one gets it and one doesn't.

Stick to what you know, be being a fop haired route one Ronnie who wouldn't know a football if it hit him in the bass.

April 22

Thursday, once the Stonewall certain day of the week when there is no decent football played. Everybody not of professional standard and of playing age trains on Thursday night. Then the UEFA Cup gradually made inroads into football's 'holy' day and this has now been changed probably forever.

Foregoing the two televised matches on offer, I turn up at Wealdstone's The Vale, for the second time this season. They must win tonight, as must their opponents, Tonbridge Angels, to stand any chance of making the play offs.

Last night was the testimonial dinner for the Stones long serving manager Gordon Bartlett, one of the only free evenings available as their fixture congestion takes a grip. In this neck of the woods this is because of the poor winter weather, allied with successful cup runs, and has meant games on Tuesday, Thursday, and Saturday for the last two weeks.

Tonbridge take an early lead, and thankfully their faithful don't start belting out the Robbie Williams hit as I feared. They are originally named after a local hotel 'The Angel'.

A cracking game ensues, both teams committed and it's good to hear banter from the crowd at close quarters, the only noise louder is the swearing from the players. The usual players shouts of 'winners', 'feet', and 'fuckin' 'ell referee', are only trumped by the call of 'two sugars' when a nutmeg is partially successful. Only one sugar then, no milk, decaff.

Level at the break, we haven't quite finished downing our pints in the clubhouse when the home side take the lead.

They hold onto this, setting up a grand finale for the weekend, only a win will do, in conjunction with one of the three teams above them slipping up. I'll keep my fingers crossed.

Should this go to plan, and Wealdstone then come through in the play offs, they would find themselves in the Blue Square South. This would only be allowed with the inevitable ground improvements. Here, this would entail a large amount of work, new and separate turnstiles for the away supporters, and extra roofing/covers for much of the ground.

One promotion further and a whole new set of regulations must be put into place; much of this then is seating and segregation. You can understand why some clubs are just happy to stay as they are, with a decent cup run every now and then to propel them into the limelight.

We have a sunny St George's Day, an event which has rightly grown in popularity in recent years. If were lucky in a decade or so, we may even get a bank holiday, probably at the expense of Mayday.

Myth as the legend of our patron saint is, most would be surprised to know where the 'real' George is buried. This I discovered on England's away game in Israel in March 2007.

Our cabbie, who was akin to having Jackie Mason for a driver, pointed out not too far from Tel Aviv Airport his whereabouts. What amazed me was that no one from seemed to notice this detail from the FA, if they did it was kept under their hats, possibly under the auspices of political correctness.

After drinking the host city dry we also made a trip to Jerusalem, which to those of you who've never been, could be under described as interesting. Don't let this put you off taking a look at one of the planet's craziest places, but give me 'those dark satanic mills' every time. I'm being literal I know, but when on April 23rd you get emotional whilst singing Blake's hymn, I'd rather we don't build Jerusalem in our green and pleasant land thank you very much.

April 24

The weather is not the only thing hotting up. This is a good time of the year to pick a match that has a great deal of significance to its outcome. My selection is deep in the Essex countryside at the end of the branch line from Liverpool Street, Braintree.

Just into the journey, I get a look at the Olympic site at Stratford which has moved along at a cracking pace. It's a vast area, and the stadium, if not quite

Wembley, is impressive enough. It looks too big for West Ham or most clubs to move into.

Arriving near kick off at Cressing Road, I'm greeted by a flock of sheep. Not just you're run of the mill Derbyshire Merino, if there is such a breed, but Welsh Homo sapien. This lesser known pedigree are lining up at the turnstiles, complete with white PVC chemical suits and 'Dolly' masks. Whereas Newport's boys are all dressed as sheep, I notice as I enter the ground, the remainder of their supporters are dressed head to toe in orange, more reminiscent of Holland than a team from Gwent, officially, the actual kit colour is amber.

They deserve to celebrate in style; they've stormed the Blue Square South and are now only one division from their long quest to regain league status, lost in '88, followed by bankruptcy the year after, and no longer playing at their original ground, Somerton Park. Like Chelmsford City in this league, their new premises may be council owned with an athletics track, but it's a better than nothing.

The last occasion I saw Newport County play was in an FAC second round tie at Harrow Borough in December '83, when a certain John Aldridge scored twice in a 3-1 away win.

Now, as the last game of a successful season kicks off, they are already on a century of points, and twenty eight clear of their nearest rivals Dover Athletic.

Dean Holdsworth, whom I never thought of as management material, watches his charges steam roller the home side with two goals from set pieces in the first twelve minutes.

This match is just as vital to Braintree Town, who need a point to cement their play off spot.

At half time the high jinks continue, with impromptu penalties being taken against an agreeable steward by ovine takers, shepherded by men in orange gimp suits. Not a copper in sight, just good fun.

In the same goal, Braintree net a penalty, but it is not enough for 'the Iron', and Woking nick their play off spot. I'm informed that they have plans to build a new stadium, but I'm at a loss to explain why, as at least half the crowd of 1187 here this afternoon are from South Wales.

Once again the argument arises that Newport have deprived an English club a place in the division above and should join the League of Wales, to ply their trade against the likes of TNS and Airbus UK. I reiterate, I would not be an advocate of this, these sides have crossed swords with us bastards from across the border for over a century in most cases, and long may it continue.

My football bet goes down because Rangers decide to win their last away game at Oakwell albeit with a weakened team. Still they are wankers.

It's all happening now, Burnley and Hull are unable to halt their decline and join Pompey in the FL again.

Southend swap divisions with Bournemouth.

On Sunday, in addition to my regular reading material, I purchase The Non League Paper to check on the comings and goings of the lower divisions at this crucial time.

In a frantic battle at the bottom of the Conference, Forest Green Rovers, and Ebbsfleet United join Grays Athletic in playing at a lesser standard. All the shareholders at Myfootballclub don't seem to have helped the North Kent side much, but their problems are trivial in comparison to those of the Essex team, who have lost their ground and are unsure which league they will be playing next season.

Southport will take one of these places winning the Blue Square North title, pipping coastal rivals Fleetwood Town with ill feeling on both sides.

The results are comprehensive and I scour the pages for interesting titbits, which include Farnborough being crowned champions of what was once the Southern League, not remarkable in itself, but comic when you see the trophy you receive, the Zamaretto Shield. It takes two to lift it comfortably, and will require a special cabinet for storage, looking more akin to a public schools honours board.

Then there is the inevitable double figure defeat which takes in the Koolsport Northern Counties East League Premier Division where Scarborough Athletic put thirteen past Brodsworth Miners Welfare, this is not a shock as they've only managed two draws all season.

Best league sponsorship has to be, Ziggy's Spice House Halifax & District League.

It's good to see former members of the hallowed ninety two, picking up after years of failure, Halifax, Bradford Park Avenue, and Workington, all fall into this category.

Closer to home, very close in fact, North Greenford United look set to win the Cherry Red Combined Counties Premier Division, and with it promotion to either the Ryman or Zamaretto lower divisions, this will also involve competing in the FA Trophy rather than the Vase. A huge development for a club such as this, as kids we used to kick a Wembley Trophy about here when it was just an open playing field.

April 27

Wealdstone fall short in their play off quest. This doesn't stop me from attending the game in which they could have been playing. You must visit a ground with the brilliant name of Gander Goose Lane. Somehow this is the third time I've seen Sutton this season, without ever having seen them before and tonight has the prospect of a thriller, a derby against Kingstonian.

This is the fairest play off system in operation.

Sutton, who finished second, face the aforementioned Kingston who were fifth, over one leg because they were, of course, placed higher. Last night Aveley who were third, lost at home to Borehamwood, fourth. If Sutton win tonight, they will be at home to last nights victors, again by league position. If not, B'wood will have home advantage. This rewards the year's endeavours much more reasonably than the more well known current system. No doubt it's less of an earner, fairness has little to do with it, it seems with we are saddled with Wembley finals for good.

Alighting at West Sutton station, there is already a long queue developing and even at this level a murmur of expectation. It feels good when you start to need sunglasses for the first half at a night game.

Inside, the crowd looks larger than it actually is (1401) and I spot a few pro's both current and former who enjoy with the rest of us a frantic battle, that sees Kingstonian take an early lead only for Sutton to hit back with two before the break. I stand with friend Tony Hill, whose fiancée's son is helping to shore the K's defence together.

Half time gives the audience a chance to practice that age old tradition of changing ends, only possible now at this level, as many of the Conference grounds are either former league sides or clubs who have moved into new premises. With most they are constructed in such a way that prevents the fans crossover and the repositioning of flags behind the goal you are attacking.

The K's make their followers glad they switched around, by hitting three more, including one beauty, a volley from twenty yards, to run out four two victors. Fourth place will now play fifth at Meadow Park, Borehamwood.

The next evening, we settle down for a romantic night in. Jake is sound asleep, a good bottle of Bordeaux uncorked, chicken chorizo, goose fat potatoes, redcurrant jelly, asparagus, and the Champions League Semi Final Second Leg for dessert. Along with some Haagen-Dazs ice cream.

From different perspectives, I've been looking forward to this. The mind games of the translator against the undoubted talent of the Catalans.

The outcome shows the mortality of Barca, once Sergio Busquets, with method acting qualities Marlon Brando would've been proud of, cons the ref, this culminates in the first half dismissal of Thiago Motta. Somehow this plays into Inter's hands, and from then on switches my sympathies to the ten men Italians.

This is not totally accurate, of the fourteen players used, nine are from South America, three are Africans, and only two non Italian Europeans. Even the unused Balotelli, be honest, doesn't pass much of a resemblance to Julius Caesar.

Without Iniesta pulling the strings, Keita is a less than adequate replacement, the other two major stars, Messi and Xavi are well chaperoned, and the outcome means that Barcelona can't large it in their enemies lair, the Bernabeau, next month.

It pains me to say it, but Fulham and manager Roy Hodgson deserve immense credit for reaching the Europa League Final, extra officials and all.

Jealousy on my behalf, in that continued success for clubs local to me, could, coupled with my own teams' failure to compete, lose a generation in an area once staunchly QPR. This is pretty much what has happened to Brentford over the course of the last half a century. Chelsea I've learned to live with, but to accept a large Fulham influx in the area as well would be difficult for my selfish outlook.

No condolences however for Liverpool, losing out to Atletico Madrid, both teams shouldn't have been in this competition in the first place, having been eliminated from the Champions League, even though in that they weren't champions either. Bitter, twisted and accurate.

April 30

Bea takes Jake to Poland, attending a confirmation. Being neither a Catholic nor interested, a window has opened up for me to travel once again, especially as the skies seem ash free for now. Having amassed more BA miles, enough to make at least one way affordable, I take to the air to Budapest.

My only previous visit was during the early days of the '98 WC.

Two football related memories here, the first involved an elderly couple of American tourists who, when Iran scored against the US and I remarked, 'Good header', the lady said to her husband 'What's a header?'

He replied, ' It's when you kick a football with your head.' I've been trying to do it ever since.

The other the next evening, when a small crowd gathered to watch a crazy Englishman go mental at Graeme Le Saux's defending when Romania get a late winner after Owen's equaliser just moments before. I then headed to Lens for the Colombia game, in which you may recall a certain David Beckham bent in a free kick, his first international goal.

Geographically, Hungary is the Centre of Europe, hence Central Europe, not Eastern as my wife is keen to point out. That's that cleared up them.

World masters in the fifties, one wonders what has gone wrong, as now the national side is barely ranked in the top fifty.

You tend to be far more relaxed when re-visiting roads you've previously trodden. With this in mind I saunter into the 26°C early afternoon sunshine, to the bus number 200E from the airport to the Metro terminal and onwards to my good hotel on the eastern bank of the Danube.

It had to happen I suppose. After a season of waterlogged and frozen pitches causing postponements, and even an abandonment, here was a new knock back for me.

I arrive at the metro stop Nepliget, on the M3 blue line at about 5.15, not even out of my brain on the train, for a 7pm kick off. For tonight is the big derby,

Ferencvaros v Ujpest Dozsa. There are robocops or in local lingo, Rendorseg, as it says on the back of their armour, everywhere. Good name for a metal band.

A ticket cannot be purchased without an identity card. You had to register by five today to be entitled to one. I had previously sent an email in the week about getting a ticket, but to no avail. No matter, I'll get in somehow, I usually do.

Standing outside, hoping to grab a spare from a helpful Magyar, I notice about fifty or so blokes walking up the dual carriageway towards us. It appears that no one else is aware of this, neither the riot police nor the Ferencvaros followers, unless they are turning a blind eye. Spending my formative years in the '70s now shapes me to secure a decent vantage point and watch the proceedings unfurl. This may seem callous, but I'm immune as I watch the action take place. By the time the Ujpest boys get within fifty yards of the home crowd the police intervene, pursued by all manner of bottle throwing Ferencvarosi. It appears that everyone is fair game, hooligans and coppers alike. They don't land a single glove on each other; the batons are used to full effect. The sight of a boy no older than thirteen throwing a beer bottle is disquieting, perhaps showing why discus is a national sport here. Although aiming for at least the distance at which Usain Bolt runs in nine and a half seconds, he only manages to hit the back of the riot helmet of a Schwarzeneggar clone not more than ten yards ahead. Turning in amazement the policeman doesn't realise that mummy's little angel is the culprit saving him a hefty whack, which are being dished out liberally elsewhere. My sole surprise is that there is not a single arrest. This is the way things are done here, at home you would be lucky to escape with less than six months at Her Majesty's pleasure.

This brief interlude does little to aid my entrance to the match.

Kevin McCabe, the owner of Sheffield United, as well as having interests in China, also has control here, with Craig Short managing and a host of English players. Is this what Hungarian football has come to?

No amount of blagging on my behalf, even talking to the English staff, gets me through the gates and it looks likely that this will go on my small list of games that I've not succeeded in gaining entry to. The last was in Hanover during the 2006 WC, Angola v Mexico. Thinking admission would be a breeze, we couldn't believe it, when there were more Mexicans in attendance than present at the Alamo, with the touts charging 500 Euros for entry.

Across from the Stadion Albert Florian, under the flyover, a small crowd has gathered outside a hexagonal shaped bar to watch the televised game only a discus throw from where the action is taking place.

Disconsolate, I buy a beer, and I drink some cum. Not for the first time, but the first time from a plastic cup. Stop tittering as Frankie Howerd would have said. Zwack Unicum is the beverage in question, the local herb liqueur. Cum probably tastes better.

The purple shirted away team score and I find myself pleased. Nothing to do with not getting in.

Actually, everything to do with this. The stadium is only half full, my fiver would have made a considerable, err, not much difference at all. The biggest club in Hungary. Ha.

An eagle eyed steward nips my attempt in the bud to get in for the last ten. Wanker.

This is why the Russians invaded in '56, I yell. Well I don't, but I should have, if I thought he would have understood my outburst. Khrushchev, I picture, not gaining admittance to a fixture containing the greats of the era, stating,

'Vuk this, ve'll teach 'em', ve vill bury you.'

Why he was speaking in a faux German accent I've no idea?

Later, back in the city centre, I team up with a stag party from Nottingham, seemingly willing to pay for an attractive guide, happy to let them be convinced that they're getting a good deal for being shown around the city's bars that they would have found anyway, as she smiles and does her make up.

I leave them at a popular and big open air bar, Godor, departing at height of its popularity, at the relatively early time of one o'clock.

May 1

It gets worse. After a breakfast so large I won't need to eat again until tomorrow, I decide to double check with the concierge today's kicked off times. The couple in front of me are discussing the events of last night, where it turns out, they had VIP tickets. Fair enough, my misfortune is none of their concern, but the woman didn't enjoy the experience, and then the killer line, 'I much prefer watching rugby.'

The conversation is terminated with my contemptuous reply, 'At least in football the players usually leave the field with both eyes in working order.' That effective Partheon shot kills the dialogue stone dead, just think what I would have said if I hadn't had breakfast, or moments later when the concierge informs me that there are no matches today they were all played last night. He is adamant, checking a Hungarian website, certainly none in Budapest.

No, no, no, bollocks, no. All this way for nothing. It wouldn't be so bad if it was a virgin city for me, but I've seen the sights before, and on such a beautiful day like this, it would be a waste to go and sit in a spa.

Wait until the better half hears about this.

'What do you mean; you went all the way to Hungary and didn't see any football?' She storms, whilst clearing the swarf away from the lathe chuck.

It's a pity there's no volcanic eruption this week.

It must be karma, I think to myself. Bunking the train yesterday or dreaming about a ménage a trois with the Cheeky Girls. With their mum videoing. Directed by David Lynch. (Yes, I know they are Romanian.)

Sulking, I pass an internet cafe, and think that there must be a game on somewhere, its midday, I've still got time. I check both matches that were on my itinerary today, they are both very much on.

Thank fuck for that.

The concierge is a good example of what seems to be wrong with the Magyar game, no one seems to care. Asking directions is equally as frustrating. The universal mime for football, volleying an air ball, doesn't get you very far either. Especially in the hotel lobby. I point out the error to the man behind the counter with gusto, bet he'd have got it right if I'd wanted to go to the opera.

Feeling justified, I head to the first leg of the days entertainment, fourth versus second in the Hungarian top division.

On my previous visit here, I paid a visit to the Nep (Peoples) Stadium, as no one seemed to know when the opera was showing. Now it's named after the nation's most famous son, Ferenc Puskas. It is the location of the 7-1 thrashing of England and also where a pre sir, Trevor Brooking stuck one in the stanchion. The vicinity around the ground is filled with huge statues from the communist era, and as for the arena itself, think of the Nou Camp with one tier less.

This time I make a different homage in the same district, to watch MTK at another ground named after one of 'the' team, Nandor Hidegkuti. Here in 1981, a monumental event took place that shook the world of football. The best/worst film about eleven a side ever conceived, Escape to Victory was filmed, in parts, at this very ground.

ETV taught me so much. Before it was released, did you know that Ipswich shot stopper Laurie Sivell was a full German international? That Kevin O'Callaghan had to become an outfield player after breaking his arm playing in goal for this game? That Paul van Himst should be included in the list of famous Belgians? That all Americans are goalkeepers? Obviously we all new that Bobby Moore was a POW and escaped, it makes sense, he was England captain after all. However, I never knew that Max von Sydow was actually a Nazi? He has never ever played a similar character.

Unusually for me, I become a 'shirt' for the day, wearing a navy QPR third team shirt in hope of receiving feedback from the locals wise enough to know the link between our two clubs is Akos Buzsaky. Of course this doesn't happen.

No trouble getting in today, you would be hard pressed to know there is a game on here at all.

Pushing the boat out, I pay about six quid for the best ticket, and get given an MTK wristband to get me into the upper part of the main stand. The support is paltry. The two terraced stands behind each goal are closed. Opposite, the Debreceni followers, numbering about one hundred, of an 800 crowd, sit in the sun. They are the current Hungarian champions, and played in the CL group stage finishing bottom behind Liverpool. Sponsor apart, their kit is exactly the same as the Scousers, and has brought them about the same amount of luck this year, as they lost all six matches.

This is similar to watching a Sunday league final being played at a professional stadium. The few that are scattered about are, more than likely, munching on sunflower seeds, plain or probably paprika covered.

MTK's squad numbers are amusing. The ten outfield players are numbered as follows: 10,11,17,20,24,25,39,55,77 and 86. It seems that they have been selected by raffle.

The hosts are two up, prompting the chant of 'Em-tee-ka', in truth it should be five at half time.

I sip a lager convinced that this game will only go one way.

Sure enough it does, 3-2 to Debreceni, what do I know? Fuck all.

As I leave just before time, I swear there's an announcement over the loudspeaker in German. My grasp of the lingo has improved to an extent that I think he says,

'Will all Gestapo units be on the look out for a small black man wearing a beret, an overcoat and football boots, if approached with the words 'Good Luck', he will answer 'Obrigado'.

Pele, or Edison Arantes do Nascimento as he prefers to be called was captured and starred in 'Escape to Victory 2, Extra Time' but the project was shelved due to Robert De Niro being unavailable to play offence.

Forgach Utca on the M3 line is the next location for a 5.30 kick off, a five minute stroll to the Illovsky Stadium, the home of Vasas, famous in the '60s, at home in a Budapest derby against the team who inspired European club matches, Kispest, or as you and I know them, Honved.

Expecting even worse than previous, I pay 1300 Forints, just over four quid, right as the ref starts proceedings. If Vasas translates from Magyar into English as 'dilapidated ground', then I wouldn't raise an eyebrow. At least the crowd is livelier, and larger (2000) with terracing open this time.

After taking the lead with a curling free kick, the home side then concede twice. The first of which I hear a cheer whilst taking a pee, then thinking that there will be a brief lull in the proceedings, Honved score again as I grab a beer. Probably a diving header from fifty yards.

The away terrace has flags hung on the perimeter fencing that include a St Georges Cross, and the symbol of the wannabe hooligan, the Stone Island badge. It looks about as cool as VW car insignia did on Beastie Boys followers.

Vasas level to force a 2-2 draw, a result which leaves both teams near to safety in the lower reaches of the table, not that most seem too concerned.

Back to the nightlife of Pest, which is livelier than the other half, Buda. It's noticeable how upmarket that they are trying to make the city now. Prague does the whole Gothic/Baroque thing better, so perhaps they are aiming for a different market. The beggars have gone, prices have risen, considerably more when they go into the Eurozone. Wondering how to spend my evening, I stumble across the Balaton Wine Festival, bang in the middle of town, fenced off in a small park, a fiver in with free glass, with wine tokens available to buy cheap, decent vino and a better than average live band on to get drunk to. None of your Bulls Blood rubbish here. Or goulash for that matter, but local cheese and pork products, perfect to soak up what I am about to receive.

Whilst on roughly my fourth glass of red, happily watching the better than expected band play an electric flute and mandolin version of Rage Against The Machine's 'Killing in the name of', my right ear gets a surprising blast of 'You 'R's'. Now if I was in London or the South East this wouldn't come as too much of a shock, but in Hungary? It turns out to be Bill, an Aberdonian who supports QPR, and is here on a short break. He then proceeds to show me his match ticket for tomorrow's game, probably carrying it with him for just this eventuality. We share a few schooners, then he gets an early night leaving me left to talk gibberish to anyone who'll listen, even more so as I'm given more vouchers by friendly locals less interested in getting pissed than me.

My karma must have improved drastically during the course of the day, buying a train ticket, not making a voodoo doll of the concierge, and thinking of my beautiful wife and son.(Not at the same time) Directed by whoever does Disney films these days. Pixar probably, it would be animated. Hope they don't over accentuate my jaw line.

May 2

Bill and I bore the other passengers with matters football all the way to arrivals at Terminal 5. The final day of the Championship, all fixtures are 1pm kicking off, and we are playing the title winners.

Sheffield Wednesday versus Crystal Palace is the only game of the day worth watching, and BBC has stolen the thunder from Sky, who are showing Liverpool v Chelsea. The discerning viewer, I would hope will opt for the former, the all or nothing, despite the fact that it isn't the Premiership.

Chris Hughton, the Newcastle manager, deserves a large amount of praise for returning the Geordies from whence they came. Certainly, I did not expect them to live up to their tag of title favourites as convincingly as they have. They win by the only goal and finish with over one hundred points, with West Brom in a comfortable second.

In contrast, we finish thirteenth, our season promised a great deal but delivered little, although at least we now seem to be a bit more settled for August, and season ticket prices have been reduced in an effort to reconnect with dispirited fans.

As with the opening day, so with the last, another bingefest. The final straggler leaves my abode an hour before my wife returns on the Monday afternoon. No amount of cleaning and airing can hide from a woman the fact that ' I had a few mates round.' That and the fifty bottles and cans in the recycle bin outside.

There is trouble on the pitches at both Hillsborough and Kenilworth Road after both games finish.

The only reason I raise an eyebrow at this is these incidents is that in this age of closed circuit television, the perpetrators are being foolish to think that they will not be seen, identified, caught and sentenced, at the very least banned from following the team they probably love.

Without defending the actions of those involved, it would be wise for the relevant authorities to ensure that the away team and its supporters, having either just been relegated or denied promotion for the home side, don't over celebrate at the local fans expense. Surely, if it is any time for emotions to run high it would then? Or is this just stating the bleeding obvious?

A run of the mill end of season night game between Man.City and Tottenham is now afforded greater than cup final significance, as the winner is likely to grab the fourth Champions League spot.

Sky builds it up as game of the decade, and Spurs run out winners.

The fourth highest in the Premiership, only the third highest in London.

Portsmouth's debt is now £138 million, by the end of the month no doubt, it will be up to £200 million. Surely the Serious Fraud Office must get involved soon, he says once again, or have they got a sweepstake running and are holding out for a quarter of a billion?

Another minor event taking place this week is the General Election, from which you qualify for the Europa League. Up all night to discover we have a hung Parliament. Play offs it is then.

May 8

Munich. Home of BMW, Editors best song, city of the Champions League Finalists, and as I land at the airport, the place that both ruined and made Manchester United in equal measure. How would England have fared in the 1958 World Cup had Duncan Edwards and company had played?

The last weekend of the German Bundesliga, as it is back at home, my main reason being here is for a game tomorrow in the second division, today however, without wishing to bust a gut travelling too far, I manage to find a cheeky third division fixture only an hour or so from the airport, Unterhaching, not an at all a German sounding name.

As often comes up in conversation,

'Ever been to Unterhaching Mel?'

'Do you mean the suburb south east of the city centre of Munich?'

'That's the one, under ten years ago they were in the top division, and defeated Leverkusen, which stopped them becoming champions, don't you know!'

This is hard to believe now, as I dash on line S3 to the Generali Sportpark.

A kindly fraulein hands me a complimentary ticket for the main stand as the kick off is early for the whole division at 1.30, and the game has already started. She probably gave me the freebie as a reward for finding the place. My good fortune encourages me to splash out on a match magazine for ein Euro.

Not a bad little ground, a 15000 capacity, which reminds me, somehow, of a US college stadium.

It's hard not to like a club with a badge adorned with a four man bobsleigh instead of the usual coat of arms/football motif.

My sausage craving is sated with a decent bratwurst priced at only one and half Euros, and I spill a combination of mustard and tomato sauce all over my notes in my over enthusiasm to stuff it into my greedy gob.

In Germany as in much of mainland Europe, the lower leagues often feature the second string of the major players in the top division. Here, most of the big clubs are represented in the third or fourth divisions (the fourth tier is regionalised).You expect the main stadium to be used, however, as I discovered when flying to Bremen to watch Union three years ago this is not often the case. Walking, I assumed to the Weserstadion with Bernd, I found it hard to hide my disappointment when we continue straight past and follow the river down to what isn't much more than a training ground with viewing facilities, where the second eleven play. So, I've never visited Werder Bremen's main ground, but I've seen their stiffs run around, and paid for the pleasure of doing so. The fucking Ryanair flight was delayed four hours on the return journey as well.

The spectacle in front of me is the perfect end of season game cliché. Comedy goals, though only 1800 are there to see it. Forty of these are followers of Wehen Wiesbaden, (yes, I counted them!) gutted, as they were 3-1 up, only to lose 4-3. Tobias Schweinsteiger, older brother of the more famous Bastian, scores twice after coming on as substitute, a good effort for a pig climber. Expensive though, if your son wants his name on the back of his replica shirt.

This is the most goals I've seen in any match this season, though this is only just over half as many as were seen at Fir Park in the six all midweek draw between Motherwell and Hibernian.

Back to the city centre to rendezvous with the visiting Berliners and with some of the Charlton lads who have also flown over.

Meeting in the popular Hofbrauhaus, Bernd is getting drunk enough to start a Putsch on his own. We then head to the end of S2 line to Erding. This feels like the equivalent of going to Epping at the end of the Central line on the London Underground.

Our destination is what we assume to be the bar of a former Union player, Sebastian Bonig, but this turns out to be a sports centre and over 500 Union supporters and exiles have turned up, which is not bad as Berlin to Munich is over 300 miles.

A drunken evening ensues, drinking variations, pils, weiss or dark of Erdinger, which of course, is brewed next door.

We meet Christian Beeck, one of the team's coaches, and the club President, who stays mixing with the noisy Berliners all night. Would this type of event have taken place at home? Perhaps, but not with same success at this distance, and we are not talking about a club the size of Bayern Munich either. Bayern have the title confirmed today, overcoming the challenge of the eternal bridesmaids Schalke in the last few weeks. Munchen will be lively tomorrow.

May 9/10

The omens are not good. There are no baked beans available with my breakfast. Smoked salmon is just no substitute for the prairie strawberry.

In the Marienplatz today, Louis van Gaal's champs will be celebrating their title in front of the Bavarian faithful. Last season he won the Dutch title with an unfashionable club, AZ Alkmaar, and now his side are on course for an historic treble in his first season, he must have some sort of idea of what it takes to win. I wonder if he takes his inspiration from playing Football Manager on X box. Not that I would know too much about computer games, being of voting age.

As the crowds start to gather, we leave before we get caught up in the mass of people who either want, or don't want to be there. The Union supporters don't want to be here, as I would imagine the TSV 1860 Munich fans prefer not to be here either, to have their noses rubbed in their bitter rival's success. Ironically where we go to escape is, the Allianz Arena, on the U6 line to Frottmansing, home to Bayern and TSV 1860.

My last visit to this great city was the weekend when Beckham's goal beat Ecuador in Stuttgart; unfortunately I missed the 5-1 in 2001 as I was on a stag do in Cork. Though I did take a look around the original stadium on my last visit, with its strange design, and stare eerily at what was the Olympic village and the events that took place there in 1972. The newer ground is equally unique, a spaceship that lights up red or blue in the evening depending on who is playing at home. Living in the shadow of Bayern can't be easy; TSV will struggle unless they can get back into the first league. Finance is an issue, which explains the dearer entrance fee of 14 Euros, not extortionate by any means. However, these tickets are all sold for the away end, and we have to pay 28E for the next section. Roughly 3000 Berliners have made the trip which swells the crowd to over 20000, still only making the arena less than a third full. Impressive as the stadium is, it is the most corporate of German grounds, and adopts the card system for refreshment; hopefully this will not become the norm in the rest of the country, or become compulsory back home when it is introduced under the banner of concerns over health and safety or some such nonsense.

A goal down at half time, midway through the second half there is a loudspeaker announcement followed by a groan which I don't understand until the fateful words 'Munchen Flughafen' are flashed across the scoreboard. The only reason for this is the cloud of ash which has caused the closure of the fucking airport. Calling and messaging occurs at a frantic pace. On the pitch, Union earn a penalty, but contrive to miss, and then concede again, but I'm only half watching. At least next season with the relegation of Hertha Berlin, Union have a derby to cherish, the 'Bundehauptstad', strictly speaking is the first ever between the two clubs, and the first east versus west clash since 1950.

My wife thinks that I've done this on purpose to gain more time away from babysitting Jake, the rain dance obviously did the trick.

I say my farewells, their six hour drive doesn't now seem so daunting, and head back to my hotel to collect my bag. When there I enquire as to whether or not they can keep the same rate if I require another room tonight. I am politely refused, and the increase is 100 Euros extra. My answer is not so polite, and I head off to Franz Josef Airport to see where I stand.

The queue at the information desk seems to stretch to Salzburg and looks ominous. I steel myself and head to the BA check in. They confirm me on a flight at 4.20 tomorrow afternoon.

'Alright, but what I am supposed to do about accommodation?'

'If you care to wait for a minute, we'll discuss this.'

Expecting the worst, I look around the empty terminal and picture myself slumped on the floor with a sleeping bag. Next to a few coins scattered in a Tupperware box beside my feet. My faithful mutt 'Loftus' whimpering with hunger pains.

My sleeping rough thoughts are broken by the voice of the kindly lady behind the counter.

'We'll book you in the Holiday Inn Express, with an evening meal and breakfast. Take the shuttle bus outside which leaves in ten minutes.'

This takes the wind out of my sails. All primed ready to explode, I murmur a thank you and walk to the bus stop, almost disappointed that I've had to keep my pram full of toys.

Of all the fellow stranded passengers I get to speak to, it seems that only BA and Lufthansa have afforded their passengers this courtesy. With most other airlines it's fend for yourselves, and pay full price for whatever beds you can find.

It is ironic, that on the previous BA flight home from here four years ago, Danny and I were bumped off, as the flight was overbooked. It did however only take four hours longer to get home via Brussels, and I was paid £170 for the inconvenience.

That night in the hotel bar 'The Silent Sigh', or certainly that is what feels appropriate for drinking in this type of establishment under these circumstances, an unexpectedly pleasant evening ensues. With everybody in the same boat, or to be more specific, not on the plane home, the comradeship has the 'well, there is bugger all we can do about it' spirit.

They keep the bar open as long as there are customers, of whom there are few, but we are willing, and the Erdinger is more than palatable.

The drinking party consists of a couple of audiophiles, Simon and Steve, over for an exhibition, able to tell your nose from Bose, myself, and a hairy biker with his spouse. Dave Myers is the mobile chef stranded like the rest of us.

His story is just one of many in a desperate need to get back. After trying all manner of route variations to return to host a show at the Blackpool Tower, he succumbed to the inevitability of time and distance. Turns out they'd been to see The Scorpions last night, but this 'Wind of change' didn't do any of us any good, and his sold out show with his oppo Si, on The Golden Mile had to be cancelled. (Much preferred Scorpions in their early years with Michael Schenker and Uli Jon Roth) He hails from Barrow, and does give me a surprise when letting me know that they had beaten favourites Stevenage to win the FA Trophy the previous day. Good on them.

The next morning after a Spartan but free breakfast, I decide to make use of my spare time and finish off my trip with a visit to Dachau. There is nothing like a visit to a death camp, to spend a cheery couple of hours and realise that one, as it turned out, not so bad night of your life, is nothing compared to the misery that took place here. This may not be the most infamous, but it was the forerunner of the notorious Polish based killing camps.

It's not often that I would say that I would rather be indoors scoffing a bowl of crunchy nut, with Jake flicking Petits Filous at me, but this morning it's true.

This weekend was the 65th anniversary of VE Day, so it does seem the right thing to do.

True to form, after nearly an hour and a half on the train I arrive to find that the museum is shut. This shouldn't raise an eyebrow, as if Monday isn't bad enough without a visit to a concentration camp. Only part deterred, the Dachau Aldstadt beckons. It is a quaint Bavarian town, and begs the question, why put a prison here? The answer could be just that.

This is best illustrated with a Terry Jones female voice, in German of course, a Marlene Dietrich style doesn't work.

'Where are they sending you again?'

'Somewhere called Dachau.'

'Oooo, that's a lovely place, you'll like it there. If you work you may be set free.'

A five star jail, complete with en-suite firing squads.

Returning home, I discover the fates of the ninety two plus.

Chelsea, have won the minor prize. Leeds finally stumble over the finishing line.

Gillingham fall back from whence they came, and Grimsby finally succumb after leaving it too late.

Fleetwood and Bath both reach the Conference, winning their relevant play offs.

The initial thirty man England squad is announced; the only surprises may come when this trimmed to twenty three.

Many of the pre-season friendlies are being announced already, and I have to smile when the first for QPR is in the West Country, they day after the World Cup Final. Whether you want it or not, you now have a 365 day season.

One, albeit for me reluctantly, has to take your hat off to Fulham. Roy Hodgson is deserving of the LMA manager of the year award, and to get the Europa League Final beating Juventus, holders Shaktar Donetsk and Hamburg is no mean feat. In the final they are done for by the class of Aguerro and Forlan, however my sympathy wanes, first with images of Hugh Grant, and then Lily Allen crying. It makes me smile.

May 15/16

Ryanair, much criticised, often by myself, do sometimes have their uses. You can take advantage of genuine low fares without always having to sell your soul to Michael O'Leary.

For about £90, Bea, Jake and I are winging it to Santander for the weekend. Spain, or Spanish speaking nations, always gets the vote of approval from the wife as she is fluent in their native tongue, thus a Hispanophile by design. This has been handy in the past, stopping us getting fleeced by taxi drivers in Colombia, or negotiating ticket purchase at the Azteca in Mexico City.

Since the age of six, the only FA Cup Final that I have not watched was in 2004 when you just knew that Millwall would get comfortably beaten by Manchester United, so, my then girlfriend, now wife, and I went to Bilbao. We met, by chance, a young Fernando Torres in a hotel, complete with screaming teenage girl audience peering through the window. Later watching him score twice and miss a penalty for Atletico Madrid at Atletico Bilbao. My recommendation to the powers that be in London W12 to sign him up fell on deaf ears and an empty cheque book.

The night before we arrive I try and book a room, expecting this to be easy. I'm unsuccessful, and leave it to chance the next day. It turns out there is a doctor's convention in town. After traipsing around for an hour or so, a friendly bar owner finds us a fourth floor pension for 32 Euros. Cheap but clean, no en-suite bathroom, or cot for the baby. Jake will try and interrupt our sex life again, especially after last time when he alerted security in the supermarket after we got frisky at the cold meat counter.

Santander, in the region of Cantabria, is more renowned these days for its global bank status, but it is still a port, but not a large one. The residents of both Portsmouth and Plymouth may have taken advantage of the ferry service that runs across the Bay of Biscay.

After a breakfast that includes tortilla, which I love to the extent that I am surprised that they are not part of our staple diet in the way that onion bhajis now are. I'm not advocating a 'Tortilla-u-like' chain or the like, but they are so simple to make that they would make to a perfect addition to full English.

My wife says that they are better than sex. Sex with me. With Jake trying to watch.

Cuisine tip over with, the top chefs having taken note for their next cookbook, I make tracks to the ground to ensure entrance, and pick a ticket up for 10 Euros. This is just as well as the opponents are Sporting Gijon who may hail from eighty plus miles up the coast in the next province, Asturias, but it is close enough to still be considered a derby.

Racing are threatened with relegation today, fortunately for them there are three clubs on the same points that can suffer the same fate, but their opponents are the top three of Barca, Real Madrid and Valencia.

Many Gijon followers, mainly families, have made a day of it and rightly so. The beaches are superb; the popular 'El Sardinero' area also contains the stadium. England played a friendly here in 1992; I recall David Bardsley winning a cap, unusual as the capacity of this tight all-seater is only 22000.

With so much to play for it is a full house, and a carnival atmosphere for the friendliest derby I've ever seen. There are pockets of red and white shirted 'away' supporters dotted all around the stands but in complete safety, without a hint of animosity. Even the Gijon players get warmly applauded when they are substituted. Two nil to home side both scored by the unfortunately named Tchite. The last game for the nineteen year old Sergio Canales, who is Real Madrid bound for a fairly large fee.

Barcelona are the Champions, though only one trophy this year, and send Vallidolid down in the process. Tenerife are the other fall guys.

The next day we manage to fly home without any problems, despite temporary closure of many British airports. There has however been another storm brewing over the weekend that could have a significant effect on our bid to host the 2018 WC.

It is revealed that Lord Triesman is another in a long list of dirty stop outs, and the famous quote about hell having no fury like a woman scorned is once again proved correct. Except that three hundred years ago tape recorders, Max Clifford and 'The Mail on Sunday' would not have been involved. This time, you have to question the morals of the participants, and if this does derail the bid, I hope that Ms Jacobs ends up a lonely spinster struggling to feed her cats.

Oh, Chelsea win the FA Cup, and as suspected, Oxford return to the Football League, defeating York City in the Conference final.

England winning the 20/20 Cricket World Cup in Barbados is great, but I can't help feeling that it is similar to the football team winning a five a side trophy. Test cricket is far superior. Heretics.

May 19

The play offs are in full swing, and whatever you opinion on their fairness, they are compelling to watch. Compelling enough in fact for me to want to go to at least one of these fixtures. After almost no deliberation whatsoever, I decide that Rotherham v Aldershot is the game for me.

Nowadays, until their new ground is built, even though the old one, Millmoor, is still in a playable condition, the Millers have to play at Sheffield's Don Valley Stadium, the biggest athletics track in Britain, and venue of the World Student games in 1991.

The last train back to St Pancras would mean having to leave at half time, so I post a message on the Aldershot fan's website, and within an hour receive a call and ponce a lift from Steffan and his son Lee, who previously hails from just two miles away from where I now reside.

It seems to be forgotten how the Shots have managed to climb back up the mountain they fell from when being dissolved in 1992, a la Accrington. Ironically, they were the first ever team to win promotion via the play offs, when they knocked out Wolves in 1987, then run on a slightly different format.

We make good time up the M1, parking up just after five in Attercliffe, two minutes from the stadium. Make no bones about it; this area of the Steel City is about as run down as it gets in England. Boarded up properties, dereliction on a grand scale, you try and picture the scene when British industry was in its heyday.

After trying a few pubs that wouldn't make it into 'The Good Beer Guide', we find one that should be if it isn't already, 'The Clifton'. My hosts stay only for a short while, leaving me to share a few extra pints with a genial bunch of locals.

Eventually, I make it to the match and part with £18 to sit with the Aldershot supporters. The ground is only about a third full (7082) , but I shouldn't complain about the running track, as it is an athletics stadium, certainly not conducive to watching eleven-a-side.

The first leg, at the Recreation Ground, had ended with a dreadful last minute back pass being punished by the lively Adam Le Fondre.

Just before half time he adds another to a prolific season, making the Shots task even tougher, he looks as if he can play at a higher level.

The interval music over the loudspeaker makes me smile, 'Into the valley' by The Skids, because it's apt, and I haven't heard it in years. RIP Stuart Adamson.

Aldershot press forward, but are caught on the break to make the tie irretrievable.

The Millers now plan for Wembley, where they will play the Daggers, leaving the poor old Shots left to dream of next season.

All the vehicles nearby have had their windscreens leafleted by a local entrepreneur already advertising coaches for their big day out. This is why the play offs are unlikely to change from their current format, the visit to the London Borough of Brent. The lure for clubs like these is just too great. Having walked to the old Twin Towers when Rangers were there in '82 and many trips before and since, its allure for me is not as great. Appreciating the magnetic draw of Wembley should not be underestimated, a novelty only recently available to every team, apart from a select few, over the last couple of decades.

The first of these days in the sun follows on Saturday, with the game billed as football's richest, the winners earning up to ninety million from all derivatives.

I'm convinced Cardiff will win, as it is their turn, but Blackpool overturn the odds and reach the land of milk and money after a fantastic first half, from then on the future is bright, the future is tangerine. Ian Holloway, of whom all QPR followers have a soft spot, will no doubt be in his element with the media at full throttle, enjoy it while you can.

The football express continues into the evening with the other big earner, The Champions League Final in Madrid. On a weekend for the first time, to attract more families, say UEFA, although for once I have to agree, it is more convenient for travelling.

Only one team of the two will complete the treble, and thanks to Diego Milito's brace it is Internazionale. They were both finished well, but, did you notice the second goal? The defending from Bayern's Daniel Van Buyten was questionable to be polite, but being blunt, bloody awful. The turning circle of the Ark Royal closely resembles his inaction, I doubt whether the Belgian Naval Component has any aircraft carriers, or too many large ships, perhaps as I've mentioned in the famous Belgians section before, called the Jean Claude van Damme, the Rene Magritte, the Jan Ceulemans, or the one there should be, the Phillipe Albert. The fisheries vessel the King Leopold II is more likely, the murdering bastard from the Congo's heart of darkness. If you get my North Atlantic drift.

Perhaps in watching videos for a game of this magnitude, realising that Milito is all right foot, led Van Buyten into a false sense of security, as he turned on to his left, but still tucked it away with the outside of his right. Bluff, double bluff, and me drinking when studying the game in too great a detail, late at night.

Still, it was the turn of an arthritic elderly gentleman, after a visit from the twenty four hour head to toe plaster of Paris service, and downing three bottles of Polish vodka, who then had to escape from Everton's Marouane Fellaini's Afro. Try saying that after several pints of Fuller's ESB.

Mourinho accepts the thanks and joins Real Madrid. Another feather sticking out of his cap, along with another trophy under his coat.

May 24

Advertised as 'The Tickets for Troops International', it's almost like waving goodbye to the Ark Royal from Southampton Dock. The media frenzy is gathering pace and tonight is our last chance to sing 'God save the Queen' on these shores until, er, August when we host Hungary in a celebration of being World Cup winners. It has got to happen one day hasn't it?

Wembley is bedecked in T-shirts; or rather fans wearing them, mainly white, some red, originally draped on the seat backs, that create, it must be said, a very impressive cross of St George covering the whole stadium. Mine is white, as I'm in the cheap seats, for once they've got something right, as the size of this pound shop top is XXL, meaning either they know wear I sit and have got my measurements, or they are one size fits all, because they've got our number and we are all fat bastards.

I think it's the former, as I'm special. Special needs says the wife.

It is nice to feel so relaxed at the lull before the storm, even the Mexicans join in their eponymous wave.

A comfortable 3-1 victory, then its back to the Alps for the squad. Peter Crouch, flat track bully or not, has an international goal scoring record that many better players would be envious of, as he increases his tally. Tactically it doesn't yet look right, but for once, let's get it right when it matters; this is more than just overdue. The nation is positively aching, as is my stomach after eating some of the food on offer at half time.

UEFA announce Michel Platini's financial fair play scheme which will try and enforce that clubs must reach a break even requirement by 2012. This will be assessed in the 2013-4 season, and the idea is 'to protect not punish'. Oh yea! In theory, I'm all for it, but in actuality I have my doubts. If these honest men gave me a racehorse, I would send it to a veterinary dentist.

Michel was also in the news this week, when he was the man who opened the envelope that said that France would be the hosts of Euro 2016. Talk about under the radar, they beat the Turks by a single vote, but no-one has seemed to notice. They held the tournament in 1984, but this must count as the last century as it is that long ago that Platini has forgotten collecting his winners' medal in Paris.

May 30

One of the problems with booking a trip at this stage of the season is that you have to second guess the importance of the fixture well in advance, unless you're prepared to pay through the nose for travel costs. Taking a flyer on this one has worked out well. Having seen them in their opening match today could be the last in Serie B for some time for my latest adopted team Cesena. The alternative would be the dreaded play offs as discovered by Swindon yesterday in their defeat to Millwall, rectifying last years Wembley heartache for Zampa the Lion, and Kenny Jackett for that matter.

There are no problems with my BA flight to Milan Linate, even though the cabin crew are in the middle of industrial action which they are perfectly entitled to do.

Public opinion these days, has no sympathy with strikes, the attitude is one of selfishness. Much as I'm glad to board the Airbus with no difficulties, and we even land early, the right to do what they feel is appropriate should not be questioned by not many of us not well enough informed. Try and put yourself in their position and don't believe the hype or 'The Daily Mail'.

Removing my Wolfie Smith hat, I jump on a 73 bus not to Tooting Broadway but to San Babila to then take the Metro to the impressive Central Station.

This takes me back nearly 18 years to when I was last here, meeting my Anglo/Italian amico, Francesco Quaranta, who, although living in Italy at the time, hails from the same manor as me, London, not Londinium.

We procured tickets for Internazionale v Juventus, known as the derby of Italy, in which I recall East German Matthias Sammer being man of the match in a 3-1 home win in one of his few appearances there. Those were the days when it seemed like an epic travel adventure to attend such a far flung fixture. Nowadays it's just down the road. Or it certainly feels that way. The advent of the internet has made obtaining information a doddle, throw cheap air travel into the mix and it's now as easy as scoring a penalty against a goalkeeper from St Dunstans.

The 12 Euros 'quick' train fare takes about 45 minutes to Piacenza. Be careful if you get somebody trying to assist you buying a ticket. The friendly exterior that will deprive you of your correct change, in a way that you probably won't even realise until you are comfortably ensconced in seat to your chosen destination. What amazes me is that even the locals seem too taken in by this scam, and that no official presence is about, or concerned enough to do anything to stop it. If you cotton on to the skulduggery, it is almost as if you are creating an unnecessary fuss, and you would more than likely to be the one arrested.

Geographically, Piacenza has a significant importance, being located at the confluence of the rivers Trebbia and the more importantly, the Po. In footballing terms though, not so much.

I'm directed straight off the train on to a waiting bus which is full of Cesena followers. Not sure if I'm meant to pay for this privilege, but, I'm the last one to board, and an over the top escort by the carabinieri takes us to the Stadio Leonardo Garilli. Just as well for me as it seems that the arena is nowhere near where I'd alighted.

Setting the scene, Cesena lie in third, three points behind the leaders, and a point behind the second, but with better goal difference than both. Lecce, who are top, are at home to Sassuolo (not the Phil Collins hit), who lie in fourth. Second placed Brescia are away at relegation threatened Padova.

Piacenza are mid table with little to play for, so, in theory at least the Seahorses have the easier of the ties.

As I disembark from my convenient bus journey with the catchy sound of Biffy Clyro's 'Bubbles' ringing in my ears, Marco greets me like a long lost brother, instantly handing over a bottle of beer, match ticket, a scarf to wear, and a straw trilby type titfer that every other supporter seems to be wearing.

With no bars in the near vicinity, we enter the ground at a time that the authorities recommend you take up your seats, but that most of us ignore to quaff another pint. With no alcohol officially on sale, I buy a handful of 33.5ml Borghettis. These are 20% proof, coffee liqueur shots sold by supporters that are fairly insipid, but like the last bottle of Martini left at a party, serve a purpose.

Another uninspiring communal stadium with an athletics track, sparsely populated except for the south stand, filled with 6000 black and white clad promotion chasers. Not bad for a crowd that turns out to be 8066.

Shirt off, beer belly prominent, and that's just the ladies. Two minutes in, a tsunami of cheers around the Curva Sud, Padova have scored. Much looking skywards and praying takes place and the mood is now so upbeat to the extent that the Pavarottis are in fine voice.

'My mother, and brother, all follow Cesena,
And if you don't like it, we'll shit in your gelati,
Then place our thumbnail under our front teeth,
In which we flick in your direction.'

At least that's my translation, or in fact completely fictitious, but nonetheless I join in as best I can oblivious to what is being sung. One tune I do recognise, oddly enough, even if the adapted words mean little, is 'Moonlight Shadow', by Sally Oldfield. Weird to hear this at a game this side of the Iron Curtain. Weird to hear this at all.

Just before half time the jungle drums beat faster still, Padova have got a second. I do my best to calm down the temperamental Italians around me by stating the bleeding obvious, that Brescia have now got to score three to go up.

It gets better. Two minutes into the second half, Cesena finally take the lead through Marco Parolo, who will probably go down in local folklore. The stands go Radio Rental.

From then on, true to the spirit of Italian calcio, Cesena's defence, the most miserly in the division, close and bolt the door, put up the grill and padlock the shop firmly shut.

A quarter of an hour from time, we hear Brescia have pulled one back from the penalty spot. Even I start glancing at my watch, as fingernails are bitten to the quick, the tifosi gather around earpieces attached to pocket radios.

Near the end of the ninety, word gets out that the sprinklers have gone off at Padova, delaying the finish and heightening the tension.

The final whistle is blown here to muted celebrations, as both the players and fans alike look to the heavens for divine inspiration, or for another Padova goal at least.

There's no need as promotion is confirmed a couple of space minutes later, Serie A beckons. There are more men crying than at the world onion peeling championship, as the team do the now familiar run and dive in front of the massed ranks. Lecce have scraped home with a goalless draw that gives them the title, but nobody is too concerned about that.

Outside is air horn city, as we make our way back to the car park where a nine seater is waiting, complete with ice cold beers to transport us home, dropping me at Bologna Airport on the way.

I'm genuinely pleased for my surrogate team and friends, now an honorary fratelli for life with the promise of free beer every time I visit in future(unfortunately not with flight thrown in). As I say arrivederci with a team photo at the airport, leaving them to depart with another effective parting gift, pissing on rival Bologna's ground, without any encouragement from me whatsoever, in anticipation of next season, where I may well join them, continuing my love/hate relationship with Italian bladder ball.

My perfect day, without sangria in the park, or even heroin for that matter, is only spoiled by a two hour delay on the Ryanair flight back.

England complete their friendlies with an apparently unconvincing win over Japan in Austria, but a win is a win, and I'm sure Fabio knows what he wants and we hope, this is what he will get.

Dagenham & Redbridge finish the last match of our domestic season victorious and in the third tier, not bad for a pub side as they have been called.

Except for a few odds and ends around Europe, or in Scandanavia where much of the season is played over the summer, that's it in anger until August, there's never any serious football in June.

This year there is a trivial international tournament taking place in the African continent for the first time, nothing to concern you with.

The deserts of Sudan, the wilds of Borneo, Eskimo, Arapaho (Ian Dury's lyrics are too good to not be used elsewhere) will be engrossed in a tele-visual feast of association football. No other sport can surprise, or be so simple to improvise with only one piece of equipment, a ball.

Not content with ever being free from controversy, a brand new match ball from Adidas is being used for the first time at the World Cup. The Jabulani translated from Zulu means rejoice, which is far from what the reaction is by many of the goalkeepers practicing with this aerodynamic sphere of pleasure.

Coupled with the thin air at altitude, I'm left with visions of 40 yard rocket shots swerving as if radio controlled, whizzing past Alan Rough, circa 1978 Argentina.

The final twenty three are announced, with the main bone of contention being the choice of wingers. Walcott and Johnson are left at home in favour of Lennon and Wright-Philips. This is surprising as Theo would seem ideal as an impact player, especially after his hat trick in Croatia earlier in qualifying, and new kid on the block Adam Johnson has been ahead of Wright-Philips in the Manchester City pecking order, Aaron Lennon has only finished 90 minutes for Spurs once this year, being out injured after his early season promise. This is why Capello is manager, seeing things the rest of us mere mortals are not privy to, and making decisions based on this information. Of course this won't cease the amount of opinions and soundbites on television, by celebrities who were either not old enough, or know little about the subject matter put in front of them to make a valid comment worthy of any recognition.

Luck will play a huge part in the destiny of the trophy, and only one training session into the adventure, England's already starts to desert them. Our captain tears his left knee ligaments and is out for six weeks. Steven Gerrard takes over the armband from Rio, with Michael Dawson flown in as cover. Let's hope that this early setback is the only one that effects are chances from now on.

Misfortune is not just restricted to us; Drogba, Robben and Nani are amongst other world stars already facing a potential enforced holiday.

June 11

So in the words of a chant not sung for years except in television productions of football realism, here we go. The first WC in Africa, and the only feasible place on the continent likely to do so. Can you picture in the future the tournament taking place in Nigeria or the Congo?

Nearly five weeks of wall to wall replays, of which I will be attending, but not from the off, that really would be grounds for divorce.

The Bafana bafana (The boys) get us underway. Siphiwe Tshabalala with a dream finish sets Soccer City sound levels to maximum. ITV's coverage gives us the reaction to the goal from Soweto, they jump around. Well there's a shock. Sometimes it is amateur hour, even though they now have the affable, one of us, Adrian Chiles now at the helm. The Mexicans are no shower and deserve their leveller, which briefly quietens the vuvuzelas, but not, unfortunately Jim Beglin, whose co-commentary grates.

Always used to like Barry Davies myself, back in the day. Whenever that day was?

Can someone also answer me when did it become essential to show the manager's reaction to a goal? What do TV producers think will happen? He'll merely continue removing dirt from his fingernails?

Later in Cape Town, France look disjointed in their bore draw with Uruguay. Am I the only one unimpressed with Frank Ribery? We are not talking about a Sacha Distel lookalike competition here.

June 12

On paper we should beat the Yanks, yet we play on grass not paper. History should not repeat itself in Rustenburg, sixty years on from the disaster in Belo Horizonte, Brazil. That's the logic over and done with. It's nice of Mr World Cup fixture computer to put us on Saturday night. It seems that every other person you pass in the street is wearing some sort of item of English regalia. To say anticipation is high is an understatement.

The South Koreans set the tone for the day, giving the Greeks are hard time. How on earth did they ever win Euro 2004?

Argentina are the team who worry me. They don't look so assured at the back, but have spare talent, and you can easily envisage Maradona having that 'I told you so' look at the post match Final press conference.

Every World Cup seems to throw up a word that has never before been much used in everyday language. Petulant and metatarsal are two of the most recent incumbents.

Vuvuzela, or plastic trumpet to us, is the latest.

If Australia gets awarded the 2022 WC, are they going to use the didgeridoo or wobble board to the same extent?

I wonder when the first casualty will be from one of these irritating toys, either from eardrums just giving up the ghost and exploding, or, by gangs of tinnitus sufferers clubbing a noisy bastard to death with one. They could then carry on and do that to the England Supporters band as well.

The stage is set, let the play begin. Come on England.

June 13

The morning after the night of the mistake before. Calmer now, and on reflection not too perturbed.

Even your gran could have saved it. Or at least pushed it round the post. No, saved it.

You would certainly not be envious of Green, up to a tenth of the world saw or will see that error of errors. At least though, it is unlikely that most of the population of the United States won't have seen it. ITV HD viewers also missed the action, like Green they both switched off at crucial moments.

On a positive note, Gerrard played like a captain should, Heskey, finishing apart, was typically unselfish, and I lost count of the times that we got in behind their full back only for a poor ball to be played in.

Credit must be given to the Septics, who ran themselves into the ground, but it was noticeable how strong we finished.

Television stated that the Americans had sold 8000, and England 6000 tickets for the match in Rustenburg. The actuality is plain to see, at what looks like the first capacity crowd; well over half are from these shores.

If you check Ebay for tickets, you can purchase hundreds from the States, it is illegal to do so over here, maybe this should tell you something.

Watching Algeria lose to Slovenia today reminds me not to cancel my flights.

Whilst you can have sympathy with Robert Green, they same cannot be said of Serbian Zdravda Kuzmanovic, whose idiotic handball cost his team a likely point against Ghana, and, possibly, much chance of reaching the last sixteen, after seeing the Germans destroy the swimming cossies.

I'm now itching to get out there, if only to escape from watching the James Corden football show.

June 14

Much as it is vaunted as a celebration of football, we are also watching some of the largest marketing campaigns in the history of the planet.

You cannot fail to notice the Nike orange and purple boot. Golden slipper more like.

Visiting their website informs me that Vapor (sic) Superfly II Elite's colours have an 'increasing focus of peripheral vision' assisting players to 'spot a team mate quickly for a game changing pass.' This is all well and good as long as the opposition aren't wearing the identical boots. Didn't think that through did they?

Retailing at £275.00, one would assume that complete with them, you get a Thai masseur, for dubbing purposes. Not that matches are played on mud any more.

The Dutch beat the Danes, the Japs upset Cameroon, an African country, God forbid, but since 2002, any England fan that travelled to the WC there, more than likely has a soft spot for Japan, I certainly do.

In Group F, the holders Italy look ordinary as they did when they won it four years ago, and are held by Paraguay.

June 15

There are no mugs at the Finals any more, apart from the fans. Gone are the days of the double digit defeat. However, pre-tournament, you got the feeling that the Kiwis might be the last of this dying breed, the pushover.

Having battled bravely through a four team qualifying group, that included six times Pacific shrimper champions Vanuatu, New Caledonia, where if you happen to be on holiday and can do more than fifty at keepy uppy you should get at least a substitute appearance, and Fiji, even losing to them once. Then they overcame Bahrain over two legs to get to South Africa, and qualify for the first time since 1982.

So, knowing this, will they rollover as one suspects? Nope, they'll equalise in the last minute against the Slovaks.

There is always a 'group of death'. The most fancied Africans, Ivory Coast, cancel out the penalty nemesis of England, Portugal.

The main event brings a strange romantic air to J'burg. The unknown quantity in every sense is North Korea, up against the overblown Brazilians.

Watching the national anthems, I find it hard not to laugh as North Korea's is played, thinking that it would be Kim Jong Il singing 'I'm so roanrey' from 'Team America'. It's difficult not to stereotype the underdog, and you can't mention them either, or they will be under the grill.

They don't disgrace themselves, but, unfortunately no repeat of '66, but will the poor man on the streets of Pyongyang be aware of this? He won't even know that they aren't finalists from the 1970 competition yet.

June 16

The first round of matches comes to an end with a shock, Spain the favourites, are beaten.

Hopp Suisse.

They won't find it easy against Chile, who beat Wigan or Honduras as they are otherwise known, and have become their feeder nation. Odd that they have a scouting network in Central America based in the weirdest capital name Tegucigalpa.

A distinct lack of goals, except by the Germans who have been practising with this ball a year longer than anyone else. Not a single free kick of note so far, and no one player has yet scored more than once.

You would expect a break in proceedings of at least a day, but it's only two and a half hours until the local boys play once more.

South Africa get found out, by a Forlan inspired Uruguay, and will almost certainly exit as quickly as FIFA has slapped legal proceedings on Bavarian lager for its 'ambush marketing'.

It's unusual for the hosts to go out so early, and one hopes this won't affect the rest of the football festival in a negative way.

Ironically, the beer in question is brewed in Eindhoven, next to PSV's stadium, and more than a well aimed piss to Southern Germany. Better than Budweiser though.

June 17

To great hoo ha, at nine in the morning, next season's fixtures are announced. They over egg Blackpool's lot, as they did with Burnley last year. It's difficult to get as excited as usual when there is nearly four weeks of this little cup to get through.

Back in the southern hemisphere, Group B, has the potential for an interesting finish, where it is quite feasible that the team that finishes second behind Argentina will only have three points, each side having lost two of their games.

Ireland points its collective bottom in the general direction of France, who stand off the Mexicans to the extent that they play like they're almost guilty to be there.

Surely the Uruguayans will tango with the Mexicans to secure a draw, as the Austrians and Germans infamously waltzed into the next round in Gijon, Spain '82. Sending home the hosts and bidding au revoir to the 2006 finalists.

Strange to see players wearing mittens during tonight's spectacle because of the cold, but from a footballing perspective, the gloves are off. After a tentative start, the competition is up and running, let's hope England run with it.

June 18

After scintillating ties earlier in the day that see the Germans lose, and the Slovenes impress before being pegged back by the battling Americans, the expectation is high on Friday night for something special.

That couldn't be further from the truth. I've been racking my brains trying to pinpoint what went wrong. As of yet, I don't have any answers. In my forty years of having a vague idea of how the game is played, I cannot remember England ever playing as badly. Algeria could not believe that defending could be as simple. Luckily they didn't decide to attack

Sometimes it is best just to remain silent, pending further futile analysis.

As I sit disconsolate, an old slapper with fake tits beckons me to talk dirty to her on late night Babestation TV. Piss off you ugly cow, don't you know what has taken place tonight?

June 19

A virtually empty bottle of Smirnoff vanilla flavoured vodka stares back at me as I half watch the Netherlands edge out Japan. Generally I don't drink spirits, but if ever there was a time to deviate from my own maxim, it was last night.

Watching the 'highlights', BBC commentator Guy Mowbray gets it right with, 'Why is it always such an ordeal watching England?'

The realisation that England might not make it through to the last sixteen must now be considered.

I had never taken this possibility seriously before; even the inconvenience of coming second in the group seemed unlikely. At the moment I'd probably settle for that, and the pain in the ass of having to travel to Bloemfontein rather than Rustenburg. Better than not travelling at all.

Ten men Australia keep their hopes alive with a battling performance against Ghana, and it is as clear as it is likely that Raymond Domenech would win a popularity contest, whom England may play in the next round. Should we progress. I hate having to say that.

Cameroon, so often Africa's leading lights, even with Samuel Eto'o, become the first side definitely on the way home, after defeat to Denmark.

June 20

After seeing Paraguay look very comfortable earlier in the day, I let out a yell as Smeltz puts the Kiwis ahead, albeit from an offside position. My wife and son are startled, so apart from apologising for making Jake cry, I also have to explain that my joy will only be fleeting as the Italians are certain to fight back and win by two or three goals. Bea says they might not, only to be chastised by my one hundred per cent certain self. Luckily I decide against taking the wager of wearing stockings and a suspenders down the pub in the event that I am wrong, as they can only manage a discreditable draw.

Are the Italians destined to join England and France in the self imploding club?

Fabio Capello has a clear the air meeting with the players which can't be a bad thing.

As for the French, well, Nicolas Anelka is likely to spearhead a blockade of Calais, and will the rest of his team mates join the air traffic controllers on strike?

Brazil begin to look like, well, what Brazil are meant to. Useful.

June 21

Portugal face North Korea without Eusebio to rescue them this time. No need of course, seven are put past the poor, financially at least, keeper Ri Myong-Guk.

Hope he doesn't end up like the Colombian own goal scorer, Andres Escobar.

Following on from the dubious dismissal of Kaka yesterday, the Saudi official, one, Khalil Al Ghamdi, takes pickiness to the next level in Chile's defeat of the Swiss. One off, nine more only one card away from a suspension at least.

'It's only a game', an epithet that would never be levelled at the murderers of Escobar, nor in 1969 at El Salvador or Honduras who fought in what became known as the 'Football War'. You wouldn't want to ref that one, which cannot take place, potentially, for at least another couple of years, in qualification for the 2014 WC, as the latter lose to an improving Spain and can prepare to go home.

June 22

At 5/2 for a 0-0 draw the odds are a bit skinny, but I feel my score is a good investment for Mexico versus Uruguay, who are both guaranteed a place in the last sixteen if they decide to do so.

Given a choice of matches to watch, I opt for the above and am shocked at what I watch.

Both teams are trying to win! This is not in the script. After an end to end battle, Saurez puts me out of my twenty pounds misery. This is how it remains, which is not enough for the Bafana Bafana who go out on a high defeating international football enemy number one, France. The Group A table is pretty much the polar opposite of what was expected. Domenech will be about as missed as a verruca, and his parting gift is to refuse to shake the hand of South African coach Carlos Alberto Parreira.

Argentina lay in wait for Mexico, and the happy South Koreans take on the smaller neighbours of Maradona's boys across the River Plate, Uruguay.

June 23

Slovenia has a population smaller than that of West London, which doesn't count for much today. Only been there the once, to the capital Ljubljana and along their tiny coastline at Portoroz. Let's hope that there is no need for a football war after 5pm today.

Let me hope that as I am flying out, the team are not flying back, in economy. Like the French.

Better. Better get a bucket I'm going to be sick.

Relief. Then panic. Jermaine Defoe's solitary goal is just enough.

One team from Uruguay, South Korea, USA or Ghana is going to be in the semi final.

For England to get that far we now have to beat Germany, I think we might, but the improvement will have to be considerable.

Then, more than likely Argentina, to get to the last four against Spain or Italy or Portugal.

Winning the group was extremely important; the only people who are happy are the media.

They will now go into uber overdrive, and should we get past this kleine hurdle, they will then wax not so lyrical with the handy opposition.

Bloemfontein, as I feared is now actually going to be a pain in the ass to get to, but better there than nowhere, also it seems there is little accommodation available, I'll just have play it by ear from now on.

Landon Donovan has a lot to answer for. Didn't he used to be in 'The little house on the prairie' or one of those seventies shows, proving how little viewing choice there was available back then.

June 24

Typically, as the temperature is meant to soar into the nineties here this weekend, so I have to pack long sleeved tops for the cold evenings at altitude, or so the reports tell me.

Bea's parents fly over for a break and to look after the now proper handful Jake. Bless 'em.

As I hastily pack, or throw things in a suitcase as it should more accurately be described, I have one eye on TV, watching Slovakia realise that Italy are actually that bad, and put three past them. So it's arrivederci to the holders, and farewell to the terra firma of this sceptred isle on flight BA55. Eleven hours on a packed

Jumbo, in an economy middle row seat. It's times like these that all the Lilliputians who have to stand on tiptoes at matches or gigs get their own back.

June 25

Red eyed, we land at Oliver Tambo International Airport, Johannesburg.

As a rule, when you are at the WC you don't actually see much of it. This was the case in Japan 2002, where it was sometimes difficult to find bars to watch games, as I found out in Kyoto where I spent an hour searching for a bar to watch the opening game between France and Senegal.

Hopefully, this WC will be as memorable as that one was for me.

Japan, incidentally, overcame Denmark I learn, to earn a place in the last sixteen.

First things first, I find the FIFA ticketing centre easily enough, and insert my credit card into the machine. Almost instantly, four tickets for England v Germany are printed out, without me inputting any password or pin number. Should I ring the Daily Mirror about another lapse in security? Perhaps I will get free stadium access if I do, and have a chat with Becks to share a drink; quite possibly, he can recommend me a tattooist.

The next BA flight lands a couple of hours after mine, with Eddie Roberts and son, young Ed, aboard, who are greeted by my ugly mug rather than Archbishop Desmond Tutu and are to be accompanying me for certainly some of this trip.

We buy a couple of cheap mobile phones then get an expensive cab to the capital Pretoria, or Tshwane as it has now been renamed. A half sleep in a poor hotel, then out for the evening's entertainment. We walk through downtown Pretoria and eating burgers and drinking our first bottle of Castle lager this trip. Heading to the floodlights of the Loftus Varsfield Stadium, I should feel at home with a name like that, and the last game of Group H, Chile v Spain. Having already bought a couple of Category 3 tickets at cost from a fellow England fan, Chris, at Canary Wharf, we manage to get another one also at face value, there don't seem too many about.

Inside, there is chaos, I end up watching the whole ninety minutes standing up with the boisterous Chileans, the stewarding is clueless, and this suits me fine. This is a football match not a night at the opera.

After a good start in the tightish ground, Chile let in dreadful goal, then another, in which Torres feigns injury/cheats, resulting in the South Americans being reduced to ten men. My loyalties from this moment on are with the men from Santiago, Viva Chile. Viva Zapata I shout as they pull a goal back, which is not enough, but they qualify anyway as Switzerland can't find the Honduran net.

All the South American teams have made it through, but only one from Africa.

In the nearby bar, Eastwoods, where you don't have to drink Budweiser as you are forced to in the stadia, 'brewed over beech wood' mixed with it more like, the atmosphere is good.

This is until my day isn't made when my camera gets stolen. Quite a tasty one as well, a Panasonic Lumix. Stupid of me, putting it a jacket pocket just for a minute because of ease. I think I know who did it and when. Three mouthy Afrikaaners who had already vanished when I noticed it was missing after only about five minutes.

If I'm wrong in my assumption then I apologise, if not, then I'm glad we invented concentration camps.

June 26

The choice is get a return coach back to J'burg, or hire a motor and drive the 350 miles to Bloemfontein, and carry on from there. Toyota Corolla it is then.

We leave the Gauteng region, formerly the Transvaal, for Free State. A clear road, punctuated by signs for weird and wonderful towns and game parks. Seeing springboks next to the road is a novelty, however not as much as the speed camera trap we are allegedly caught in by a lone patrolman, on an empty road. Strange how he accepts an offer of a lesser amount than the 750 rand requested, with no receipt. How many of us are prepared to call their bluff and insist on making matters official?

Uruguay v South Korea sounds enthralling in the rain according to the radio, with Saurez netting a great winner to send the original WC winners through.

With Mr Blatter's sons company Match, commandeering many of the hotel rooms, potential beds are looking limited. 350 miles later, we are in Bloem, as it is known.

To gauge the price and availability, the first central hotel we see is the Queen's Park Lodge. It's a house that has bedrooms, and has rooms for tonight but not tomorrow. We check other ropey hotels but decide to take our chances for somewhere better tomorrow night, and opt for the QPL. The proprietor, Deon van Zyl, extends us warm hospitality, and sorts us out beds at his friend's house for the Sunday.

A short stroll past the cricket and tomorrow's showdown ground the Free State Stadium, and then turn left lakeside to the Waterfront, a modern restaurant/shopping mall area. We shovel down steaks whilst watching Africa's remaining hope, Ghana, overcome the Yanks in Rustenburg. From here to the lively Second Avenue, where a few more Castle lagers and back to be fresh for the re-enactment of El-Alamein, not, we hope, Dunkirk.

Back at the lodge, with the nights turning chilly, our host turns back the years and the beds, by leaving electric blankets turned on. For me, it's thirty five years since I've had the pleasure of sleeping on one. If only he could have left a bottle of Cresta in the fridge as well. Near to my monkey boots.

June 27

Match 51, Round of 16, Germany versus England, my ticket tells me. Just another game, between two footballing nations with no previous history, or axes to grind.

After a late breakfast in the shopping mall, with no beans, a bad omen, we park the car back at last night's hotel after being driven to the new accommodation. As the lodge is in such a prime location, Deon and sons make hay while the sun shines so to speak, and sell tins of beer and South African hot dogs to the passers by; this is the last encounter in Bloem.

Not even ten minutes and you're at the stadium, en route I'm interviewed by Greg Krumbock, MP with the Democratic Alliance and Shadow Minister for Tourism. He asks my opinion on how I feel the tournament is progressing; he has bumped into the wrong bloke here. Ask me in a few hours I should have said.

We meet the lads in a packed Barba's bar on Second Avenue for a nervous few, before the sunny afternoon's confrontation. Due to awkward location of this fixture, and that many had banked on England winning the group, tickets are available at half price near kick off.

So, to the main event. There can't too many reading this that missed the action, for the only game this season here is my less than in depth analysis.

We've got good seats, Cat 2, Row 2 $150 US, top tier, dead in line with the eighteen yard line of the goal that England are defending in the first half, I say that loosely, because that's exactly what the goals we conceded were, loose.

The National anthem was sung with gusto, though I believe 'Land of hope and glory' should always be used where England are concerned.

After a nervy start, it seemed that we were just settling down when we concede from a goal kick, one bounce and Klose sticks out a leg to prod it past James. Our two centre halves look like the Chuckle Bros with their indecision, if that was conceded on Sunday morning by an under nines team, questions would still be asked. Deep breath, heads up lads, plenty of time. To go two nil down.

In truth, from a German viewpoint, the second was well crafted, and well finished by Podolski, another Deutsche Pole. We're being cut to ribbons. Fucking hell.

Then, after Defoe hitting the bar, albeit offside, Upson nods us back in it, then seconds later, quite possibly the single biggest contributing factor to a change in technology to be used in future matches.

I was a considerable distance from Lampard's volley, but thought, rightly, that it was in. There was a strange split second of uncertainty in the stadium, the referee looked towards his assistant, the crowd looked towards the television screens for a replay which was not forthcoming, nor was the finger towards the centre circle. In fact, in the melee, the Germans nearly scored again.

Once it wasn't given, my mind instantly turned to thoughts of the Russian linesman from '66. In actuality, the man in question, Tofik Bakhramov is Azeri, the national ground in Baku is named after him, ironically built by German PoWs, one of the better England trips from six years ago.

Back then, the debate was whether the ball had crossed the line, now there is no argument, it did.

You can't lay the blame on the Uruguayan officials, only the head in the sand attitude of FIFA, which, surely, has to change now.

The English in the stadium, and probably the Germans for that matter, receive a multitude of text messages. I get four. 'Over the line', ' One yard over the line', 'Two yards over the line', and the final damning verdict, 'Further in than a cod in deep sea trawlers nets.'

Two each approaching the break, with England in the ascendancy and we would have bitten your hand off ten minutes ago. As it turns out, the optimism is still with us at half time, where we now have the moral high ground knowing that we've already been cheated. There's always something isn't there?

We have to chase, and get caught twice on the break, with Schweinsteiger and Mueller playing perfect matches. Losing is easier to take, when you know that they have done their utmost, trying until they are bleeding with exhaustion. If this is physically possible? If not, it should be.

Numb with defeat, alcohol just doesn't make any difference; we grab a pizza and watch the evening game to see who we won't be playing in the quarter final.

A dreadful decision for the first goal put in by Carlos Tevez, makes the victors a foregone conclusion in the Argentina versus Mexico game. Worse still, is when the Mexicans, walking off for half time, spot on the scoreboard replay, just how far offside the Man.City forward was when flicking the ball in. Their furious reaction won't resolve the outcome, but you can't blame them. As with the earlier ruling, another fateful judgement that could and should have been correct, but that would mean using 21st Century technology by a panel of officials stuck in the 19th.

We are indoors by eleven, something I've not done since that outbreak of Black Death. At least I've got an electric blanket for 'cold' comfort.

We're out having only scored three goals, our lowest since 1950.

The fallout from today will last for some time, two errors that will live long in the football memory. To try and apply comic effect does not seem appropriate, as none of us are laughing. England aren't the best team in the world, yet they are a team that most don't want to play, unless you are Argentina, Brazil, Germany or Portugal. The only teams we have lost to at the WC for a significant time, significant, meaning my life time. Has there been a hex on us since 1966? Sometimes it's difficult not to think so.

La tristesse durera.

June 28

After stocking up on important items such as currency, crisps and deodorant, we leave late in heading down the N1 to Cape Town, the Vortrekker route. We're flat, and undecided. I'm in favour of a trip to Lesotho, just to tick it off among the places where I've been, but I'm not really fussed, so I go with the flow and resign myself to the thousand kilometres drive south west.

Driving down this single lane highway, you are reminded of the Mid-West, America not Wiltshire, farmland, wind turbines, grazing cattle and sheep, and herds of wildebeest blocking the road.

We leave early afternoon, stopping to look at the Gariep Dam, another on the list of unimpressive dams I've seen this season.

The afternoon commentary game is Holland v Slovakia. Radio has never really agreed with me when concerning football. Rangers defeats in big matches when I was a boy have left there mark, haunting me ever since. Sneijder sounds like he scored a good winner, but it come of been a tap in for all we know. Throw ins become one on ones, shots fizz just past the post are in fact just past the dugout. You know what I mean.

As it's getting dark we stop in Colesberg, population 29, and settle on a room, or an apartment at the Horse and Mill English Pub. £40 or thereabouts, for all of us, including electric blankets. If Colesberg did value for money overnight stops........................

Here we eat and drink with various travellers, and watch Brazil demolish the Chileans, this does not look like the year of the underdog.

June 29

Four o'clock, FM Radio 2000, live commentary on the game of the afternoon. Today its Japan v Paraguay, as we pass through Oudtshoorn, the ostrich feather and meat centre of the world. In a short space of time our routine is not complete without the voice over accompanying the match. My aversion to radio football is tempered by the equivalent of John Bird playing the mouthpiece of Idi Amin in the '70s, or the Zulu warrior from the Silk Cut cinema ads of the same era, but reporting on the game. 'What a shot, (lengthy pause) miles over de bar.' 'Good tackle, oh no, de ball is free again.' Harmless fun, needed today for the Paraguay v Japan fixture, which isn't the most gripping.

Extra time and penalties for the first time that we watch in a converted railway carriage called 'Zanzibar' in the town of George (After George III). The barmaid has a cleavage that follows you around the room. Ironically the Japs were based here, but can now pack their up possessions and wave sayonara.

We press on to Knysna down the Garden route, base to Denmark and the disgraced French. The Royal Hotel is our roof for the night, and as we are out of season, and not near a ground, the prices are as they should be, reasonable.

Out for the evening, we have stumbled on the Marie Celeste of towns, finally managing to see Spain win the Iberian Peninsula derby, by an offside goal from David Villa.

June 30

The first break in matches for seventeen days. It feels somehow hollow being here now. No sense of anticipation or even worry to occupy your mind. A radio report states that the expected amount of visitors during the WC was 450,000, but in actuality, less than half that figure has arrived. Whether or not this is a success or failure it's hard to tell, but you lose track of the amount of times that the natives ask you if you having a good time, not understanding that it would be good if your team weren't shit and still competing.

Driving by the towns of Wilderness and Mossel Bay, it's not hard to see why the settlers fell in love with the place, and why they're reluctant to give it up. Time constraints stop us visiting the southern most tip of Africa, Cape Agulhas, so we stay on the N2 to Cape Town.

Bea texts me to say that Jake has had his first poo in a potty. I wish I was there to see it. Then I picture him in the future, mortified at a moment such as this has been laid down in print.

Arriving after dark, without having booked rooms in advance, we head for the centrally located City Lodge. At reception, they offer us the full price rate, no discount, only when I point out that the internet cost is far cheaper, does the girl let us use their computer to book at this reduced amount. This is only a massively ridiculous system. I crash in with Fleetwood, and Stuart from Preston via Saudi, where he works, who have just flown down from J'burg.

News that the Nigerian President Goodluck Jonathan has suspended his trustworthy nation's FA for two years following their dismal showing. Perhaps our equally righteous non-elected leader can hurry through a bill giving the same powers concerning our under achieving tossers.

July 1

Cape Town is a fantastic city. A confession here, the wife, then five months pregnant, and I, were here in February 2009, one of the best breaks we've had, and almost an unintentional reconnaissance mission for me.

The attractions are plentiful. The one thing you can't miss, literally, is the imposing Table Mountain. Robben Island, reached by hydrofoil, Mandela's 'home' for eighteen years. Then the Cape of Good Hope, which does feel like the end of the world at Cape Point. Camps Bay and the Twelve Apostles to see and be seen. The Winelands including Stellenbosch and Franschhoek, strongly recommended for everyone who likes a drink, and by many who don't. Then there is the District 6 Museum, satirised in Peter Jackson's film District 9, though not on the feel-good list of most.

We also went on a Desert Safari, and visited a uranium mine in Namibia, but that is a two hour flight away.

Before you think that none of this has anything to do with football, I got a sneaky game in at the Athlone Stadium. Ajax Cape Town v Amazulu. One of the most wacky games I've ever been to, because that's what half the crowd were smoking, and which culminated in my cabbie getting beaten up by other drivers for not being from round these parts. We got out of there faster than I did that time we tried to take the Stretford End wearing dresses and stiletto heels.

Trouble is, I've experienced the majority of this before, but none of the other lads have. At least I will get a lie in for the next few days, and stroll at leisure around the tourist orientated V & A Waterfront, full of bars, restaurants and shops. There is a signpost that gives world distances near to the old clock tower. The South Pole is 6131km away which surprises me, as being at the bottom of the continent one feels that it could never be that far. If you are into astronomy, you would imagine that being here gives the stargazer a completely different perspective than the view from up north, as in hemisphere. I can't locate Orion's Belt for a while, which comes as no great shock, I can't find my leather one most mornings. As you can patently tell, I've got too much time on my hands, astral planing won't help win us the gold pot.

July 2

The V & A is buzzing as the first quarter final is anticipated. Left to my own devices with most of my mates sightseeing, I settle down to watch the Brazil v The Netherlands in Den Anker, the Belgian bar/restaurant with a prime location dockside. A good choice as it turns out, the staff are decked out in orange, well, half the country speak the same language, Flemish that is, not Afrikaans.

Amongst the strong beer available is Kwak, 8.4%, an instant driving ban served in a yard of ale style glass, which I had as a knockout nightcap on my last visit 18 months ago. There's a slight difference here. You have to hand over one of your shoes if you want to down one. The reason is so that you don't run off with the item as a souvenir, something I was inclined to do as a younger man, until I'd collected about fifty but wasn't quite sure why? It is also the reason that the Cape Town and District bunion, corn, and verruca darts league don't play here any more.

As the match gets underway, Brazil threaten to steamroller the Dutch in the first quarter of an hour. Thinking that will be the final outcome I get chatting to the two Germans next to me at the bar. As they are Berliners, I give the only greeting I know, 'Eisern Union', which leaves them incredulous, the only Englishman they've ever met who knows their team, so their holiday snaps are complete mit ein Tommy. Listening in are four Melbourne Aussies of Greek descent, Sam, Manny, Theo and George who are out here with a mentality similar to mine and a thirst to match.

The foregone conclusion changes in the second half, with the previously untroubled Brazilian defence looking shaky, the Dutch running out two-one winners. Free drinks all round.

Continuing on, the United Nations drinking team head for Long Street for the evening. There is a feel like Bourbon Street, New Orleans here. Much better than the sanitised V & A district.

Unlike any other tournament, the whole continent is being supported here in the shape of the old Gold Coast nation, Ghana. Cynical me doesn't share their enthusiasm, and whilst accepting that the power base of world football may shift in the coming decades, at the moment if you add Brazil and Argentina to the Euro tournament you've got better than a WC.

All the bars are busy down Long Street, which isn't particularly long, and we settle for standing room only in the British style Stones Bar. There were many offers of tickets for this tie, for free in some cases, but it's taking place at Soccer City, a mere nine hundred miles away. It seems I'm in a minority of one siding with Uruguay, who from a population of only three million are the real underdogs.

Then in the last minute of extra time, with the score at one all, the ball is looping in to the South American net only to be palmed out by Luis Suarez. Penalty. Red card. Correct decision, these are the rules. Now if Asamoah Gyan had scored, nothing more would be said, even if Ghana had won the ensuing shoot out, no problem. However, he missed, and the Uruguayans in the penalty decider, bar one, did not, and went through to the semi final. When the initial kick was missed, the cameras managed to locate Saurez celebrating at the tunnel entrance. So what, he was punished, he is suspended for the semi. Have these people ever played football? Ghana were cheated. No they weren't, they missed from twelve yards. You strike the ball cleanly, paying special attention not to lean back when making contact with the ball.

There are a lot of Argentinians out for the night, ebullient at Brazil's defeat, so much so, they have a mocked up coffin with their bitter rival's name on it. This leads to the first skirmish I've seen during the WC, not an England fan in sight. We are all watching from the balcony of the trendy Cape to Cuba bar. Here, a large community of English have congregated, mainly those like us who aren't going home yet, BBC employees working here, their WC base, and a selection of sports journalists.

Now I rarely read 'The Sun', and this works to my advantage as I stumble into a round with Rob Beasley without knowledge of his work, therefore unable to criticise him for past misdemeanours or have any preconceptions of his writing, and we drink until the small hours talking the usual football bollocks.

July 3

Today, I'm mostly being German. Union Berlin T-shirt, Puma XC Favo trainers is the most Teutonic clobber that I can muster from my suitcase. Its moments such as this that you wish the Freddie Starr Hitler get up was still politically correct, if indeed it ever was. I've got no bayonet to sharpen with the Argies, certainly I'd recommend Buenos Aires and the Iguazu Falls as places to visit, and there is none of that Malvinas patriotism to contend with. The truth is we've much more in common with the Germans, perhaps the lowering of borders has finally made subconscious Europeans of us after all? Or again, just me?

After a drought on the ticketing front, suddenly a downpour of availability. A hundred quid gets me a Category 3 entrance, off Dave Gates, a red Manc, just checking in to the City Lodge as we are about to leave for the day. He's now got the pleasure of my company for at least ninety minutes, which I'm sure he'll enjoy.

The Aussies have a couple of spares which Ed and son take off their hands in our meeting spot, Den Anker.

There's bad blood from the last WC, the same QF stage finished with an on the pitch set to, and I'm fully expecting this to carry on at the 70000 capacity Green Point Stadium this afternoon. The location of the new arena is perfect in so far as location is concerned, near the coast with the Table Mountain backdrop, and easy walking distance from the waterfront.

Once inside, through security that takes thirty minutes, our seats behind the goal afford us a view of Signal Hill above the roof of the stadium. To prove they do have a sense of humour, the Germans have placed a red, orange and black flag high up for all to see.

They also have a publication to rival our Free Lions, the fanzine provided by the Football Supporters Federation, theirs is called 'Helmut'.

Maradona prowls the touchline, playing with rosary beads, resembling a man wearing somebody else's suit, and looking as if he's itching to play. As it turns out, he couldn't have done as worse job than his defender Demichelis, who is given a torrid time and should have known what to expect as he plays for Bayern Munich. Muller scores after only three minutes, and from then on Lahm, Khedira, Mertesacker, and Schweinsteiger are faultless. My first time of seeing Messi in the flesh as it were, and I'm left without having viewed the full range of his talent. He either didn't receive the ball, and when he did, a size eleven took it off his toe.

Ein, zwei, drei, fir – nul. In the quarter final of a WC! On the large screen, we're left with the image of Angela Merkel applauding as Miroslav Klose continues his fantastic scoring record, by banging in the fourth.

Speaking as a bad loser, the Argies are the same, and they are not so cocky out on the town tonight.

We grab stools in the Long Street Cafe for more of the same we hope, as Spain take on Paraguay.

Spain, I'm convinced have their name on the trophy after the events of tonight. They have both luck and skill in equal measure, convincing this pundit that they are destined to be champions.

Referee Carlos Batres, from the footballing hotbed, Guatemala, deserves a lot of credit for being brave enough to correctly give decisions that many would have baulked at. Giving the first penalty, that Paraguay then missed, and subsequently making Spain's Xavi Alonso retake for encroachment after netting his first kick. David Villa their talisman, eventually gets them to the last four, perhaps now they'll justify their favouritism.

A long day finishes with in a hot and sweaty nightclub called Zula with the Aussies, with a feeling of mortality and the saying, too old to rock'n'roll, too young to die, ringing in my ears along with drum and bass.

July 4

Another break in games, sort it out FIFA. There are only so many re runs I can stomach. It is wall to wall TV footy, and I'm complaining! Harambee, a TV show featuring the comments of John Barnes and Gary Bailey, inspiring about as much as do the comments of the presenters of Talk Sport back home.

Other irritations from this WC include the various items of plastic.

Your honour, may I present exhibit one, the vuvu-bloody-zela. Contrary to popular opinion, they are not part of an historic cultural tradition, but a more recent Chinese made addition to entertain fans with the attention span of a goldfish. At yesterday's game I threatened an Argie nearby (or someone more than likely following them for the day) with trumpet cone side first vuvuzela anal entry, but there was no need as the Germans got a third, and the drone ceased.

Exhibits two and three are of the more visual annoyance variety, the makarapa with or without Elton John type coloured glass frames to show how crazy you are. The former is not a dance, but a safety helmet cut into angles and painted in teams' colours. Even funnier is they are fifty quid, and we actually saw an England supporter purchase one, which felt like seeing somebody actually wearing a T-shirt with the legend, 'I like the pope, the pope smokes dope'. As for the lens less glasses, your guess is as good as mine. Like face painting all of this is acceptable if are you a child or have special needs, but if this is what people are meant to expect as a football experience then you can keep it. Remind to change my surname to 'killjoy' upon my return.

Doing my damnedest to keep out of pub, my weakness only lasts until just after lunch when I bump into Beefy and his wife Shirley along with Tranmere follower Goldie, and a day of abstinence is bade farewell.

Den Anker to the Paulaner Brauhaus then to the Ferryman's Tavern. Eighteen months ago, a bottle of Savannah Dry cider, was roughly a pound. It's doubled in price since, nothing to do with the WC of course. In here, working for Irish TV channel RTE, we meet Ray Houghton and Trevor Steven. Both are veterans of two WCs each, Houghton, famously scored the winner in New York against Italy, whereas Steven appeared in both the 'Hand of God' game in '86, and the semi in Turin '90. This is not forgetting the league and cup medals they both accumulated with high profile clubs, the volume of which would not look out of place on the chest of a American general. Being roughly the same age, I have watched them enough times over the years to recall their golden moments, especially ones against my side. What is good about their company is a genuine love of the game which we evaluate over a few pints. It's nice to chat with stars, not self obsessed or too big time to afford you the time of day. I'll bet they couldn't wait to leave!

In what has now become almost a ritual, we walk to Long Street for the final time this trip, and meet up with Mick Gabriel, over from Shepherd's Bush for his fiftieth birthday, with his South African cousins, whom can't understand a word I say, the hearing is mutual.

So long then Cape Town, hope to see you again one day, next time under different circumstances, a test match at Newlands.

July 5

Advertised as the warmest place to be during the WC, coupled with the lure of the semi final, I say my goodbyes to the lads returning home, and set off for the region of Kwazulu Natal.

A two hour flight with Mango, a 50 Rand bus fare and I'm by the beaches of Durban.

My hotel is reminiscent of those you would imagine frequented by gumshoes in those film noirs from the 1940s. Only after checking in and paying for a cheap no frills room do I read the guidebook that advises tourists not to stay in this area.

Durban seems to have made the most effort in attracting visitors during this month of excess. In fact, it is the only host city that has made this endeavour. A lot of rand has been spent on the beachfront in anticipation of football mania, the FIFA Fan fest is in a prime location, running from uShaka Beach to Battery Beach. There are only a few cities that spring to mind that would be fortunate enough to hold such an event. Combining the essential qualities of guaranteed warm weather, with sand, coupled with a football culture. In four years time Rio de Janeiro will no doubt take this to the next level, and places like Miami, San Diego, and Sydney would make a decent fist of it, whereas the Mediterranean venues have no need to attract the 'new' fan as it is in the blood anyway.

There's a large Asian influence present here, with the Jumma Musjid Mosque being the largest in the southern hemisphere. This is not my bowl of falafel, and having once taken five shoeless minutes to bowl around the Blue Mosque in Istanbul, is about all my theologically culture less mind can absorb. I'll get out my prayer mat and pray to the west, London.

Flip flops and shorts on, belly in, it is most agreeable after over doing the warm clothes option, to finally feel like you're on holiday of sorts.

Two BBC newsmen interview a man selling samosas, along with me, about how business has been during the tournament. Thieving is going quite well I inform them, knowing that there is no chance this being shown on prime time telly, except on a future edition of Crimewatch.

July 6

In the morning, I need to purchase all manner of useful items, namely socks, a disposable camera, and cash. Being camera less has been a bit of a pain, so eventually I succumb and step back to the Twentieth Century and embarrassed, buy a disposable one. Strange how you get used to everyday items, and feel lost without them. On to FNB to get some readies, straight forward enough you would assume. Wrong. After getting ripped off at a previous bureau de change, where one gets charged for administration in addition to the three per cent commission. So this time it has to be a proper bank for me.

Queuing for fifteen minutes as we once were brought up to do, but in true grumpy old man speak, this seems to be a talent less and less evident in modern manners. Then I'm taken to a kiosk to change a measly two hundred nicker in the form of ten twenty pound notes, which I hand over along with my passport. The lady disappears for five minutes, only to return informing me that my notes are no longer in circulation and cannot be exchanged any more. Digging my heels in, knowing that there is bugger all wrong, it's not as if they're white fivers, I ask to see the manager. A unit of time longer than the attention span of celebs in the director's seats passes before a different woman returns with a fax sheet stating what she believes is sufficient information to justify her colleague's actions. She was right of course, the Sir Edward Elgar note is obsolete, not the newer Adam Smith version that I have submitted. I gleefully point out that is written in bold in the fax heading. She leaves silently like a mistaken referee, to be replaced by the original Miss Jobsworth who hands over my rand with no apology an hour after I first set foot in the joke shop/bank. I wish I had slipped in a few counterfeit scores now. A smug smile crosses my face as I depart; with Elgar's stimulating piece Nimrod emanating from the bank's speakers. In my mind anyway.

This minor victory against the Durban Banking XI sets the tone for day of the underdog I hope, as Uruguay take on Holland. The home of Fray Bentos, the scuttled Graf Spee, hosts and winners of the 1930 WC, and again twenty years later in Rio, witnessed by the largest crowd to ever witness a football match, take on The Netherlands. Three years previous, I spent a solitary day in

Montevideo, choked as my flight to Sao Paolo left just as Penarol were playing at the Estadio Centenario, the venue of the aforementioned WC final in 1930. Proper football history.

Not that I dislike the Dutch, but the anti Uruguayan feeling here since the defeat of Ghana, and that they tonked South Africa, is absurd.

For the purposes of research and tiny part nosiness, I opt to watch the first semi-final on the beach at the Fan Fest. The focal point resembles the main stage at the Reading festival, with space for 30000 onlookers. Coca Cola are the principal sponsors, their logo splashed on every conceivable space. At least it isn't Bud, though the beer on sale is the brilliantly named, South African lager, and no one seems to know what it is, canned urine wouldn't be far wrong.

The MC, who cringingly got the audience to repeat the name of the most famous product on the planet, then introduces K'naan on stage. Not getting Dr Who's dog, but a live performance by the performer of the 'company' song. Give me strength, bring on the headline act.

These side events are designed for people with no interest in the ninety minutes taking place in Cape Town, and I make it to 'The Londoner' a beach pub, in time to see Giovanni van Bronckhorst hit the best shot of the competition. This is on a par with Johnny Rep or Arie Haan, and caps his illustrious career. The sky blue South Americans don't give in though and fight back to level at the break through the wily old Forlan. The second orange goal is offside in my eyes, reminding me of Brian Clough's comment that if you are not interfering with play, what are you doing on the pitch. An all European final is ensured as the red hot Dutch run out three to two victors.

Not wishing to ride the 'Congo Express' as one wag puts it, referring to the prostitutes that appear later on, the evening is rounded off with a taxi to the Berea district with its more up market Florida Road. John and Cathal from Carlow in Ireland, veterans of several tournaments, are my drinking partners and good examples of some of the people you meet from all parts of the globe without a vested national interest in the contest, Puerto Ricans, Finns and Peruvians among some of the random peoples met since I've been here.

July 7

The cooler temperature today is perfect for kicking a Jabulani around for ninety minutes. Can't say I noticed what type of ball was being used in my dream, but I awoke after being sent to the stands by the referee, my wife, for a minor offence in the U21 topless, female cup. What would Freud make of that?

England played here in Durban in 2003 at the Natal Sharks Kings Park, next to the new eye catching Wembley like arch design, South African flag inspired, Moses Mabhida Stadium. He was former head of the Communist Party and ANC member, one of the more 'militant' associates. Can't believe that they didn't share the arena name with prominent white supremacist Eugene Terre Blanche killed earlier in the year. It really would be the rainbow nation then!

Chris, from whom I'd bought the two Chile v Spain tickets in London, has a couple more spares for tonight, at cost. Pete, the Wealdstone announcer is having the other. Category three, two hundred and fifty dollars, the most I've ever paid to watch a game, slightly more than Evander Holyfield v Lennox Lewis at Madison Square Garden in '99. I should read the small print on the ticket to see if you receive a free whore at these prices. Does FIFA translate in any language to PIMP? Normally we'd take our chances at the ground and get in cheaply, but as it is now down to the last three in the world, and I've travelled all this way, too far to watch from a bar.

Germany, as both West and united, have now featured in the last four in nine of previous twelve tournaments. An impressive record, though Spain have one over them after their victory in the final of Euro 2008.

Pete and I gulp a few in the early evening, he's been on a coach trip with fellow England fans which has continued regardless of the fact that we're out. Nearing the venue, despite already having tickets, like Dirty Harry, you just gotta know how much you could have got in for. As it turns out, a lot less, top seats at under half what we've paid. Flaming telepaths couldn't predict it.

Inside, it's hard to believe you are attending the spectacle you are. A large Asian presence, who if they are not supporting Sachin Tendulkar or Liverpool, have chosen to nail their colours to either a German or Spanish mast. Nothing wrong with this, but one gets the distinct impression that most really are there because they feel they should be, as its taking place in their own backyard and they won't experience it again. Being spoilt, both in where I was brought up, and in lifestyle, this is alien to me. Like going to Twickenham for the rugby, I'm just taking the place of someone who really wants to be there ahead of someone, ie me, who is nonplussed by it all.

In a poor game, the Spaniards stifle the Germans, but get a goal from an unlikely source, Puyol, and never look back from then on. To underline my earlier point, a couple sitting to my left, bedecked in Deutsche clobber, start cheering when Spain score.

Pete and I just shake our heads, probably subconsciously wishing that we could be as impartial.

There will be a new name on the list of WC winners, and I think it will be 'Viva Espana' and not 'Tulips from Amsterdam' blasting from the bad taste jukeboxes that still remain on the Costa del Sol.

July 8

A free day in which to relax. A much needed lie in, then a late breakfast, otherwise known as lunch, of bunny chow, which, is curry stuffed into a loaf of bread. This is fairly typical of my diet whilst I'm away. Good intentions are disregarded in favour of convenience. Burgers, sausages, pizza, and chips with everything give me a virtual Atkins diet. I am beginning to feel like a guinea pig for 'Supersize Me'. Football can never be said to give salad days, Wimpy is still popular here, which says it all.

Whilst eating my way towards a sixteen stones record, looking out to the Indian Ocean, where container vessels the size of the Channel Islands pass on the horizon, I glimpse the headline from the local rag, 'What a shambles.'

It transpires that many scheduled flights were significantly delayed landing at the brand new King Shaka Airport, only opened two months previously. I thought that for semi final that there were too many empty seats, the crowd was only 60960 was the lowest of the seven games played here, the previous low was South Korea v Nigeria at 61874. The airport was unable to cope with the increase in traffic, mainly unscheduled private jets landing willy-nilly for the game. There were near riots on some of the flights, and who can blame them. Some were late, some were diverted miles away, but thousands possibly missed it. It's nice to see that the celebs made it, and that the priorities were accurately given. Charlize Theron made it, but didn't answer my text about sharing a cheeky glass of pinotage or ten after. Picture England fans being in the same boat or plane, the under used song 'let's go fuckin' mental' would have been appropriate, especially if I was one of the late arrivals. This was why it was so cheap to gain entrance by the gates last night.

Unfortunately, my intention to visit the famous battlegrounds of Isandlwana and Rorke's Drift, if only to say in my best Michael Caine voice, 'Don't you, throw spears, at me', has been scuppered by time, distance, cost, and my lack of forward planning.

However, opposite the Kingsmead C.C, where England beat SA on the last tour, I stumble across a tiny museum, dedicated to the Memorable Order of Tin Hats, non sectarian or political, basically fighting soldiers from everywhere. It has some fairly unique material inside, my favourite item is from a WWII PoW camp, Stalag VIII 'C' Sagan, where the inmates held a lottery guessing when they thought D day was likely to take place. Two were only a day out, one not feeling too positive when predicting was three years out. Entry is free, but you can make a donation to help the friendly custodian Charles, with the upkeep.

Down by the beach, I browse for knick-knacks, but as is so often the case, nothing jumps out at me, a wooden shrunken African head isn't much use to man or beast.

Later, by a chain of events that would upset my wife due to my stupidity; walking around lesser known Durban streets without an automatic weapon, I end up at the Suncoast Casino drinking with more Germans, at prices more in line with what should be expected pre WC. It's no Sun City, but then Sun City is no Las Vegas. I've had enough and want to go home.

July 9

Another new airline flown, this time, 1Time gets me back to Jozi. Only forty quid, but flying for the first time on an airline with this title does make you feel a bit uneasy.

After collecting my case, I head to the BA ticketing desk to see what the options are for changing my flight home. Weighing up the options, it becomes clear in Yank speak, that it is a no brainer.

Firstly, the alteration to fly home tonight will save my marriage. I think she now knows that England are out. Someone must have grassed.

The hundred quid fee will be chicken feed compared to the amount I'll have to spend to stay here for another five days, which frankly, I can't face anyway.

Then there is the added expense and worry of trying to get a ticket for the final.

In US Dollars, the prices are as follows: Category 1 900, Cat 2 600, Cat 3 400. If you are lucky enough to reside in South Africa, then a Cat 4 will only set you back 150. I'd buy a hat full and flog the lot. Sorry, is that not in the spirit of the game?

This is cost, so minimum price if you are lucky. I'm not going to pay about a monkey to watch two teams of whom I care little. I sit too much? By miles, but by the same token, how much would you pay to see England in the final? Or whoever your team is? They've got us by the short and curlies and they know it.

Back home it is then, but with six hours to kill until the critical check in time that I usually take to the wire, and with 500 Rand left, a cabbie, Themba, agrees to take me to have a look at Soccer City and throws Soweto into the bargain. Accompanying me on this mini excursion is Flying Dutchman Pat van der Pol, whom we collect from his hotel, having just flown in from Bangkok. He is after a ticket, however, I dissuade him from paying 15000 Rand off a tout, convincing him that he'll get in cheaper than that. For his sake, I hope I'm right.

The First National Bank Soccer City Stadium is located on the edge of Soweto, set apart from pretty much everything, as are the new stadiums at home, but on a grander scale. It is unique there is no doubt. We take snaps, and I know that it is exceedingly unlikely that I will ever return to see a game here. This will host derby matches between Kaiser Chiefs and Orlando Pirates in future, South African internationals and little else. Perhaps ANC rallies. It is shaped like a huge bowl or calabash, an African cooking pot to you and me. It is certainly unique, with an unusual colour scheme, and what look like random holes which are actually deliberately spaced to help with ventilation. Security won't let us get too close, but a police patrol car passes as we take photos from the highway, illegally parked, but give us the thumbs up, and to their credit, the massive police operation has been very low key for the whole of the competition.

On to the South West Township to name it correctly, somewhere until recently not on a par with the Taj Mahal as must sees to visit. Even the Taj Mahal curry emporium in Southall was higher on the tourist index. Pretty much like Auschwitz, it's become one of those places you should visit if you are in the near vicinity. Expecting a huge swathe of corrugated roofed shacks, I'm pleasantly surprised when we are taken to an area that doesn't appear to destitute. This is Orlando West, where Nelson Mandela lived, also the flashpoint area of the '76 student uprising, where we visit the Hector Pieterson museum. He was a thirteen year old boy shot dead early in the struggle, mostly recognisable worldwide from the evocative photograph of his lifeless body being carried by his brother.

Now the area seems fairly sedate, and an earner for Winnie as we share a few bottles of Hansa at Sakhumzi's bar, watching the tourists turn up in droves.

Back to the airport we drive past what I am informed is the largest hospital on the globe; it seems to take five minutes to drive the length of it.

If I had to give an overview of this country, I would have to give it the thumbs up, although you can't help but feel there is an undercurrent of something more sinister around the corner, which I felt more on my first visit than this, has this just been temporarily postponed during this festival?

They say that the people here are friendly, which is true, as it is of most places around the world, with the exception of Paris, Moscow or Yorkshire.

My Fisher Price toy, or South African mobile phone, I give to an airport cleaner who accepts with a massive smile making me feel warm, and surely this gesture of goodwill must ensure me an upgrade on the journey home, my karma being in a positive place. No such luck, not even the promise of showing my tackle to the stewardess works.

She doesn't know what she's missing; you don't often get to see a blue and white hooped penis. Except in Madagascar.

July 10

Landing in a middle of a heatwave at Heathrow, leaving the aircraft is delayed as a passenger at the back has a suspected heart attack. The paramedics rush on, and you realise that it's good to be at home at Heathrow where you take the rapid response procedure like this for granted.

Scheduled flight number 343 of my forty six years, which after a Huckridge reunion and sleep, I log in to flight memory to record this feat being the part time statistician that I have become. For the benefit of those unaware of this websites wonderful features, you input all your flight history and then view maps containing trails of where you have flown, along with data like how many times you have circumnavigated the globe, or, how many flying hours you've accumulated. Neil Armstrong's diagram must look good.

Is this enough advertising to get me and the family first class to Sydney for the Ashes at Christmas?

In what now seems like a pointless exercise, the Germans edge Uruguay 3-2 in Port Elizabeth to claim third place without the bronze medal to show for it.

Paul the Octopus match predictor, who hails from Oberhausen, coincidental for me this season, should be offered a contract with ITV, at least he seems to understand football.

July 11

The eleventh of July, a date that will forever be etched on the memories of the football supporters of Amsterdam or Madrid. I would love to say that I'm not envious, but I am.

Yesterday it's estimated up to a million people demonstrated in Barcelona asking for greater autonomy for the Catalan region, however tonight they may feel a bit more Spanish than they'll care to admit, as seven of the starting eleven are employees of their most famous export, Barca.

Jake, a chip off the old block, refuses to go to sleep, and unwittingly starts to watch the first of many finals I hope. His wailing is probably similar to my protestations in 1970 when aged six, my mother sent me to bed with Brazil-Italy delicately poised at one all. I distinctly remember saying, 'But mum, I must watch the second half otherwise I'll miss Carlos Alberto's goal which will become one of my favourites.' Unfortunately my gift of foresight didn't last until I reached betting age.

We all watched it, and have our opinions, here are mine.

Well at least we've got a foot hold in the final, with the appointment of English officials.

If goalkeepers are all crazy, then referees must be considered masochists. In fact, it's surprising that they don't enter the field of play wearing a gimp mask and rubber suit. All the drugs in Colombia wouldn't get me to do their job at this level. So before criticising, sympathy is deserved if not forthcoming.

Howard Webb did his best, and for a while at least, did well, but after hefty challenges from both sides, De Jong's Bruce Lee kick on Xabi Alonso should have seen red, so much so that an attendant should have been waiting by the dugouts with soap and a towel.

From that moment on, the eyes of the world watched on as a catalogue of errors take place, most of which were key to the winning and losing of the trophy. Still I found it compelling.

After their exploits in the Seventies, my leanings were with the Dutch, and the decision to mix it, was quite possibly the correct one. Winning a trophy is better than being remembered as gallant losers, and the Spanish midfield is arguably the most accomplished on the planet at this moment in time, so don't let 'em play. The Clog is often as effective as it is disliked.

The BBC pundits toed the company line, unashamedly failing to hide their bias towards Espana, with their lovely neat triangles, failing to notice that all along one nil, Italian style, was all that you were likely to get.

Van Bommel, lucky to stay on against Uruguay was fortunate to survive once more, as was Puyol, both hatchet men. Iniesta too, booked for disrobing having scored the winner, was merely spoken to in an earlier off the ball incident, where mere mortals would have been unlikely to receive such leniency. Terrific player as he is, he also goes to ground quicker than a seasoned up hyena, and he has the irritating habit of brandishing air cards to the ref.

We also learned that David Villa can't finish on his left side, one on ones must be taken, and the jeering of Sepp Blatter was as pronounced as was the cheering for Nelson Mandela.

Spain are the new World Champions, a good side without playing well, scoring only eight times, half the German total, the lowest of any winner ever by three.

My comment to a friend at the outset that Spain would not win without a fit Torres proves that I know bugger all, and that Fernando, like Samson, should have kept his lady boy hair.

The only unbeaten team of the whole tournament, as I had always thought likely, is, New Zealand!

Perhaps I've been over analysing with the emphasis on anal, but hasn't this WC been littered with contentious decisions? When I say contentious, I actually mean bad.

The positive outcome should be that the bunch of cunts in Switzerland will now do something about it after they have finished counting the money and patting each other on the back for another heist well executed.

So ladies, fish and gentlemen, that's it then. A long year of erratic observation comes to a close.

I've tried to cover everything that has sprung to my itinerant mind in and around the world of football.

The contradictions, both mine and footballs', cannot mask the depth of feeling that millions, even billions hold for the game.

If I had attended the final or another match over the course of the season, I would have seen one hundred matches or bits of them at least. I suppose I did get to see the WC winners, twice, but I don't think they will be remembered as such a great team in years to come.

Never mind, it's only a number, and Sepp will probably invite me as his special guest for the next one, or I'll go to the 2034 Final in India and watch Jake get the winner for England.

This is only because public pressure demanded his reinstatement after his alleged involvement with all twelve of the Queen's Park Rangers cheerleaders. The court case cleared him of all wrongdoing. It was only eleven. Good lad.

If it wasn't for 'third parties' I would have attended many more.

Inclement weather, volcanic ash, the missus, over zealous stewarding, over priced ticketing, sloppy planning, televised matches, England being inept, and conversely England being less inept, as this would have been more convenient for me to watch more ties. If that makes sense. Being single would also have seen me visit far more way out locations and drink myself into an early crematorium.

Already the friendlies have started, my lot play at Tavistock in Devon tonight, and later this week there is Champions League Preliminary Qualification, as mentioned, it is now 24/7/52 footie. In fact the season will probably be a few weeks old by the time I receive my refund from FIFA for the matches that England decided to do me a financial favour and not participate in.

In conclusion, if I am to make any, and there is a design for a footballing watching life, it surely must involve fan ownership to a far greater extent. Does anyone actually believe that new owners from outside these shores have the best interests of whichever club they buy into at heart? We all dream of a huge lottery windfall so we can fritter a substantial amount of it on the purchase of a new cantilever stand or an overpriced Brazilian forward. At very least pay enough so that you are allowed to come on as substitute for the last few minutes and take a penalty if you are leading by a comfortable enough amount. This is what genuine supporters with a bit of money would be prepared to do for no financial return. For every investor with no allegiance to his step team, it is definitely money, influence and power, possibly with fame and prestige thrown in, that are the motivating factors behind any involvement. There is also a small chance that the monies are from sources unknown, and are only laid out to assist with complex laundering purposes. Ring any bells?

Hand in glove with these money driven shysters are the players, and their likeable agents. The Bosman ruling may have seemed a ground breaking decision at the time, but it has since paved the way for salaries beyond the wildest dreams of most players let alone the ubiquitous man in the street. The superstars of the game may well deserve the large rewards along with the accolades they receive. However, the old adage that the career of a footballer is only a short one holds no water any more, certainly for a large amount of the top level pro's. Many mediocre, one footed, average athletes now are comfortably earning in excess of one million pounds per annum, that they do not deserve. Foreigners are more than just keen to gain a Premiership contract, knowing that securing a four year deal, means they can put their blistered feet up back home for life when it is paid up. No wonder they kiss the team badge so convincingly. Gordon Taylor and the PFA will no doubt disagree, but they would wouldn't they? We are not talking about a full back from Cheltenham Town, who has to retire due to injury, here.

Paying for the blacked out windows of our increasingly greedy player's 4x4s is still us, one way or another. If you are happy to pay Sky for live matches and have access to all manner of replays and viewing angles from which the majority of our opinions are shaped, then that is your prerogative. However, preferring to attend a live game has become increasingly expensive, to the extent that Premiership tickets can now be considered luxury items too many households, especially in these days of recession. The working man's game is becoming the preserve of the rich and privileged as we are priced out of the market.

Ordinary millionaires aside, the organisations that run the game are too often given the benefit of the doubt when they should be held to far greater account. FIFA, UEFA and most of the larger FA's pay lip service when questioned about corruption or any other matters that threaten to undermine the status quo.

Despite all my trepidations concerning all the major collaborators involved in running the game at its highest level, there is still much to love from the top down of the simplest sport known to man.

When Ivan Pavlov experimented with his dogs a century ago, he missed a great opportunity for far greater kudos and fortune. Instead of ringing a bell to send the canines into a frenzy of expectancy, what he should have done was blown a whistle. In substituting football spectators for Rover and Sheba, (although the exception would be Pickles, the mutt that found the World Cup) the Russian scientist could have saved himself a lot of time and trouble and have seen that some of us are already conditioned. Admittedly, you can interchange the whistle with the sound of a beer tap pouring. We tend to salivate or more accurately slobber at the prospect of both.

This is a roundabout way of showing that unless the product is tampered with to such an extent that it loses all resemblance to what we are brought up to love, then there will always be unfaltering loyalty when concerning football attendance and its related culture.

Ring that bell, switch on the light, pull that pint and blow that Acme Thunderer. There is no other sport that even comes close. Continue watching your team, at whatever level they play, especially so if they are perennial failures. One day they may not be.

As to what Schrodinger's cat would make of it, after all he was Rangers, or still might be...............